D0622536

WITHDRAWN
UTSA LIBRARIES

Handbook of
Hybrid Instruments

Wiley Series in Financial Engineering

Risk Management and Analysis vol. 1: Measuring and Modelling Financial Risk
  Carol Alexander (ed.)

Risk Management and Analysis vol. 2: New Markets and Products
  Carol Alexander (ed.)

Implementing Value at Risk
  Philip Best

Derivatives Demystified: Using Structured Financial Products
  John C. Braddock

Implementing Derivatives Models
  Les Clewlow and Chris Strickland

Advanced Credit Risk Analysis: Financial Approaches and Mathematical Models to Assess, Price and Manage Credit Risk
  Didier Cossin and Hugues Pirotte

Derivatives for Decision Makers: Strategic Management Issues
  George Crawford and Bidyut Sen

Currency Derivatives: Pricing Theory, Exotic Options, and Hedging Applications
  David F. DeRosa

Options on Foreign Exchange, Revised Edition
  David F. DeRosa

The Handbook of Equity Derivatives, Revised Edition
  Jack Francis, William Toy and J. Gregg Whittaker

Interest-rate Modelling
  Jessica James and Nick Webber

Dictionary of Financial Engineering
  John F. Marshall

Handbook of Hybrid Instruments: Convertible Bonds, Preferred Shares, Lyons, ELKS, DECS and Other Mandatory Convertible Notes
  Izzy Nelken (ed.)

Interest-rate Option Models: Understanding, Analysing and Using Models for Exotic Interest-rate Options (second edition)
  Riccardo Rebonato

Volatility and Correlation in the Pricing of Equity, FX and Interest-rate Options
  Riccardo Rebonato

Derivatives Handbook: Risk Management and Control
  Robert J. Schwartz and Clifford W. Smith, Jr.

Dynamic Hedging: Managing Vanilla and Exotic Options
  Nassim Taleb

Credit Derivatives: A Guide to Instruments and Applications
  Janet Tavakoli

Pricing Financial Derivatives: The Finite Difference Method
  Domingo A. Tavella and Art Owen

Handbook of Hybrid Instruments

Convertible Bonds, Preferred Shares, Lyons,
ELKS, DECS and other Mandatory Convertible Notes

Edited by

Izzy Nelken

Super Computer Consulting, Inc.
www.supercc.com

JOHN WILEY & SONS, LTD

Chichester · New York · Weinheim · Brisbane · Singapore · Toronto

Copyright © 2000 Izzy Nelken and individual contributors as indicated on chapter title pages

Published by John Wiley & Sons Ltd,
Baffins Lane, Chichester,
West Sussex PO19 1UD, England
National   01243 779777
International (+44) 1243 779777
e-mail (for orders and customer service enquiries): cs-books @ wiley.co.uk
Visit our Home Page on http://www.wiley.co.uk
    or http://www.wiley.com

All Rights Reserved. No part of this publication may be reproduced, stored in a retrieval system, or transmitted, in any form or by any means, electronic, mechanical, photocopying, recording, scanning or otherwise, except under the terms of the Copyright, Designs and Patents Act 1988 or under the terms of a licence issued by the Copyright Licensing Agency, 90 Tottenham Court Road, London, UK W1P 9HE, without the permission in writing of the publisher.

The Editor and Contributors have asserted their right under the Copyright, Designs and Patents Act, 1988, to be identified as the editor of and contributors to this Work.

Other Wiley Editorial Offices

John Wiley & Sons, Inc., 605 Third Avenue,
New York, NY 10158-0012, USA

WILEY-VCH GmbH, Pappelallee 3,
D-69469 Weinheim, Germany

Jacaranda Wiley Ltd, 33 Park Road, Milton,
Queensland 4064, Australia

John Wiley & Sons (Asia) Pte Ltd, 2 Clementi Loop #02-01,
Jin Xing Distripark, Singapore 129809

John Wiley & Sons (Canada) Ltd, 22 Worcester Road,
Rexdale, Ontario M9W 1L1, Canada

Library of Congress Cataloging-in-Publication Data

Handbook of hybrid instruments / edited by Izzy Nelken.
    p. cm. – (Wiley series in financial engineering)
  Includes index.
  ISBN 0-471-89114-2 (cased)
  1. Convertible securities.   I. Nelken, Israel.   II. Series.

  HG4652.H36 2000
  332.63′2044-dc21   99-088565

British Library Cataloguing in Publication Data

A catalogue record for this book is available from the British Library

ISBN 0-471-89114-2

Typeset in 10/12pt Times by Kolam Information Services Pvt. Ltd, Pondicherry, India
Printed and bound in Great Britain by Bookcraft (Bath) Ltd, Midsomer Norton
This book is printed on acid-free paper responsibly manufactured from sustainable forestry,
in which at least two trees are planted for each one used for paper production.

Library
University of Texas
at San Antonio

This book is dedicated to my father,
Dr David Nelken,
with much appreciation, love and affection

Contents

Contributors

LINDA E. CARLISLE
White & Case LLP, 601 13th Street NW, Suite 600 South, Washington, DC 20005, USA

LAWRENCE CAVANAGH
Value Line Publishing Inc., 220 East 42nd Street, New York, NY 10017–5891, USA

T. ANNE COXE
First Vice President, Merrill Lynch Convertible Research, World Financial Center North Tower, New York City, NY 10281–1319, USA

BADARI S. ESWAR
Morgan Stanley Dean Witter, New York, USA

GARY GASTINEAU
New Product Development, American Stock Exchange, 26 Knollwood Road, Short Hills, NJ 07078, USA

MARK KRITZMAN
American Stock Exchange, 26 Knollwood Road, Short Hills, NJ 07078, USA

COLUM McCOOLE
c/o Morgan Stanley, 25 Cabot Square, Canary Wharf, London E14 4QA, UK

WILLIAM T. MOORE
University of South Carolina, USC-D, 1705 College Drive, Columbia, SC 29208, USA

IZZY NELKEN
Super Computer Consulting Inc., 1070 Westfield Way, Mundelein, IL 60060, USA

JOHN POIGNAND
22 Crosby Drive, Bedford, MA 01730, USA

About the Contributors

LINDA E. CARLISLE

Ms Linda E. Carlisle practices international and domestic tax law, concentrating on the taxation of financial derivative products, securities and commodities, the taxation of flow-through entities, such as partnerships, limited liability companies and Subchapter S corporations, intercompany pricing issues, and legislative, regulatory, and administrative tax matters. Among the recent tax issues in which Ms Carlisle has participated are the US tax treatment of hedging transactions and "safe harbor" trading transactions; tax analysis of financial products, including OID issues, and dividend-received-deduction issues; intercompany pricing issues under section 482 and section 6038A recordkeeping requirements; and the corporate "spin-off" of international subsidiaries as a predicate to a public offering. Ms Carlisle was instrumental in the inclusion in the Internal Revenue Code of the provisions dealing with the taxation of master limited partnerships of a section providing an exemption for commodity trading partnerships and the independent contractor status of securities broker-dealers, the revision of Treasury regulations dealing with the securities and commodities trading safe harbors, and the inclusion in New York State tax regulations of an exemption from corporate franchise tax for partners of commodity investment partnerships. Ms Carlisle was in government service with the US Department of the Treasury as an Attorney-Advisor in the Office of the Tax Legislative Counsel during 1984–85 and as the Special Assistant to the Assistant Secretary for Tax Policy during 1985–87.

LAWRENCE CAVANAGH

Lawrence D. Cavanagh is Editor of *The Value Line Daily Options Survey* and Senior Derivative Securities Analyst with the *Value Line Convertibles Survey*. Before joining Value Line in 1991, Mr Cavanagh was an options strategist for Capital Market Technologies, helping design long-term and "exotic" option replication foreign currency and gold price hedges for corporations in the Eastern US and in Canada. Prior to that, he was Director of Foreign Currency Options for the Chicago Board Options Exchange. Other work experience includes Dean Witter Reynolds (Senior Currency Analyst), European American Bank (Director of Currency Forecasting) and the Federal Reserve Bank of New York (Assistant Economist). Mr Cavanagh holds BS and MBA degrees, both from the New York University.

T. ANNE COXE

T. Anne Coxe has been the manager of Convertible Research at Merrill Lynch and Company since the beginning of 1994. Since joining the firm, she has led her group in building a comprehensive global research product with analysts in New York, London and Tokyo. In 1995, 1996 and 1997 she earned the number 1 ranking in Institutional Investor's All-American Research Team. In 1998, she earned the number 2 ranking. Anne is recognized as a convertible market authority; her work has been cited in several publications including the *New York Times, Fortune, Forbes* and *Barrons*. Her television appearances include CNBC, CNN and Wall Street Week. Her research team has continued to develop and expand the Merrill Lynch Convertible Indices, which are widely acknowledged as the industry standard. Her reports on themes, trends and convertible structures have found appreciative audiences with both investors and prospective issuers. Prior to her tenure at Merrill Lynch, Anne was a portfolio manager—this range of experience has given her a well-rounded market perspective. She was with Prudential for six years and managed several funds including Convertible Securities fund, the top ranked Natural Resources Annuity Account, and a Global Natural Resources mutual fund. Anne spent four years with Franklin as a money manager and analyst in her home state of California. While at Franklin she managed the Convertible fund and co-managed the Gold Fund. She earned a BA from the University of California at Davis, and an MBA from Columbia University, where she graduated first in her class. She is a Chartered Financial Analyst and a member of The Chicago Quantitative Alliance.

BADARI S. ESWAR

Badari S. Eswar is currently a member of the Global Convertible Research Group at Morgan Stanley Dean Witter. Previously he worked at UBS Securities LLC where he helped develop and implement a complete Convertible Analytics, Sales and Trading System. Prior to joining the Trading Research Group at Merrill Lynch, he worked as a Senior Programmer Analyst at Sun Microsystems and was a Member of the Technical Staff at Bellcore where he was involved in Research and Training. He has a Masters degree in Computer Science from San Jose State University and a Bachelors degree in Mathematics and Physics. His research interests, in addition to Convertible Securities, have been Visual Languages, User Interface Designs and Internet Technologies and application of these in Financial Engineering and E-Commerce.

GARY GASTINEAU

Gary Gastineau joined the American Stock Exchange in 1995 as Senior Vice President of New Product Development within the Exchange's derivative securities division. Mr Gastineau oversees the creation and development of new products, as well as the creation and calculation of AMEX-listed option indexes. Mr Gastineau is a specialist in risk management and derivatives applications. He has prepared and published research for S.G. Warburg, Swiss Bank, Salomon Brothers and Kidder, Peabody. Mr Gastineau is the author of *The Options Manual* (Third Edition, McGraw-Hill, 1998) and co-author of the *Dictionary of Financial Risk Management* (Fabozzi, 1999), as well as numerous journal articles. Mr Gastineau is a frequent speaker on risk management policies and techniques, execution costs and regulatory issues. He serves on the editorial boards of the *Financial Analysts Journal*, the *Journal of Derivatives*, the

Journal of Portfolio Management, Derivatives Quarterly and *Financial Practice and Education*. He is a graduate of both Harvard College and Harvard Business School.

MARK KRITZMAN

Mark Kritzman is Managing Partner of Windham Capital Management Boston, which specializes in currency hedging and asset allocation. Previously, he held investment positions at the Equitable, AT & T, and Bankers Trust Company. Mr Kritzman is a Director of the International Association of Financial Engineers and the Institute for Quantitative Research in Finance. He also serves on the Review Board of the Institute of Chartered Financial Analysts' Research Foundation, and the editorial boards of the *Financial Analysts Journal*, the *Journal of Alternative Investments*, and the *Journal of Derivatives*. He has published numerous articles in academic and professional journals. In 1993 he was a recipient of a Graham and Dodd Award in recognition of an outstanding feature article in the *Financial Analysts Journal*, and in 1997 he received the Inquire Europe 1997 first prize for his research. He is a co-author of *Currency Management: Concepts and Practices, The Dictionary of Financial Risk Management*, and *Quantitative Methods for Financial Analysis*, and the author of *The Portable Financial Analyst* and *Asset Allocation for Institutional Portfolios*. Mr Kritzman has a BS degree from St John's University and an MBA with distinction from New York University.

COLUM McCOOLE

Colum McCoole is an international convertible strategist at Morgan Stanley Dean Witter focusing on Europe, Asia and Japan. Before joining Morgan Stanley (in 1996), he worked for W. I. Carr in Hong Kong on convertible and equity research. McCoole received his MBS from the Smurfit Graduate School of Business, University College Dublin, and a BComm from University College Galway.

WILLIAM T. MOORE

William T. (Ted) Moore is a Professor of Finance with the Darla Moore School of Business, the University of South Carolina, and holder of the David and Esther Berlinberg Chair. His current research interests involve valuation of hybrid securities as well as strategic use of such securities in firms' capital structures. Ted's extensive scholarly research has been published in leading academic journals including the *Journal of Finance*, the *Journal of Financial Economics* and the *Journal of Business*. He has also published a monograph, *Options in Corporate Finance*, for use in a graduate level derivatives course. Recently Ted was named Executive Editor of the *Journal of Financial Research* and he will assume that duty in January 2000. Ted served as a US Army infantryman in Vietnam and is a 1982 graduate of Virginia Polytechnic Institute.

IZZY NELKEN

Izzy is President of Super Computer Consulting Inc. in Chicago which specializes in exotic options, convertible bonds and other complex derivatives. Izzy holds a PhD in Computer Science from Rutgers University and was on the faculty at the University of Toronto. He is editor and co-author of *The Handbook of Exotic Options, Option Embedded Bonds, Volatility in the Capital Markets, Implementing Credit Derivatives* and *Pricing Hedging and Trading Exotic Options.* Izzy teaches numerous courses and seminars around the world on a variety of topics including: credit risk management and credit derivatives exotic options, financial engineering, volatility and correlation and hybrid securities. He is also a lecturer at the prestigious mathematics department at the University of Chicago. Izzy's seminars are known for being non-mathematical. Instead they combine cutting edge analytics with real world applications and intuitive examples.

JOHN POIGNAND

John Poignand, residing in Chatham, MA, is currently an independent Marketing/ Product Consultant for Moody's Investor Services assisting the derivative products group with the launch of a better means of classifying Mutual Funds. John held the position of Vice President of Data Product Management at Interactive Data Corporation. In this capacity he was in charge of the Data Product which included extensive information on Fixed Income instruments. During his 23-year employment with Interactive Data, IDC, John held various positions including: Vice President of International Marketing and Sales, Director of Business Development and Planning, Director of Decision Support financial and econometric applications, and various sales and sales management positions. Prior to leaving Interactive, John was responsible for assessing Interactive's market opportunities within the Fixed Income investment community. John brings a unique prospective that combines extensive data knowledge, knowledge of user community requirements, and knowledge of the strengths and weakness of information sources. He may be reached at *poignand@msn.com*

Introduction

IZZY NELKEN

I.1 GENERAL

This book discusses the so-called "Hybrid Securities". These are essentially bonds with an equity component. The owner of such a security has a position in a bond. The owner is also allowed to trade the bond for a position in equities. In this case, we call the bond a "Convertible". In some cases, the bond holder is obligated to trade the bond for a position in equities. Such bonds are known as "Mandatory Convertibles". There are many different types of hybrid securities. Several of them have very inventive names such as DECS, PERQS, Reverse convertibles, and so on.

Consider, for example, a convertible bond. The convertible pays a fixed coupon and is convertible, by the holder, to a fixed number of shares. In addition to the convertibility feature, the convertible may be callable by the issuer, putable by the investor and may also contain other pertinent features. Similar instruments may be issued in the form of "preferred shares". Some issues contain reset clauses while other issues may have a "negative pledge" clause. Many bonds incorporate a "screw clause" and many issuers may "force conversion" on the investors. The list of possible variations is virtually limitless.

Hybrid instruments hold much promise to investors, issuers and financial institutions alike. For the investor these instruments hold the promise of participation in future equity market rallies. For the issuer, the hybrid may be a cheap source of financing. For the financial institutions, these instruments may be used to create huge returns via specialized hedge funds. Alternatively, the institution may invest its clients' money via an investment management regime or the institution may invest their own capital in such an investment fund. In addition, since these instruments are generally quite complicated to analyze, they may offer some arbitrage opportunities. Taking advantage of these opportunities typically requires analytical prowess as well as trading skills.

A manager of an investment fund once mentioned that there are occasions when he sells convertible bonds to hedge funds. Some of these win/win transactions make sense for both counter parties since they have differing objectives.

It is obvious that there are numerous types of hybrid instruments being used for many purposes by different parties. The field can get quite complicated and, at times, bewildering.

In this book, we have gathered some of the very best experts in the field and asked them to share their knowledge on this fascinating topic.

I.2 IMPORTANCE OF ADEQUATE ANALYSIS

Due to the tremendous complexity and diversity of hybrid instruments, adequate analysis tools are crucial. Quantitative tools are especially important in this market since most issues are not very liquid and it may be difficult to establish an accurate market price. The problem is made even more difficult since the market for hybrid instruments is quite fragmented. Users of hybrid securities come from several groups. On the sell side, users of hybrid security models include:

1. Issuers—these are the companies which issue convertible bonds.
2. Corporate services departments—they advise issuers on the type of options to include in the security.

On the buy side, users of such analytical systems include:

1. Investment managers—they have two main concerns:
   (a) find "attractive" securities;
   (b) build portfolios with limited risk exposures.
2. Hedge funds—they look for arbitrage opportunities between the convertible bond and the common share.

The issuer would like to sell a bond with the lowest possible coupon, highest conversion price, etc. On the other hand, the bond has to be attractive enough to sell. The issuer can look at similar deals that have been done in the past few months. This is not going to be very revealing as stock prices are different, the volatility has changed and probably the interest rate yield curve has shifted.

Investment managers purchase hybrid securities for several reasons:

• Risk averse equity managers purchase hybrids to reduce the risk as compared to a share purchase.
• Income oriented equity managers purchase hybrids due to the fact that the coupon is higher than the dividend rate on the stock.
• Convertible specialists manage funds that specialize in hybrid securities.
• Fixed income bond managers seeking equity "kickers" may buy hybrid securities due to the fact that their price can appreciate much more than a non-convertible bond.

Hedge funds typically invest in hybrid securities since they often allow arbitrage between the hybrid and the underlying common share. Since the market is fragmented and not so liquid, hedge funds feel that there are tremendous profits to be made with hybrids.

The importance of good analytical tools has been recognized early on. Figure I.1 is a replica of a convertible bond calculator circa 1973. This was implemented as a circular slide rule. Of course, the art and science of modeling these instruments has made rapid advancements. The book includes a CD ROM with a sample of the ConvB++ software.

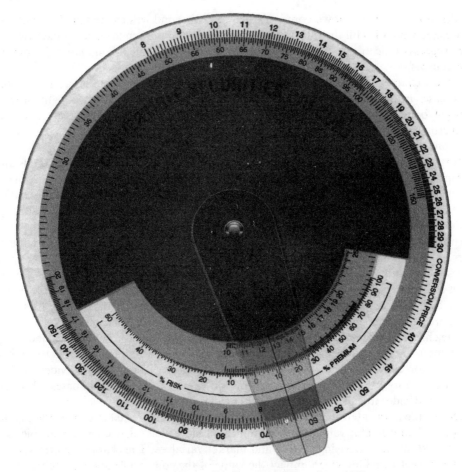

Figure I.1   A convertible bond calculator from 1973

I.3   DESCRIPTION OF THE CHAPTERS

I.3.1   Eswar Badari

Eswar Badari of Morgan Stanley has written a general introduction to hybrid instruments. He has managed to describe the instruments and the markets for them as well as convey an intuitive sense of how they are used by the different parties. He examines in detail the roles of the investor and the issuer and explains the relative advantages and disadvantages obtained by purchasing or issuing convertible bonds. Badari's chapter also contains a short terminology section. A separate part of the chapter is devoted to mandatory convertibles. Badari's chapter briefly describes the different structures and highlights the differences between them.

I.3.2   Anne Coxe

Anne Coxe of Merrill Lynch has allowed us to include the "Convertible Special Report". The report highlights the recent developments in the hybrid markets. It begins by describing the first known convertible bond. This bond was created in 1881 and was associated with J.J. Hill the railroad magnate. The chapter then takes a detailed view of the progress of the market and its evolution to the current $350 billion market for hybrid instruments.

Coxe's chapter begins by analyzing a straightforward convertible issue. This is the base case. In a somewhat simplistic fashion, the convertible can be thought of as a straight bond plus an equity option. Since the investor essentially owns a bond, the convertible provides some protection against stock market declines. On the other hand, the convertibility feature will allow the investor to participate in equity rallies.

It is quite instructive to study the historical return measures of convertible bonds and compare them with historical return measures of other asset classes. It is also possible to compare the volatility of the convertible index with the volatility of other alternative investments. It turns out that on a relative basis, convertible bonds have had high historical returns coupled with low historical volatility numbers. In a sense the convertible is an instrument with equity like returns and fixed income like volatility numbers. The combination of these two facts makes such instruments very appealing to investors. A measure of that appeal is the Sharpe ratio. A high Sharpe ratio indicates an asset class with high excessive returns and low volatility. Historically, convertible bonds have had very respectable Sharpe ratios. The chapter also contains graphics that compare the return on a convertible bond vs. the return on a common stock.

The chapter also describes the various other features related to convertibles, including the famous "screw clause". This clause is common to convertibles and means that when the investor converts, they will not be entitled to accrued interest or dividends. The chapter describes this clause and the confusion caused to investors in cases when the company decides to call the bond in its first call date.

One of the most interesting problems faced by anyone interested in convertibles is the proper valuation. The valuation is complicated since the value of a convertible is a function of many underlying factors and market variables. The chapter describes some of the market variables which impact the value of the convertible and also some of the valuation techniques that have been used by market professionals.

Coxe's chapter describes many of the variations on the basic convertibles: LYONs, TOPrS, MIPS, PERCS, DECS, PRIDES, Feline PRIDES, STRYPES and other security types are described in detail. Valuation methods, accounting and tax implications are also explained. The Ingersoll–Rand Feline PRIDE issue is described and analyzed in detail. This helps explain the theoretical concepts described in the chapter. Finally, the chapter ends with a description of the various acronyms which are so prevalent in the field and a glossary.

I.3.3   William T. Moore

William T. Moore of the University of South Carolina has written a chapter which examines the following three questions:

1.   Does public issuance of convertibles have an effect on the firm value?
2.   What are the effects on the stock price of an issuer of calls on warrants and convertibles?
3.   How do the call provisions impact the price of a convertible?

While these questions are related to convertibles, they are crucial to almost anyone including even plain equity investors. The chapter describes the curious fact that convertibles made up about 40% of debt issuance in 1929 yet almost disappeared from the scene during World War II. In a perfectly frictionless market, the company should not care how it raises funds. However, the markets are not frictionless and the chapter describes the different theories that have been used to describe the effect of various financing methods on an issuing company.

When a company decides to issue a convertible bond, it has to pay underwriting expenses and other fees. However, if the share price declines due to the fact that the company has issued a convertible bond and the information that is conveyed by this issuance, then the cost of the issue is higher than just the direct fees.

The chapter also provides an analysis of when an issuer should call a convertible bond. There is a comparison between what should happen to the underlying stock vs. what actually does happen. This analysis is made difficult by the fact that when an issuer announces an intention to call, the investors have a right to convert their bonds into shares. The issuer must take the conversion right into account. In short, the issuer will not call the bond for cash, but will force conversion on the investors. In practice, there is typically a delay between the call notice and the actual call. That delay averages approximately 30 days. During the 30 days, the underlying share price will fluctuate and may impact the convertible bond holders' decision whether to accept the call or convert into shares.

The chapter also describes the difficulties in assessing the impact of call provisions on the price of a convertible bond. The valuation can get quite tricky, some methods rely on complex binary or even quadranary trees. Other methods involve solution to various partial differential equations. The chapter correctly concludes that no simple model of Warrant value with embedded deferred calls has been made available. Modeling efforts will doubtless continue in the future.

I.3.4   John Poignand

John Poignand has written a chapter which describes one of the dilemmas of convertible bond professionals. Even if a model is available, it still needs much input data. The chapter describes the various data elements which are relevant to convertible bonds.

I.3.5   Lawrence Cavanagh

Lawrence Cavanagh of Value Line has written a chapter that describes the performance of some of their convertible bond indexes. Historical evidence suggests that convertible bond indexes have done very well. The *Value Line Convertible Survey* ranks more than 600 US convertible bonds and 120 warrants. These are ranked by comparison to a theoretical model. In addition, Value Line also ranks common stocks. If the underlying stock is ranked, the convertible is also ranked by a combination of a rich/cheap analysis combined with the stock ranking.

Cavanagh's chapter first describes the convertible bond indexes published by Value Line and then examines the returns of the highly ranked convertibles. The question at hand is the value of the convertible ranking scheme. This is evaluated by comparing the "Especially Recommended Convertibles" index with the "High Risk Group", the

"Above Average Risk Group" and the "Low Risk Group" indexes. Cavanagh's results are quite interesting since they span a substantial historical period of more than 17 years.

I.3.6 Linda Carlisle

Linda Carlisle of White & Case LLP examines the usage of DECS within a tax plan for high net worth individuals. There have been many cases where private individuals received payment in the form of a block of shares. For example, we may think of an entrepreneur whose company has been bought out by a large company. The large company paid the entrepreneur with shares. Now the entrepreneur has a large block of shares of the large company. Such an individual might consider issuing a mandatory convertible bond, such as a DECS, to hedge his exposure to the underlying stock. An integral part of this strategy would be the study of its taxation implications. Carlisle goes on to explain how some of the newer mandatory convertibles have been created mainly as an answer to various provisions of the tax code.

I.3.7 Colum McCoole

Colum McCoole of Morgan Stanley Dean Witter has written a chapter about reset convertible bonds. These have been especially popular in Japan with the issuance of ten jumbo Japanese bank bonds between 1995 and 1998. Rather than having a fixed conversion price, the reset bonds allow the conversion price to reset on specific dates based on the price of the underlying common stock. In some cases, the reset may be both downward and upward. In other cases, the conversion price may only be reset downwards.

In the mid-1990s the Japanese banks were faced with a worsening operating environment and deteriorating capital ratios. The banks faced a need to raise more capital. Conditions in the bond markets were not favorable. Nor were conditions favorable in the equity markets. In order to raise the required capital, the Japanese banks issued convertible bonds. The reset feature was designed to attract investors. At the time, investors were reluctant to buy normal convertible debentures issued by Japanese banks as they were concerned with the possibility of a drop in share prices. The reset feature was designed to alleviate these concerns. McCoole presents three reset convertible bonds as case studies. He uses these case studies to describe the effects, pricing and trading implications of the reset feature.

In summary, the reset convertible was a viable instrument. Even though it was criticized as being too complex, there was adequate issuance and a liquid market with strong turnover was created.

I.3.8 Izzy Nelken

Izzy Nelken (me) of Super Computer Consulting, Inc. has studied reset convertible bonds in detail. These bonds caused massive losses at UBS (formerly, before the merger, Union Bank of Switzerland). These losses were caused due to difficulties in hedging these bonds.

Indeed, at Super Computer Consulting, Inc., we've developed the first (and to date, only) publicly available model for Japanese style reset convertibles. Such bonds cannot be evaluated using standard approaches. The difficulty is that the conversion price changes and fluctuates over time. The conversion price, in fact, depends on the path of prices taken by the common stock. Hence, the reset bond is a "path dependant" derivative. These are known to require special techniques. Using our model, we were able to compare two bonds. One is a normal convertible with a fixed conversion price and the other includes reset clauses. It is interesting to compare the price differences between the two bonds and their delta hedge ratios. It turns out that the reset bond has a negative gamma. The negative gamma was also observed by McCoole in the previous chapter. In this chapter we also look at the difficulties faced by hedge funds when trying to hedge reset convertible bonds. In particular, the hedging activities of these bonds often lead to "short squeezes". In such situations, money making hedge strategies can quickly turn sour and cause big losses.

While discussing convertible bonds, we also mention two curious features of these bonds:

1. The duration of convertible bonds.
2. How correlation affects convertibles.

Consider normal non-convertible bonds. The duration of a high coupon bond will typically be smaller than the duration of a low coupon bond. At the extreme, the duration of a zero coupon bond is equal to its maturity. As the coupon is increased, the duration decreases. Convertible bonds do not exhibit this behavior. High coupons in a convertible may lead to large duration numbers.

This chapter can be seen as a companion chapter to the previous one. While McCoole describes the market for reset convertibles, we concentrate on the modeling aspects of these instruments.

I.3.9 Gary Gastineau

Gary Gastineau of the American Stock Exchange has allowed us to incorporate parts of his glossary in this book. We have taken the items in the glossary which pertain to hybrid instruments and included them. The hybrid instrument field has so many terms and variations, it is quite useful to have them all in one place.

I.3.10 Appendix—ConvB++

There is no question that hybrid securities require special analysis tools. Such software is required to assess fair value prices, hedging parameters and special situations. The book includes a CD ROM with a sample software of ConvB++ one of the leading softwares for hybrid securities. ConvB++ is implemented in Excel and is very easy to use.

I.4 SUMMARY

The hybrid instrument markets are quite challenging. The markets have evolved and so have the analysis tools. This book includes some of the latest thinking on the markets by top-notch experts.

1

Hybrid Instruments: Advantages and Disadvantages

BADARI S. ESWAR

1.1 INTRODUCTION

Convertible Bonds or Hybrid Securities have been in existence for several decades. Over the years the Convertible Securities market has grown to stand on its own today. There is a huge niche for trading in these securities in both domestic (United States) as well as international (Europe, Asia and others) markets. The last few years have seen a tremendous boom in trading activity and product innovation and underwriting, including several billion dollar issues.

Convertible instruments are interesting hybrid securities lying in between Fixed-Income Securities and Equity or Common Stock. By nature they are both Bear Market and Bull Market instruments. They participate in both Fixed-Income as well as Equity Markets. Convertible Bonds are sensitive to interest rate fluctuations and at the same time they are sensitive to stock volatility and moves in the equity market.

Convertible Bonds offer advantages to both the issuers and investors. Issuers are able to finance their debt via Convertible Securities at lower interest rates than via comparable straight debt instruments. Issuing a Convertible Security enables issuers to sell equity at a premium on a deferred basis. Issuers are also able to take certain tax advantages facilitated by Convertible instruments.

Investors are attracted to the dual nature of Convertible Securities. Investors can participate in both Fixed-Income and Equity Markets. The fixed-income nature of the Convertible Securities provides investors with a downside protection while the equity link lets them reap the benefits of upside potential of the underlying stock.

Convertible Securities are interesting and at the same time sophisticated financial instruments. In this chapter we try to explain their nature, their advantages and disadvantages to both the issuers and investors. We also explain the terminology associated with Convertible Securities and finally explain some of the twists introduced into their basic structure by various investment banks in their trademarked products.

1.2 WHAT IS A CONVERTIBLE BOND?

A Convertible Bond is a hybrid financial instrument combining attributes of both fixed-income securities and equity. On the financial instrument spectrum, Convertible Bonds lie somewhere in between pure equity and pure debt instruments.

Handbook of Hybrid Instruments. Edited by Izzy Nelken. © 2000 Badari S. Eswar. Published 2000 by John Wiley & Sons Ltd.

The hybrid nature of a Convertible Bond comes from its Conversion Feature. A Convertible Bond can be converted into the equity of the issuer at any time at the option of the holder. The time period in the life of the bond when it can be so converted, and the number of common shares of the issuer into which it can be converted, are both determined at the time when the bond is issued.

A Convertible Bond pays a Coupon on a Principle. As such it is a debt or fixed-income instrument subject to the effects of interest rate fluctuations in the market as well as to the credit rating of the issuing company. Similar in nature to corporate debt, a Convertible Bond can have a Call Schedule, a Coupon Schedule, a Put Schedule and a Sinking Fund Provision.

Convertible Bonds are usually debentures or preferred shares that are generally convertible into a specified number of common shares of the issuing company. Occasionally a Convertible Bond may be convertible into common shares of a company other than the issuer. In such cases, it is called an Exchangeable Bond. There are also Convertible Bonds in existence which have different kinds of conversions such as conversion into equity plus cash, conversion into straight debt, conversion into units of different currency or currencies and so on.

Convertible Bonds can be structured to take advantage of various market conditions and anticipated moves in the market. They can be structured to meet tax and accounting needs and strategies.

In a simplistic way, a Convertible Bond can be viewed as a combination of a straight debt instrument or bond along with a call option on equity. The holder of a Convertible Bond also in concept holds an option to buy (convert into) a certain number of shares of the company at a specified price (strike price) in a specified period of time (time to expiration). The debt portion of the bond needs to be evaluated just like any other straight bond, subject to the interest rate environment and credit risk. The evaluation of the equity portion of the Convertible Bond is subject to the volatility of the common stock. As such, Convertible Bonds are often classified as an Equity Derivative.

1.3   THE ISSUER

As mentioned before, Convertible Bonds can be structured in a way such that various tax and accounting strategies and needs can be satisfied. As such, Convertible Bonds are attractive financing vehicles.

Convertible Bonds begin life as debt instruments. They appear on a company's balance sheet as debt. They are evaluated as any other straight debt instrument except they pay a much lower coupon owing to the conversion option they offer. Therefore issuers can raise funds at a lower financing rate or interest expense than by issuing straight debt or fixed-income instruments.

Convertible Bond issuance can also be considered as a forward sale of equity at a premium price. Convertible Bonds are priced at a premium to their conversion value or the parity of the bond, which is the current market value of the number of shares of common stock that the bond can convert into. Thus an issuing company is able to raise more funds per issued share compared to an equivalent stock issue.

Thus using a Convertible issue, a company can raise equity capital on a deferred basis. When a company issues equity, it typically increases dilution. When a Convertible Bond is issued, the dilution of equity is postponed until the bonds are converted. Convertible Bonds are issued with the idea of having the bonds converted into equity rather than being redeemed at the time of maturity. Issuers also retain the right to call the bonds when it is advantageous to do so. Bonds are typically called when the market conditions favor conversion into stock, so that the holders opt to convert rather than redeem.

Convertible Bonds also offer certain tax advantages to the issuers. For instance the coupon paid on the Convertible Bonds is considered as and it actually is an interest expense for the company. As such it is tax deductible. On the other hand if a company were to issue stock to raise an equivalent amount of capital and paid dividend on the stock, it is not considered as a tax-deductible expense. As mentioned before, compared to raising equivalent capital via debt issues, Convertible Bonds have lower yields and therefore lower coupon payments than straight debt instruments. Issuing Convertible Bonds thus lowers the gross interest expense for the company.

Starting life on the debt side of the balance sheet, Convertible Bonds move to the equity side when they are converted. When bonds are thus converted, they reduce the debt to equity ratio. However all accounting is done on a fully diluted basis when the bonds are issued.

As mentioned earlier, an issuer of Convertible Bonds actually sells equity at a premium to current market prices, at a future date via the conversion of the bonds. Convertible Bonds usually have lower volatility than the underlying common stock. Dilution is deferred until conversion. The conversion price is adjusted for capital distributions such as stock splits, stock dividend payments and rights issues. In some instances Convertible Bonds also come with a feature to reset the conversion ratio or the conversion price, on certain dates to maintain a premium level. This feature provides a protection against unfavorable stock performance in the market.

Convertible Bonds have the following advantages for the issuer:

1. Reduced interest cost since Convertible Bonds typically have lower yields than equivalent debt securities.
2. Full tax deduction of coupon payments made on outstanding Convertible Bonds when compared to dividend payments on equivalent outstanding stock, which is non-deductible.
3. Equitization of debt, which occurs when Convertible Bonds are converted.
4. Reductions of debt to equity ratio when Convertible Bonds are converted.
5. Forward sale of common stock at a premium price to market value.

1.4 THE INVESTOR

Parity is the market value of the number of common shares a Convertible Bond converts into. In other words it is the product of the conversion ratio and the current market price of the underlying common stock of a Convertible Bond. Investors pay a premium over this parity value. Convertible Bonds are typically priced at a premium over parity at the time they are issued.

Convertible Bonds are similar in characteristics to other Corporate Bonds in that they pay a fixed coupon on a stated principal amount and they have similar cash flows. However due to the fact that they have an embedded option for the investor to convert them into common shares of the company, the coupons on Convertible Bonds are lower when compared to Corporate Bonds of similar maturities. The yield on Convertible Bonds is lower than on similar fixed-income securities.

Thus the premiums investors have to pay over the parity value and the lower fixed-income yield given seem to bias the Convertible Bonds away from the investors. However Convertible Bonds have features that make them attractive investment vehicles to meet different objectives.

Investors in Convertible Bonds are able to participate both in the fixed-income markets and the equity markets. Convertible Bonds are also considered to be both Bear Market as well as Bull Market instruments due to their fixed-income and equity attributes respectively.

Investors in Convertible Bonds can take advantage of the upward potential of the equity part of the bond. Convertible Bonds facilitate perfect hedging of short sale of a well-performing common stock. An investor can short the stock at a price higher than the conversion price of the bond. The conversion feature of the bond covers the short position in stock.

For a well-performing stock, as the stock price appreciates in the market the corresponding Convertible Bond begins to perform like the stock. No doubt investors pay a premium over parity at the time of issue but as the stock appreciates so does the parity and the premium narrows.

The advantage of holding the bond rather than the stock in this scenario comes from the coupon yield of the Convertible Bond. The coupon rates of Convertible Bonds are typically set such that the yield on the bond is much higher than the dividend yield on the underlying common stock. This is known as the yield advantage on the Convertible Bond. Moreover dividend on common stock is paid when declared while the coupon payments are company obligations and are therefore paid periodically without fail. Interest on Convertible Bonds also accrues unlike dividend payments on stock.

Many Convertible Bonds also come with put features. The put feature gives the investor the right to put the bond back to the issuer at a premium over par. With this feature an investor can voluntarily redeem the bonds on certain dates if it is advantageous to do so.

What happens when the stock price declines? At high values the price of the Convertible Bond declines with the decline of the stock price. However when the stock price declines below the conversion price (par value of the bond divided by the conversion ratio), it becomes advantageous to be holding the Convertible Bond rather than the underlying stock. This is due to the fixed-income nature of the bond. A Convertible Bond always retains the value of its fixed-income cash flows. It never trades below its investment value. Thus a Convertible Bond provides the investor with a downside protection. The value of a stock holding can potentially go to zero whereas the value of a Convertible Bond does not go below its investment value.

Thus with a holding in Convertible Bonds, investors can participate in the upside potential of the underlying stock when it performs while enjoying a downside protection when the stock does not perform.

Convertible Bonds are sensitive to the performance of the underlying stock. As the price of the underlying equity increases, the sensitivity of the bond to the stock price increases. When the stock price declines, the sensitivity of the bond to the stock price decreases until it reaches the investment value when the performance of the bond does not depend on the stock price anymore. For equal moves in the price of the underlying stock, the price of the Convertible Bond increases more on the upside than it decreases on the downside. This is known as the Favorable Leverage of Convertible Bonds.

Convertible Bonds have superior risk/return profiles to those of common stock. Convertible Bonds generally have a lower volatility than the underlying stock and they have higher yields than the dividend paid out on common shares. In addition Convertible Bonds typically enjoy a call protection feature. Convertible Bonds are usually not called in the first few years of their existence and then they are called when the stock has performed at a certain premium level compared to issue prices for a certain number of days. Some Convertible Bonds also have a put feature, which lets the investors redeem the bonds at a premium to par on certain dates. Investors put the bonds back to the issuer when it is to their advantage to do so.

Convertible Bonds, since they are debt instruments, are ranked higher in the corporate pecking order in case of a bankruptcy. As debt obligations they are senior to preferred stock and common stock.

Thus investors in Convertible Bonds have the following advantages:

1. A positive differential in yield over common stock.
2. Participation in the upside potential of the common stock since a holder can convert a bond into stock at any time.
3. Downside protection provided by the fixed-income value of the bond in case the stock plummets.
4. Seniority to preferred stock and common stock in case of default.

1.5 TERMINOLOGY

1.5.1 Par Value

The par value or the face value of a Convertible Bond is what the investor is paid on redemption at maturity. This is typically $1000 for coupon bonds and $25 or $50 for Convertible Preferred shares. The par value is also used as the basis for calculating coupon and dividend payments and yields.

1.5.2 Maturity Date

The maturity date of a Convertible Bond is the stated date on which all outstanding bonds are redeemed and the contract between the issuer and the investor expires. Convertible Preferred Shares often have perpetual maturity.

1.5.3 Coupon Rate

The coupon rate is the stated percentage of the par value that is paid to the investors on the days the coupon is due. Typically coupons are paid semi-annually. Coupon rates are typically lower than equivalent straight bond coupons and are set so that the yield is higher than the dividend yield on the underlying common stock.

Convertible Preferred Shares have a stated dividend instead of a coupon. Dividend is stated as a percentage of par value or in dollar amount and is termed the dividend yield. Dividends are typically paid every quarter.

1.5.4 Yield to Maturity

Yield to maturity is the single rate of interest that would make the sum of all the present values of all the cash flows of the bond equal to its current price.

Often when Convertible Bonds have put features or call features associated with them, it is the practice to calculate the yield assuming the put date (yield to put) or call date (yield to call) is the date on which the bond will cease to exist. The final cash flow for calculating these would then be the put price or the call price instead of par.

1.5.5 Issue Price

The issue price is the price at which a Convertible Bond is sold by the issuer to the investors on the date of issue. This price is usually equal to the par value of the bond. For zero coupon bonds the issue price is a function of the time to maturity, accretion rate and the compounding frequency.

On the day of the issue, the issue price is set. If this is set to the par value of the bond then the conversion ratio is set for the bond so that the bond is priced at a premium to the parity value. The issue price or the conversion ratio is typically set at the end of the trading activity in the markets and is set at a premium to the par value as calculated at the closing price of the common stock.

1.5.6 Conversion Ratio

An investor in a Convertible Bond can exchange the bond for a stated number of common shares of the issuing company. This predetermined number of common shares a bond converts into is called the Conversion Ratio.

$$Conversion\ Ratio = Issue\ Price\ /\ Stock\ Price\ (1 + Premium)$$

When an investor converts a Convertible Bond into common shares, the cash flow due to the coupon payments ceases, the investor in the bond becomes a holder of common stock in the company and thus becomes eligible to receive dividend payments on stock when declared.

1.5.7 Conversion Price

When an investor converts a Convertible Bond into common stock, a certain number of shares are received in lieu of the par amount on the bond. The price per share of this number of shares that the investor effectively pays is termed the Conversion Price.

$$Conversion\ Price = Par\ Value\ /\ Conversion\ Ratio$$

1.5.8   Current Yield

The Current Yield on the bond is defined to be the annual coupon divided by the current price of the bond in the market.

Current Yield = Coupon Amount / Bond Price

1.5.9   Dividend Yield

Dividend Yield is defined as the annual total dividend paid divided by the current market price of the common stock.

Dividend Yield = Annual Dividend / Stock Price

1.5.10   Yield Differential

One of the advantages of investing in Convertible Bonds rather than in the underlying common stock is that the yield on the bond is typically set to be higher than the dividend yield on common stock. The difference between the yield on the bond and the dividend on the common stock is called the Yield Differential. This, when positive, is also known as the Yield Advantage of a Convertible Bond.

*Yield Differential = Current Yield on the Bond / Dividend Yield on Common Stock =
(Coupon Rate / Bond Price) / (Dividend / Stock Price)*

1.5.11   Parity

The market value of the number of common shares obtained by the conversion of a Convertible Bond is called the Parity Value of the bond. This is also known as the Equity Parity of the bond. An investor can convert a bond and immediately sell the common stock in the market at the market price of the stock and thus receive the parity value of the bond.

Parity Value = Market Price of Stock × Conversion Ratio

1.5.12   Premium over Parity

As mentioned earlier, Convertible Bonds have certain advantages over common stock holdings. Because of these advantages Convertible Bonds trade at a premium over the value of an equivalent number of common stock, i.e., parity. This is called the Premium over Parity of a Convertible Bond.

Premium over Parity = [(Bond Price/Parity) – 1] × 100

1.5.13   Investment Value

If the bond were not convertible into common stock, a Convertible Bond would trade similar to an equivalent Corporate Bond. As such, the equivalent value for the Convertible Bond, with no regards to the conversion feature, is known as the Investment Value. A Convertible Bond typically never trades below this value. Also known as the Bond Floor, it defines the downside protection for the investor.

It is simple to calculate the bond value of a Convertible Bond, provided there are no call or put features associated with the bond. The value of such a bond would be simply the sum of all the present values of all the cash flows from the bond. Call and put features somewhat complicate the valuation of a bond.

1.5.14 Premium over Investment Value

Due to the conversion feature associated with them, Convertible Bonds typically trade at a higher price compared to equivalent (similar coupon, maturity and credit risk) non-convertible Corporate Bonds. In other words they trade at a premium to their investment or bond value. The difference between the price of a Convertible Bond and its investment value is termed as the Premium over Investment Value.

1.5.15 Accrued Interest

Accrued interest represents the amount of interest due to an investor to the current date from the date of the last coupon payment. Typically a buyer of a bond pays the seller the accrued interest, since the coupon payment is made to the holder (buyer) on record on the next coupon date. It is important to note that in the case of a Convertible Bond, accrued interest is almost always forfeited upon conversion. This is the infamous Screw Clause. Therefore when calculating the conversion value of a Convertible Bond, it makes sense to subtract the amount of interest accrued. Conversion value less the accrued interest is termed as the Net Conversion Value.

1.5.16 Call Feature

Often Convertible Bonds have call features, which provide the issuer a way to force conversion at a stipulated price or redemption of the bonds. When the conversion value of a Convertible Bond is higher than the call price, the issuer can issue a call notice. But for the investors it would be advantageous to convert to stock. An investor can convert a bond into stock and sell the stock immediately in the market at the market price to receive the parity value rather than let the issuer redeem the bonds at the call price, which would be lower than the parity value. Thus conversion is enforced.

An issuer can also call and redeem the bonds in order to reduce the debt equity ratio of the company. During periods of declining interest rates, bonds can be called since an issuer is then able to refinance at lower interest rates.

1.5.17 Call Protection

Call features if present reduce the value of a Convertible Bond to the investor. In order to make a callable Convertible Bond more attractive to the investors, Convertible Bonds come often with what are termed Call Protection features. Convertible Bonds with associated call schedules come with a stipulation that the bonds may not be called for a certain number of years. This period is called the Call Protection period. Longer call protection periods extend the life of the conversion feature and thus increases their value.

When a Convertible Bond is stipulated to be non-callable for a certain number of years, typically two to five years, it is known as a Hard Call Protection or Absolute Call Protection.

Convertible Bonds also have what are known as Provisional or Soft Call Protection. This stipulates that a Convertible Bond is callable provided that the underlying stock trades in the market at a certain level for a predetermined number of days. The equity price level is usually set at 130–150% of the conversion price.

In addition call schedules are set with a call notice period. Typically once the call notice is given, the investors have 30 days in which to convert before the issuer redeems the bonds at the call price.

1.5.18 Put Feature

If a Convertible Bond has a put feature, an investor in the bond can redeem the bond with the issuer at the predetermined put price which is usually at a premium to the par value of the bond. The investor is thus guaranteed to earn the yield to put. Thus a put feature also provides a downside protection to the bond holder.

1.5.19 Payback Period

Investors pay a premium for Convertible Bonds over the price of the common stock. Convertible Bonds do have an income advantage over common stock. However given a yield, it takes some number of years for this income advantage to offset the premium paid. This period of time, in years, is called the Payback period or Break-even period of the Convertible Bond. This is also known as the premium recovery period.

Break-even = (Convertible Bond Price – Parity) / (Current Yield – Dividend Yield) × (1/Convertible Bond Price)

1.6 CONVERTIBLE INSTRUMENTS

Over the years Convertible Bonds have come to be an asset class of their own. The Convertible market has shown tremendous growth. This has resulted in a boom in trading and underwriting activities and in product innovation. A number of varieties of Convertible Instruments have been structured and trademarked by various Investment Banks. Each of these products have their own names and their own twists on a few basic structures.

It is worthwhile to remember that depending upon various factors, a Convertible Bond behaves in different ways. If a Convertible Bond has a small premium over equity and a low coupon yield, it will be more sensitive to the fluctuations in the equity market and will resemble the underlying stock more closely. Such a Convertible Bond is considered to be an Equity Alternative.

On the other hand, a Convertible Bond with a high coupon rate and a large premium over equity value will be more sensitive to the fluctuations in the interest rates and moves in the fixed-income markets. Such a Convertible Bond is considered to be a Fixed-income Alternative.

A Convertible Bond with a moderate coupon rate priced at a moderate premium over equity value will be sensitive to both the equity market moves and interest rate fluctuations. Such a Convertible Bond can be said to be a true hybrid instrument.

C O R P O R A T E B O N D S	Convertible Bonds			Convertible Preferred		C O M M O N S T O C K
	Zero Coupon Bonds	Original Issue Discount Bonds	Coupon Paying Bonds	Perpetual Convertible Preferred Stock	Mandatory Convertible Preferred Stock (PERCS & DECS)	

Figure 1.1   Convertible Bond Spectrum

In spite of the numerous trademarked brand name products marketed by various investment banks, all Convertible Bonds fall under a few basic structures. Almost all investment banks have added twists to these basic structures to give them their own identity. The basic structures vary from bond like structures to those that are more or less equivalent to common stock (Figure 1.1).

1.6.1   LYONs

Zero Coupon Convertible Bonds as the name suggests have no periodic coupon payments. Invented as Low Yield Option Notes (LYONs) by Merrill Lynch & Co., zero coupon bonds are the most fixed-income like convertible structures. Typically they are priced at 10–20% premium over parity, with 15–20 years maturity. They are generally putable at 5 year intervals and have a 5 year Hard Call Protection. Again there are no coupon payments made to the investor. However the bonds are issued at a discount and they accrete to the par value ($1000) at maturity. Thus they can be said to have an effective coupon or yield rate. Accretion is treated as income and is taxed.

1.6.2   OID Bonds

Original Issue Discount Convertible Bonds, like LYONs, are issued at a discount and accrete to par at maturity. But unlike zero coupon bonds, they pay a stipulated coupon. The yield is typically lower than regular coupon paying bonds. The fixed-income nature of the OID Convertible Bonds comes partially from the coupon payments and partially from accretion. Again accretion and the coupon payments are both taxable incomes to the investor.

1.6.3   Convertible Debentures

Regular coupon paying Convertible Bonds or Debentures have the simplest structures. They most resemble a Corporate Debt. They have a stipulated coupon rate and a coupon frequency. They have Call Protection periods and call notice periods associated with their call schedules. They may also have put features and sinking fund provisions.

1.6.4 Step-up Bonds

Step-up Convertible Bonds lie between OID Bonds and regular Coupon Paying Convertible Bonds. The difference is simple to understand. After a certain predetermined period of time in the life of the Convertible Bond, the coupon rate is adjusted to a higher rate. If this is a downward adjustment then it is called a Step-down Convertible Bond. Typically this is scheduled on the same date as the first call date for the bond.

If the underlying stock of the Convertible Bond has been gaining in the market, the issuer has the option to call the bond and either force a conversion or redemption. Thus the issuer can avoid paying a higher coupon. It is the same case in a declining interest rate environment. An issuer can call the bonds and refinance them at a lower expense than start paying the higher coupon.

1.6.5 Eurodollar Convertible Bonds

Eurodollar Convertible Bonds are simply Convertible Bonds issued either by domestic (US) or foreign companies and sold outside the United States. They are very similar to other Convertible Bonds when issued by a domestic issuer except that they need not be registered. They may not be sold to US investors before a 40-day seasoning after the issue date. Coupon payments are typically annual rather than semi-annual. Almost all Eurodollar Convertible Bonds issues come with a US Rule 144A tranche so that they can be marketed in the domestic side as well.

The important factor to remember about the Eurodollar Convertible Bonds is that the principal and coupon payments are not subject to currency risks for US investors since they are both denominated in US dollars. Conversion however could be subject to currency fluctuations since the issuing company may or may not be a US company and as such the stock may or may not be denominated in US dollars.

1.6.6 Perpetual Convertible Preferred Stock

Perpetual Convertible Preferred Stock as the name suggests has no maturity date. They have a stipulated dividend rate either stated as a percentage of par or as a dollar value. The par value is usually $25 or $50. Perpetual Convertible Preferred Stock behaves more or less like coupon paying Convertible Bonds.

1.6.7 PERCS

Preferred Equity Redemption Cumulative Stock can be looked upon as a combination of holding a share of common stock and selling a long dates call option on it. Typically PERCS have a three-year maturity. At the end of three years, they convert mandatorily to common stock. There is a cap on the upside potential which is set to 30–35% and the initial yield advantage is set at 3–4% over the common stock. PERCS are priced at the market closing price of common stock on the date of issue. They are also callable at the option of the issuer with the call price payable in common shares. Dividend is paid on a quarterly cumulative basis. PERCS are also known as capped convertibles.

PERCS convert into one share of the common stock upon conversion subject to stock splits and stock dividends.

1.6.8 DECS

Dividend Enhanced Convertible Stocks are Convertible Preferred Shares that can be converted into common stock at any time at a premium, at the option of the investor. DECS convert mandatorily into common stock at maturity.

DECS typically have three or four years to maturity with a two- or three-year hard call protection. Conversion premiums are set at 20% or 25%. Yield advantage of DECS are usually at 5–6% above their underlying stock dividend rates and 2–3% above preferred stock dividends paid by the same issuer. DECS are also set to give the coupon at a quarterly frequency typically on the same date when common dividend is paid.

The issue price is set to be the same as the closing price of the common stock in the market on the issue date. The conversion of DECS is a function of the price of the common stock on maturity date. DECS can be said to have two conversion ratios, a maximum and a minimum. The maximum conversion ratio is 1, in the sense that a DECS instrument would convert into exactly one share of the common. The minimum conversion ratio is set as follows:

Minimum Conversion Ratio = 1 / (1 + Initial Conversion Premium)

On maturity date, if the price of the common is below the initial price of the DECS instrument then it will convert into one share of the common. If the price of the common stock is above the conversion price then it will convert into the number of shares of common given by the minimum conversion ratio. If on the other hand the price of the common stock is in between the initial price and the conversion price then the conversion is set on a sliding scale designed to give the investor the number of common shares equal in value to exactly the initial price.

An investor in a DECS instrument has the option to convert into common shares at any time before the maturity date when the conversion becomes mandatory. If converted before the maturity date, the number of shares of common it converts into is given by the minimum conversion ratio.

1.6.9 Other Convertible Structures

There are several other convertible structures in the market brought out by various investment banks. They are all designed to meet advantage of tax and accounting needs and strategies of issuers but at the same time give the investors alternative investment conduits. Most of them however behave in a similar manner either to PERCS or DECS and are in fact different flavors of these two structures. Table 1.1 enumerates some of these structures.

Table 1.1   Mandatory Convertible Preferred Securities

	DECS		PERCS
ACES	Automatically Convertible Equity Securities	CHIPS	Common-linked Higher Income Participating Securities
PRIDES	Preferred Redeemable Increased Dividend Equity Securities	ELKS	Equity Linked Securities
MARCS	Mandatory Adjustable Redeemable Convertible Securities	EYES	Enhanced Yield Equity Securities
		MCPDPS	Mandatory Conversion Premium Dividend Preferred Stock
PEPS	Preferred Equity Participation Securities	TARGETS	Targeted Growth Enhanced Term Securities
SAILS	Stock Appreciation Income Linked Securities	YEELDS	Yield Enhanced Equity Linked Debt Securities
TAPS	Threshold Appreciation Price Securities	YES	Yield Enhanced Stock
TIMES	Trust Issued Mandatory Exchange Securities		
TRACES	Trust Automatic Common Exchange Securities		

1.7   SUMMARY

Convertible Bonds are hybrid financial instruments that have both fixed-income and equity attributes. Convertible Bonds provide interesting and sophisticated financial strategies both for issuers and for investors. The equity link embedded in the Convertible products provides them with an upside potential in the stock performance in the equity markets. The fixed-income attributes provide a protection on the downside against a decline in the stock price. Thus Convertible products facilitate superior risk return profiles for equity investors.

2

Convertible Structures: Evolution Continues

T. ANNE COXE

2.1 CONVERTIBLE BONDS AND PREFERREDS: HYBRID VIGOR

The first convertible bond issue is associated with J.J. Hill, the railroad magnate, in 1881. Hill believed that the market was ascribing too much risk to his rail project and needed an innovative way to secure long term financing. Unwilling to sell stock until his planned expansion had reaped financial rewards, yet shut out from the traditional debt market, Hill issued a convertible bond. Obviously, since that time, there has been considerable growth and innovation in the convertible market which is now over $350 billion world-wide. However, convertibles still fulfill the same financing need they did in Hill's day. Convertibles provide a way for companies whose stocks are volatile to access the debt market.

As we shall see, convertibles can be thought of as roughly equivalent to a fixed income investment combined with a warrant on the issuer's stock. As a rule, debt investors exact a high toll for risk. In practice, this means they will demand a higher coupon from an issuer whose business they perceive as risky or volatile. If managers of such firms cannot convince investors to reevaluate the level of risk in their business, they will have to bear interest costs on straight debt higher than their own expectations would warrant. The appeal of a convertible is that, as a hybrid security, it combines features of a straight debt instrument with those of an equity warrant. As such, the different estimates of the

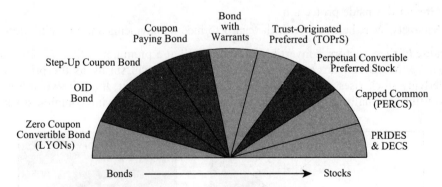

Figure 2.1 The convertible spectrum

Handbook of Hybrid Instruments. Edited by Izzy Nelken. Published 2000 by John Wiley & Sons Ltd. Reprinted by permission.
© 1999, 2000 Merrill Lynch, Pierce, Fenner & Smith Incorporated.

issuer's risk are relatively unimportant to the value of a convertible. The more volatile the business the more the warrant portion is worth, and the less volatile the more the bond portion is worth. So even if investors and management cannot agree on the risk of the issuing firm, they will be able to come to terms on the proper price for a convertible bond or preferred.

Many different customized convertible structures now exist, each tailored to fit the characteristics of specific issuers and investors. However, the basic premise that led to the initial development of convertibles has also driven these later innovations. They are essentially variations on a theme.

In this report, we will discuss the features and valuation of the various convertible securities found in the US market. Our discussion of "plain vanilla" convertibles will serve as a springboard for our analysis of the more exotic flavors of convertible financing.

2.1.1 Introduction

Convertible Bonds and convertible preferreds are fixed income securities that may be exchanged at any time for a fixed number of shares of common stock. This exchange, or conversion, feature is the primary driver of the performance for these securities. For this reason, convertibles are generally regarded as equity surrogates despite their obvious fixed income structure. In the simplest sense, the convertible "package" can be thought of as a bond or preferred stock plus a long term warrant to purchase common stock.

Convertibles by nature are hybrid securities. The fixed income aspect of the security provides downside support, sometimes referred to as a "bond floor", while the embedded warrant supplies the potential for participation with the common stock's gains. In practice, the fixed income component is not an absolute floor, because it will shift in relation to the general level of interest rates and the company's credit quality. The warrant portion is also subject to early termination since it is an embedded security and subject to refinancing risk after call protection expires.

In comparison with their underlying common stock, convertibles generally provide:

- Higher current yield
- Greater downside protection
- Seniority over the common with regard to income payments and in liquidation

Because of these factors, convertibles normally sell at a premium to their *intrinsic value* or *parity*. Moreover, this premium is not constant; it will shrink as the price of the underlying stock rises and expands as it declines. As a result, the price volatility of a convertible is usually dramatically lower than that of its underlying common stock.

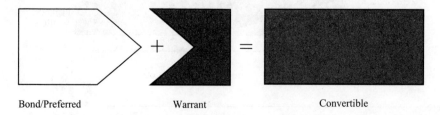

Bond/Preferred   Warrant   Convertible

Figure 2.2 Simplified convertible spectrum

2.1.2 Convertible Historical Returns

In terms of total returns, convertibles have shown considerable hybrid vigor. Figure 2.3 compares long term returns of convertibles, the S&P 500 and High Grade Bonds. Convertibles' returns have largely kept pace with those of stocks while vastly outdistancing those of bonds. The returns of convertibles over this period are more impressive when one adjusts for the relative volatility of convertibles and stocks.

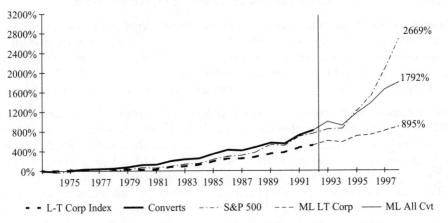

Figure 2.3 Cumulative total returns of stock, bonds and convertibles from 12/73 to 12/98

Table 2.1 Sharpe Ratio analysis

Dec 1989 through Dec 1998	Annual return (%)	Standard deviation (%)	Sharpe Ratio*
All Convertibles V0A0	13.21	8.48	0.93
All Invest Grade Converts V0A1	12.80	8.15	0.92
All Spec Grade Converts V0A2	14.42	9.18	0.99
S&P 500	17.87	12.79	0.98
Russell 2000	12.54	14.26	0.51
ML Corporate & Govt. Master Index	8.83	5.67	0.62

$$^*\text{Sharpe Ratio} = \frac{\text{Total Return} - \text{Risk Free Rate}}{\text{Standard Deviation}}$$

Risk Free Return = 5.32%

2.1.3 General Convertible Description

Convertible bonds and convertible preferreds share the basic fixed income structures of their namesakes—a fixed coupon or dividend rate, priority in regard to income and liquidation, a fixed maturity (for bonds), early redemption provisions, anti-takeover features (frequently) and put options or sinking funds (occasionally). In addition, of course, they are convertible for stock.

Typically they have the following terms:

Conversion Privilege—The conversion privilege is usually described in terms of a conversion price or a conversion ratio (number of shares obtainable by converting one share of preferred of one $1000 bond). When initially sold, the conversion price may be set anywhere from 15% to 30% above the market price of the underlying common stock, with 20–25% the most common range. Conversion, at the option of the investor, is usually permitted at any time during the life of the issue.

Coupon—Coupon and dividend rates are generally set below what the issuer would have to pay in the non-convertible market typically 300–400 bps below. The coupon or dividend rate averages 400 to 600 bps above that of the common stock.

Maturity—Convertible bonds had initial maturities of twenty years or longer as recently as the early 1980s. Today, seven years has become the most common maturity and almost none have been issued with maturities beyond ten years. Convertible preferreds are normally perpetual but a number of recent issues have included mandatory redemption features, effectively setting a "maturity date" of as short as ten years after issue.

Call Protection—Call protection was rarely included in convertible securities prior to 1982. In the early '80s, several issues were redeemed within less than a year of issue. A few were redeemed before they had been outstanding for six months, with the result that not even one coupon was paid before investors were forced to convert in order to maximize returns. Soon after, call protection became a standard feature.

Restrictions on the issuer's right to call a convert come in two forms, which sometimes are combined in the same issue. *Hard call protection* (most common) simply prohibits redemption under any circumstances. *Provisional or "soft" call protection* prohibits redemption unless the underlying common reaches a certain threshold price level. For example, redemption might be prohibited unless the closing price of the underlying stock was at least 150% of the conversion price for any 20 out of 30 consecutive trading days. The length of call protection is most often three years, but it may range from two to five years. Like other terms, this is subject to change with market conditions.

Sinking Fund—Through a sinking fund the issuer retires a portion of the issue before maturity according to a fixed schedule. The most common types of sinking funds are through open market purchases and by lottery. The issuer redeems the bonds in the open market by purchasing them on prearranged dates. On the other hand, when the bonds are redeemed by lottery they can be selected at random. Ordinarily bonds redeemed through lottery are redeemed at face value. While sinking funds tend to support bond prices they serve to reduce the value of the conversion feature.

Subordination—The vast majority of convertible bonds are *subordinated debt*, ranking junior to any senior debt, whether existing or prospective. Subordinated debt has a lower priority with regard to payment of interest or principal. *Convertible preferred*, as a type of equity, ranks below all debt but ahead of common stock in the capital structure. In most cases, it ranks equally with other preferred stocks. *Preference stock* generally ranks below other preferreds. Preferreds may be further stratified using the designations "*junior*" or "*second*", or if the terms of another series of preferred give it priority.

Taxation—As a general rule, conversion is not a taxable event. An investor's basis in the convertible is carried over to the stock received upon conversion. The main exception to this is for "*exchangeable*" convertibles, where conversion is into stock of a different corporation than the issuer. In addition, conversion into a package of stock and cash, or stock and bonds, is taxable with regard to the non-stock portion of the package.

2.1.4 Valuation

The valuation of convertibles can get quite complex as one weighs conversion premium against yield advantage, taking into account the remaining call protection, the credit quality of the issue and the merits of the underlying stock. For this reason, Merrill Lynch has developed a valuation model that combines the stock's volatility and dividend rate and the appropriate credit spread to derive a theoretical value for the convertible. In this way, we are able to combine the various factors that influence a convertible's value.

The factors which influence the Bond/Preferred component are:

- Interest rates
- Credit rating/spreads
- Coupon
- Duration

The factors which influence the Warrant component are:

- Stock performance
- Embedded strike price
- Common dividend yield and dividend growth rate
- Stock volatility
- Life of warrant/call protection

Historical Valuation Methods

One traditional method for valuing converts is to calculate a *"payback"* period, which is the length of time, in years, required to recoup the conversion premium through the income advantage of the convertible. Sometimes useful as a quick "rule-of-thumb" type of calculation, it also has its flaws. It fails to take into account changes in the common dividend and ignores the time value of money. In addition, when referred to as *"breakeven"*, it becomes even more misleading, for the total returns of the convert and its underlying common will only be equal if, in addition to the common dividend remaining constant, their prices remain unchanged for the calculated number of years.

2.1.5 Return Profile

Figures 2.4 to 2.7 present total return profiles for a convertible bond and a convertible preferred over a one year and three year horizon. Generally it is not in the investor's best interest to convert early and thereby give up the additional yield and seniority over the common. However, if the common stock's dividend has grown enough since issuance to outstrip that of the convertible early conversion may be optimal. In the vast majority of cases the issuer calls the convertible at a slight premium to par once the parity value is 10–20% above the call price. This effectively "forces" the holder to convert into common stock. Thus, the point at which call protection expires, usually three years from issuance, becomes critical.

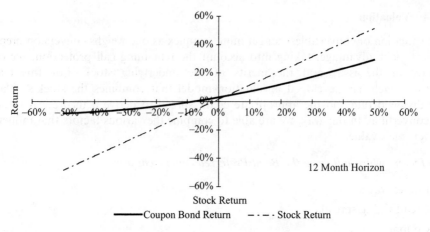

Figure 2.4   Coupon convertible bonds vs. stock total returns: one year horizon

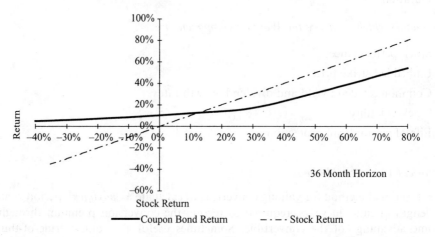

Figure 2.5   Coupon convertible bonds vs. stock total returns: three year horizon

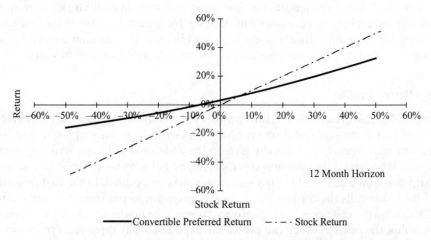

Figure 2.6   Convertible preferreds vs. stock total returns: one year horizon

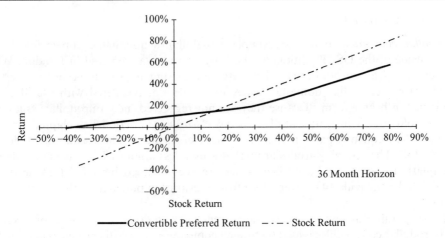

Figure 2.7   Convertible preferreds vs. stock total returns: three year horizon

2.1.6   Convertible Bond Variations

Original Issue Discount Convertibles

Original Issue Discount (OID) convertible bonds have below-market coupon levels and are offered at a steep discount to their par (or face) value. The most extreme version of an OID is the LYON or zero coupon convertible bond (discussed later in this report). In between the zero coupon and the full coupon, almost any combination of coupon and discount is possible. In recent years, we have seen a 6.55% coupon offered at 79.5% of par and a 1.125% coupon offered at 55.36% of par. The deeper the discount, the more LYONs-like the bond becomes. *Unlike LYONs, OID bonds usually do not have put options.*

The bond component of return on an OID convert comes partly from the coupon and partly from accretion of the discount. Upon conversion, the accretion is not paid, so realization of this portion of total return becomes an either/or situation. Either the stock appreciates faster than the growth in accreted value, or the accretion is paid at maturity or earlier redemption. The steeper the initial discount, the more significant this accretion factor becomes. The accretion of OID is treated as ordinary income and is taxable, just as with a LYON.

Step-Up Convertible Bonds

In the convertible security spectrum, *Step-Up* converts lie between Coupon Pay bonds and OID bonds. The distinguishing feature of these bonds is straightforward; after a certain period of time, the initial interest rate is stepped up to a higher rate. In most cases, this is scheduled to occur at the first call date. If the stock has performed well since the convert was issued, the bond may be called to *"force"* *conversion* and the issuer never has to pay the higher coupon. If the stock has not risen sufficiently to force conversion, the higher coupon may provide an incentive to the issuer to refinance. For tax purposes, Step-Up bonds are considered to have imbedded OID, creating a situation where there is ordinary income subject to tax even though it has not been received in cash form. Generally, this is a smaller amount than for most OID bonds.

Eurodollar Convertibles

Eurodollar convertible bonds are simply US dollar denominated convertible bonds sold outside of the US. Traditionally the Euro market was centered in London. When offered by US corporations, they are quite similar to domestic convertible bonds. However, unlike domestic issues, Euros are not registered with the SEC and are issued in bearer form. Because they are not registered, new Eurodollar issues may not be sold to US investors until a 40 day *"seasoning"* period has elapsed. Interest coupons are frequently paid on an annual basis versus the standard semi-annual domestic schedule. The "pure" Eurodollar market is used less often by US issuers now than in the 1980s. Today, most Eurodollar issues are accompanied by a US tranche that is offered under the Rule 144A exemption from registration pursuant to the Securities Act of 1933.

US corporate Euro issues involve no currency risk to dollar based investors. Neither do Eurodollar convertibles issued by foreign companies as regards principal and interest payments. However, the value of the conversion feature is subject to the currency risks associated with foreign stock markets.

Bonds with Warrants

If, as we have seen, it is reasonable to think of a convertible as a package consisting of a bond plus a warrant, why not create a security where the warrant is separable rather than embedded in the package? As a matter of fact, this has frequently been done, though the structure has never become widely popular. In its most common form, this structure pairs a bond with enough warrants to make the strike price times the number of warrants per bond equal to par of $1000. In addition, the terms of the issue often provide that the bonds may be applied to payment of the strike price and are valued at par when so used. *"Usable bonds"* is the term applied to such bonds. Viewed as a package, such a security is equivalent to a standard convertible bond, though the warrant may expire before the maturity of the bond.

In the secondary market, the pieces will also trade in separate markets—the *"ex-warrant"* bonds may appeal to fixed income investors, while the warrants will likely be of interest to investors in the options market. The unit is usually offered at par and the separated bond becomes an OID bond with issue price equal to par, minus the value of the warrants originally attached to it.

2.1.7 Additional Security Provisions

Change of Control Provisions

The mergers and takeovers of the 1980s exposed a gap in the protective features of the traditional convertible structure. This was most evident in cash mergers when the convert was selling well below par. In such cases, the provisions existing at the time simply adjusted the conversion feature by multiplying the conversion ratio by the merger price per share of stock. Thus, for example, a bond selling at 75 with a conversion value of 45 might have its conversion value boosted to 60 by a merger, but with all the value represented by cash so that future equity participation was canceled out. The bond would then trade as a straight bond and, depending on coupon, maturity and credit rating, might even fall in price from its pre-merger level.

As a result, various forms of *"poison puts"* were added and have become a common, if not universal, feature. The goal of these provisions is to allow the investor to exit a position at par in the event of mergers that are potentially harmful to the conversion option. There are several variations. Generally, poison puts are triggered by a *"Change of Control"*, in which a third party obtains either 50% or over 50% voting control of the company. Some simply provide for a cash put at par plus accrued interest; others aim to adjust the ratio so that parity will equal par. An all-stock merger usually does not trigger a put, nor does a merger in which conversion parity exceeds par just before the merger. Initially, poison puts only applied to hostile takeovers, but over time, they have been modified so that friendly mergers are covered as well. Because complete standardization has not yet been achieved, each issue needs to be looked at individually.

The Infamous "Screw Clause"

Most convertible investors are familiar with the provision that says *"upon conversion, no adjustment will be made for interest or dividends."* In plain English this means that when you convert, you don't get the income accrued since the last payment. Exceptions to this are extremely rare. An investor can avoid serious injury from this provision by timing. Confusion and difficulty arise most often at the first call date if the convert is in the money and the company decides to call it in order to "force" conversion. For most bonds and many preferreds, the first call date coincides with an interest/dividend payment date. What are some of the pitfalls?

- Early expiration of the conversion privilege. It is not uncommon for the conversion right to expire one or more days before the redemption date.
- Conversion before the pay date. Many issues require that if conversion takes place between a record date and a pay date, the interest/dividend that will be received has to be repaid to the company.

In combination, these two requirements create a kind of Catch-22 situation: (1) if you wait to receive your interest, you forfeit a valuable conversion feature, or (2) if you convert, you lose your interest. Investors may reasonably object if the bond that they thought had three years of call protection turns out to have only 2.5 years with regard to interest payments. In response, many convertible issues now include wording that effectively cancels out the *"screw" provisions* at the first call date. But some do not and the above example does not necessarily exhaust legal creativity. So, read the prospectus. Forewarned is forearmed.

Anti-dilution Provisions

Most convertibles protect the convertible investor in the event of actions on the company's part which might dilute their equity interest. These can include issues of equity at a discount (e.g. rights issues), scrip issues, subsidiary spin-offs, stock splits or one-time extraordinary dividends. The convertible ratio is usually adjusted upwards, pro rata the convertible investor's theoretical loss, in such events.

2.2   LYONs: A BREED APART

Liquid Yield Option Notes (LYONs) were developed and introduced by Merrill Lynch in early 1985. To create LYONs, the standard convertible bond was redesigned in two important respects: (1) the bonds were reconfigured as deep discount zero coupon instruments; and (2) one or more put options were added. The put prices were equal to the LYONs original offering price plus accrued interest to the put dates. This reduced the downside risk of the security while (at the same time) largely retaining the equity participation characteristics of traditional convertible bonds. This structure also provided issuers with tax advantages and its introduction spurred the issuance of more large investment grade convertibles.

2.2.1   Introduction

LYONs, because of their put option (five years or less after issuance), tend to be less sensitive to changes in interest rates than either long maturity bonds or preferred stocks. Their put feature also provides significant downside price support and insures holders a minimum total return equal to the yield to put, provided, of course, the issuer remains solvent. LYONs, due to their high safety level and modest equity sensitivity, are the most *"bond-like"* convertible structure.

LYONs were the first of what has become a wide array of innovative convertible structures with acronyms to match. Since their introduction, LYONs and similar zero coupon convertibles have captured a sizable share of the market.

2.2.2   Description

LYONs are zero coupon convertible bonds which are convertible anytime (at the holder's option) into common stock.

Typically they have the following terms:

Coupon/Yield to Maturity: zero coupon bonds priced at 20% to 40% of par to provide an average yield to maturity of 4–7%.

Maturity: Generally 15 to 20 years.

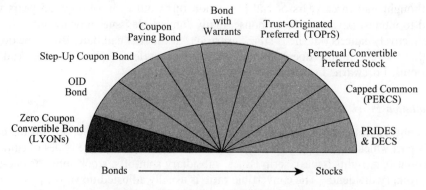

Figure 2.8   The convertible spectrum

Put Option: Putable at the investor's option on one or more dates prior to maturity. The most common put schedule provides for a put option five years after issuance and at additional five year intervals through maturity. Put options can be divided into two groups: *"hard" puts*, payable only in cash; and *"soft" puts* which the company, may satisfy with cash, common stock, or subordinated notes and, in some cases, a combination of all three.

Conversion Premium: Initial conversion premiums have ranged from 12% to 20%. LYONs are convertible into a fixed number of common shares, subject to adjustments for stock splits. In some cases, the company has the option to deliver cash equal to the conversion value, rather than deliver the actual underlying shares. This feature is most common with *"exchangeable" LYONs*. Exchangeable securities are convertible into stock other than that of the issuer.

Call Protection: Five years of call protection is the most common provision. Issuers must give 15–30 days of call notice before they can redeem the securities. This notice provides investors with the opportunity to convert or sell their LYONs if parity is above the call price.

2.2.3 Valuation

Merrill Lynch has developed a valuation model for LYONs which combines the stock's volatility and dividend rate, and the appropriate credit spread to derive a theoretical value for the security. A more simplistic, but nonetheless useful approach, is to view LYONs as a combination of the following securities:

1. A five year zero coupon bond; and
2. A five year call option.

Why should an investor treat the fixed income component as having a five year maturity rather than the LYON's 20 year stated maturity?

The LYON's put option ensures that an investor receives at least the accreted value after five years, even if interest rates have moved up and the underlying stock has declined. On the other hand, if interest rates move down the issuer is more likely to call the LYON after five years and refinance at lower rates, even if its stock has not performed well. This was a frequent occurrence in 1992–93. In this regard LYONs contrast with other convertibles, where calls primarily occur if the underlying stock has risen sharply. Thus, while it is true that LYONs are the most "bond-like" of all convertibles (see Return Profile below), because of their effective five year duration a LYON's price will actually change less for a given change in interest rates than will a coupon bearing convertible's.[1]

2.2.4 Return Profile

Figures 2.9 to 2.11 show the return profile of a LYON compared to its underlying common stock after one, three, and five years. As they show, the LYON's downside

---

[1] In statistical terms, a regression of LYONs' returns on changes on interest rates would give a higher R2 but a lower slope than a similar regression for coupon bearing converts.

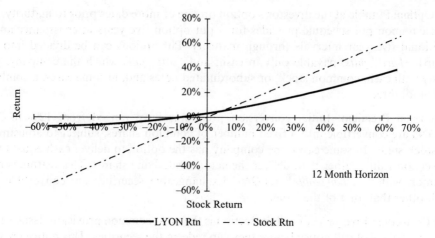

Figure 2.9   LYON vs. stock total return: one year horizon

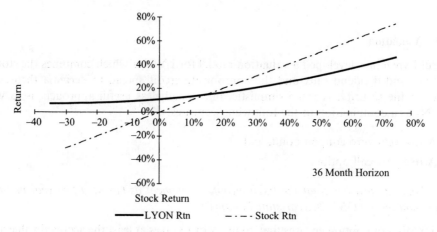

Figure 2.10   LYON vs. stock total return: three year horizon

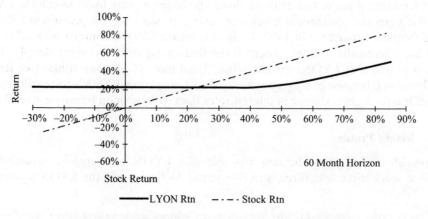

Figure 2.11   LYON vs. stock total return: five year horizon

protection relative to the underlying common increases as it approaches the put date. After one year the LYON has significant downside risk, but after three years this has largely disappeared. By the put date the return profile is a *"hockey stick"*.

On the upside, the conversion feature of the LYON will only become valuable if the underlying stock appreciates at a higher rate than the accretion rate on the LYON. For this reason, the initial conversion premium can be a little misleading. With a coupon bearing convertible the investment value of the bond rises only slowly as the bond ages. Because of this, the price that the underlying stock must exceed in order for parity to exceed investment value also remains relatively constant. However, with a LYON investment value rises more rapidly since the bond accrues interest rather than paying in cash. Thus the price that the underlying stock must exceed in order for parity to exceed investment value also rises more rapidly. Since an investor will not want to convert earlier than necessary and give up downside protection, for valuation purposes the critical date is when call protection expires (typically five years). That being said, when calculating the strike price for the embedded option investors should therefore use the investment value after five years (i.e. the put price) divided by the conversion ratio.

2.2.5 Tax Considerations

Much of the appeal of LYONs to issuers lies in their tax treatment. Issuers deduct the accrued interest, even though no cash interest is being paid, just as they do with straight zero coupon securities. Conversely, investors pay taxes on the LYONs' accreted interest (discount amortization) as ordinary income. This tax treatment holds for LYONs purchased in the secondary market, even if the purchase price exceeds accreted value. However, in this case the premium over accreted value may be deducted, on an amortized basis through maturity.

2.3 TOPrS: PREFERREDS MADE BETTER

Convertible TOPrS, or <u>T</u>rust <u>O</u>rginated <u>P</u>referred <u>S</u>ecurities, are essentially convertible preferred securities that pay quarterly dividends. From the issuer's perspective their attraction is twofold: unlike regular preferreds, Convertible TOPrS' "dividends" are tax deductible, yet the securities still receive partial equity credit from the rating agencies.

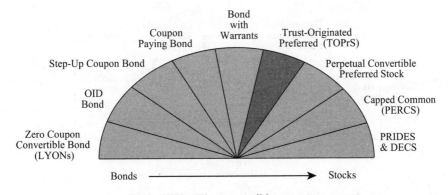

Figure 2.12 The convertible spectrum

2.3.1 Introduction

At present there are about two dozen Convertible TOPrS issues outstanding. They have been favored by issuers because of their obviously advantageous tax structure. For the same reason, corporations have found it economically viable to exchange outstanding convertible preferreds into Convertible TOPrS. A case in point is Unocal (UCL) Corp.'s exchange of their 7% series convertible preferred for a 6.25% series trust-originated preferred.

2.3.2 Description

Convertible TOPrS are preferred shares which pay quarterly dividends and are convertible into common shares of a primary issuer.

Typically they have the following terms:

- $50 par value
- 20–30 year maturity (with possible extensions)
- Three to five years of call protection
- Conversion premium of 20–25%
- Convertible any time at holder's option into a fixed number of shares
- Quarterly dividends paid in arrears
- Dividend payments not eligible for Dividend Received Deduction
- Yield advantage of 4–7 percentage points over the primary issuer's common stock

The mechanics of a Convertible TOPrS are as follows: The primary issuer sets up an entity to issue the Convertible TOPrS. The entity is a Delaware statutory business Trust which sells the TOPrS to the public investor. The proceeds go to purchase convertible subordinated debentures with terms identical to those of the Convertible TOPrS. The primary issuer owns all the common securities in the Trust; this allows for consolidation of these securities on the corporation's balance sheet.

Interest Deferral

The primary issuer may defer interest payments on the convertible subordinated debentures for up to but not exceeding 20 consecutive quarters, or five years. However, during

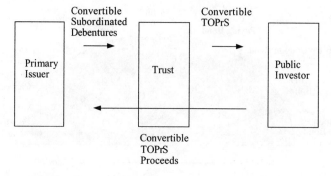

Figure 2.13   Simplified convertible TOPrS schematic

this period dividend payments will continue to accrue and compound quarterly and the primary issuer would be prohibited from paying dividends on its own common or preferred stock. So the Convertible TOPrS and the convertible subordinated debentures are essentially at the same level in the capital structure.

Since the primary issuer has sold convertible subordinated debentures to the Trust, it is entitled to deduct the coupon payments for tax purposes. However, the debentures do not appear on the primary issuer's balance sheet. Instead, the primary issuer consolidates its financial statements with those of the Trust and the Convertible TOPrS show up as a minority interest. This consolidation allows the primary issuer to receive partial equity treatment from the rating agencies.

TOPrS, like many convertible securities, are issued under a variety of brand name acronyms. For a list of TOPrS-like products, see page 50.

2.3.3   Valuation and Return Profile

From a valuation standpoint, Convertible TOPrS are almost the same as traditional convertible preferreds. Hard call protection is often four to five years, more generous than the standard three years. Also, the fixed maturity of Convertible TOPrS should make them slightly less interest rate sensitive and bolster their investment value. This effect is negligible for 30 year maturities, but becomes more significant with shorter maturities.

For a taxable corporate investor the loss of the *Dividend Received Deduction* will, of course, make a Convertible TOPrS less attractive than an equivalent traditional convertible preferred. Therefore, such investors may compare Convertible TOPrS to traditional convertible subordinated debentures. The return profile for a Convertible TOPrS is quite similar to that of a traditional convertible preferred—lagging the common stock slightly on the upside and outperforming on the downside by virtue of its enhanced yield and investment value floor. Other things being equal we would expect the TOPrS to trade with a higher conversion premium because of its longer call protection. Figure 2.14 shows the Convertible TOPrS return versus its underlying stock for a three year time horizon.

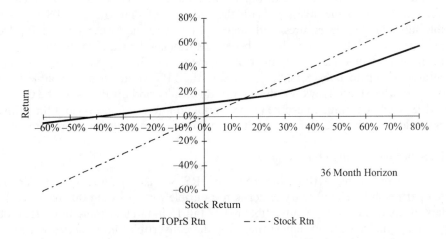

Figure 2.14   Convertible TOPrS vs. stock annualized total return

2.4 MIPS: PREDECESSOR TO TOPRS

Prior to the introduction of TOPrS, Convertible MIPS, or Monthly Income Preferred Securities, were introduced in 1994. From the holder's point of view they are essentially trust preferreds with monthly dividend payments. The most important distinction is that while TOPrS are originated in a Delaware statutory business trust, MIPS are originated in a limited partnership. MIPS and TOPrS share two advantages for issuers: "dividends" are tax deductible, and securities receive partial equity credit from rating agencies. However, because of the additional issuer requirements for limited partnerships, MIPS have been all but replaced by TOPrS in the new issue market.

2.4.1 Description

Only five MIPS issues were outstanding at the end of 1997. Convertible MIPS are preferred shares which pay monthly dividends and are convertible into common shares of a primary issuer.

Typically they have the following terms:

- $50 par value
- 30 year maturity (with possible extensions)
- Five years of call protection
- Conversion premium of 20–25%
- Convertible any time at holder's option into a fixed number of shares
- Monthly dividends paid in arrears
- Dividend payments not eligible for Dividend Received Deduction
- Yield advantage of 4–7 percentage points over the primary issuer's common stock

The mechanics of a Convertible MIPS are almost identical to TOPrS. The primary issuer sets up a *Special Purpose Subsidiary (SPS)* to issue the Convertible MIPS. The SPS, which is essentially a pass-through entity, is a limited partnership which sells Convertible MIPS to the investor. With the proceeds of that sale the SPS buys convertible subordinated debentures, with identical terms to the Convertible MIPS, from the primary issuer. The primary issuer becomes the general partner in the SPS.

The primary issuer may defer interest payments on the convertible subordinated debentures for up to five years. If this occurs the SPS would then be unable to pay dividends on the MIPS. However, during this deferral period dividends on the Convertible MIPS would continue to accrue (and compound interest monthly) and the primary issuer would be prohibited from paying dividends on its own common or preferred stock.

2.4.2 Schedule K-1 and Other Considerations

Holders of Convertible MIPS will receive an IRS *Schedule K1* because the SPS is a limited partnership. The primary issuer is responsible for providing this paperwork to holders. If dividends on the Convertible MIPS fall 15 months or more into arrears the holders have the right to exchange them for the convertible subordinated debentures held by the SPS. This provision is intended to reinforce the holders' position in the event of bankruptcy. (Since this is a fairly new security structure this provision has not been tested in bankruptcy court.) The same provision comes into effect if the tax treatment of Convertible MIPS is struck down. In that case, the economics of the structure would remain unchanged, but the primary issuer would lose the minority interest treatment and its balance sheet would show the convertible subordinated debentures outstanding.

2.4.3   A Twist on MIPS

Convertible MIPS are attractive from a tax standpoint to issuers looking to raise money de novo. However, they have also proven more attractive to companies with outstanding *"hung" convertible* preferreds—that is, converts where forced conversion is nearly impossible because the stock is trading well below the conversion price. In such a situation, an issuer may offer to exchange the outstanding security for a Convertible MIPS with identical terms. In doing so, the issuer gains the benefit of deducting the previously non-deductible dividends. In addition, rating agencies may give the issuer slightly more equity-like treatment on the new security since the possibility of five year dividend deferral gives the issuer more financial flexibility.

AMR Corp. was the first issuer to take advantage of this financing alternative. In an additional twist, AMR opted to bypass the SPS structure and offer the underlying convertible subordinated debentures directly to the existing "hung" convertible preferred holders. In doing this, management was probably motivated by the belief that rating agencies would look through the details of the structure to the underlying economics of the debt.

2.5   PERCS AND THEIR RELATIVES

PERCS are preferred shares which offer limited upside participation with the underlying stock (generally 30–35% price cap) and mandatorily convert into common stock at maturity. Thus, as Figure 2.15 points out, PERCS are among the most equity-like convertible securities and therefore offer different risk/reward tradeoffs from traditional convertible securities. Most notably, other than their yield advantage, PERCS provide no protection from a decline in the price of their underlying stock. PERCS also offer

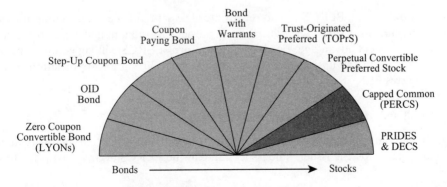

Figure 2.15   The convertible spectrum

higher current yields than traditional convertibles to compensate investors for this greater downside risk and limited appreciation.

2.5.1 Introduction

First introduced in 1991, PERCS is an acronym for Preferred Equity Redemption Cumulative Stock. Basically, PERCS and their look-alikes can be thought of as long dated, packaged buy-writes. That is, they are economically equivalent to a share of common stock with a long-dated call option sold against it.

Typically they have the following terms:

- Approximately three year maturity at which time they mandatorily convert into common stock
- Issued with an appreciation cap of 30–35%
- Initial income advantage of roughly 3–4 percentage points over the common stock
- Issued at the same price as the common
- Pay a cumulative preferred dividend, quarterly
- Callable at the option of the issuer, at a declining price payable in shares

2.5.2 Valuation

The most intuitive way to analyze a PERCS is to compare it to an option buy-write strategy. A PERCS security is basically a combination of:

1. Long one share of common stock;
2. Short one three year out-of-the-money call with a strike price approximately 30% above the current level.

The enhanced yield the PERCS offers over the common stock is essentially the money gained by selling the out-of-the-money call option. Unlike a straight buy-write strategy however, the premium is not received in an initial lump sum but is instead paid out in quarterly allotments. Thus the present value of the income advantage over the common should equal the value of the call option.

2.5.3 Return Profile

As one would expect, PERCS have a return profile essentially identical to that of a buy-write. For moderate stock returns, PERCS outperform common if held to maturity owing to their yield advantage. For high stock returns PERCS will lag common as they are capped out on the upside at a maximum of about 30% price appreciation. Figure 2.16 compares PERCS and stock returns for a typical issue.

2.5.4 Call and Mandatory Conversion of PERCS

PERCS mandatorily convert into one share of common stock[2] at maturity unless previously called by the issuer. The issuer can call the PERCS at any time prior to the

---

[2] Subject to adjustment for splits, stock dividends, etc.

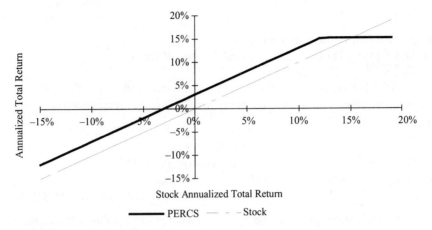

Figure 2.16 PERCS return through mandatory conversion date vs. stock return

mandatory conversion date (maturity) at predetermined call prices. The PERCS call price declines daily at a fixed rate until two months before the mandatory conversion date. Thereafter, the call price remains the same till one day prior to maturity. The call schedule insures that the PERCS holder receives payment for the remaining dividend advantage of the PERCS over the common. Further, the call schedule assumes a flat stock dividend and is not adjusted downward in the event of a decrease in the stock's dividend. Generally, therefore, the issuer has little incentive to call the PERCS early, unless the stock price rises well above the cap and the company anticipates a future decline in its stock price.

If the PERCS are called the holder generally receives payment in common shares not cash. The number of shares delivered per PERCS is given by the following formula:

$$\text{Shares delivered/PERCS} = \frac{\text{Call Price} + \text{Accrued and Unpaid Dividends}}{\text{``Current Market Price''}}$$

"*Current Market Price*" is calculated by averaging the closing stock price for the five consecutive business days ending two trading days prior to the notice date. However, if the stock price on the trading day immediately after the five-day period ("*next-day closing price*") is less than 95% of the five-day average price then the "Current Market Price" will be the next-day closing price.

This becomes clearer with an example. Table 2.2 shows two possible scenarios for the prices of an imaginary common stock underlying a PERCS issue over the period prior to a call. For the sake of simplicity we ignore accrued dividend and assume the call price on the notice date is $25.

Table 2.2 Call scenario analysis

	Determination period stock prices					"Next day closing price"	Notice date
	2-May	3-May	4-May	5-May	6-May	9-May	10-May
Scenario A	$25	$26	$24	$25	$25	$24	$24
Scenario B	$25	$26	$24	$25	$25	$23	$24

Scenario A

Average Price During Determination Period = $25
"Next Day Closing Price" = $24 (96% of Average Price Above)
Shares Received = $25 / $25 = 1
Value to PERCS Holder = 1× $24 = $24.00 vs. Stated Call Price of $25.00

Scenario B

Average Price During Determination Period = $25
"Next Day Closing Price" = $23 (94% of Average Price Above)
Shares Received = $25 / $23 = 1.067
Value to PERCS Holder = 1.067× $24 = $26.09 vs. Stated Call Price of $25.00

As this example shows, the averaging or "*Asian*" feature can cause the PERCS holder to receive shares worth an amount significantly different from the call price. This introduces risk for the PERCS holder because the issuer has the luxury of choosing the most opportune time to announce the call. The PERCS holders are, to some extent, protected by virtue of the 95% "*next day closing price*" feature.

The company can choose any date from 15 to 60 days after the notice date as the delivery date for the common shares. The company announces the delivery date when they give notice of the call. We would expect the company to choose a delivery date after the record date for the common stock dividend to avoid paying the PERCS holder a double dividend.

2.5.5 Analysis of PERCS Nearing Maturity

For illustration purposes, let's look at General Motors $3.31 PERCS. The call price on the GM PERCS declined at the rate of $0.004759 per day to $54.08 on 4/30/94. After 5/1/94 the PERCS were callable at a fixed price of $53.79. If it were not called by 6/30/94, it would have converted mandatorily into one share of common stock on 7/1/94 (see Figure 2.17).

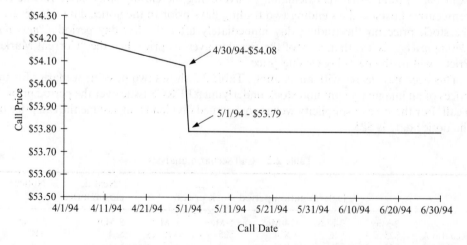

Figure 2.17   Call schedule for General Motors PERCS

If GM common were above $53.79, it would have been sub-optimal for GM to call the PERCS before 5/1/94 unless the company expected the stock to drop significantly in the near future. After 5/1/94, if the stock were above $53.79, GM may have decided to call the PERCS early. The company had to decide between the merits of saving the incremental dividend on the PERCS and potentially reducing the number of shares delivered if the stock were to move up. This was particularly problematic since the common was hovering right around the final cap price. In the case of GM, the dividend accrual on the PERCS was about 1 ¢ per day.

So, had GM management anticipated a return on the stock of more than 1 ¢ per day, it would probably have been better for them to defer conversion until 6/30/94. If GM had chosen to call early, it would have been advantageous to choose a delivery date after the common stock's dividend record date (approximately May 12). As it really happened, GM deferred conversion until 6/18/94, for 0.99 shares of common per PERCS.

To date, Texas Instruments is the only issuer to have called its PERCS well before the mandatory conversion date. This represented a windfall for the PERCS holders since they received the remaining income advantage of the PERCS over the common in an up-front payment in additional shares instead of in quarterly cash installments over the PERCS remaining life. The present value of the latter was, of course, lower. Texas Instrument's "generosity" was likely due to their desire to capture the very rapid run-up in their stock price, and to conserve cash by ending the PERCS dividend.[3]

2.5.6 The Liquidity Trap at Conversion

Many PERCS issues upon converting to stock pose significant liquidity implications for their underlying stocks as new shares are abruptly added to the float. As PERCS convert, the additional shares delivered have been known to depress the issuers' stock prices. Income-oriented investors, not wishing to hold common stock, will be better off selling the PERCS before mandatory conversion to avoid likely stock weakness. On the other hand Equity-oriented investors should be aware of the potential for stock price declines as the PERCS convert to common stock. Where the fundamental equity story remains strong, such a decline may represent a buying opportunity in the common shares.

Once again, the General Motors PERCS provide a good illustration. GM's call of the PERCS resulted in the issuance of over 17 million new common shares (an addition of roughly 2% to shares outstanding). A review of GM stock's subsequent performance will thus provide investors with some useful insights. GM's stock fell nearly 5% during the two trading days after the call announcement on double its normal trading volume. During the same period, Ford and Chrysler fell 2% and 5% respectively, but on normal volume. GM PERCS, since they were very near their cap price, still had a good deal of stock sensitivity at the time of conversion. Therefore they were not predominantly held by fixed-income investors, unlike some of the issues currently trading well above their cap prices. Because of this, the impact of the conversion on GM's stock price may have been more muted.

---

[3] GM PERCS were callable for cash or stock.

2.5.7 Related Securities

The basic PERCS structure has taken different names at each Wall Street house. Additionally *"synthetic"* PERCS securities have also been issued. In this case the security is issued not by the underlying company but rather by a third party such as an investment banking firm. Each firm of course choosing a different acronym. Below is an acronym scorecard for PERCS and related securities:

Company Issued:

- MCPDPS: Mandatory Conversion Premium Dividend Preferred Stock
- TARGETS: TARgeted Growth Enhanced Terms Securities
- YES: Yield Enhanced Stock

Synthetic:

- CHIPS: Common linked Higher Income Participating debt Securities
- ELKS: Equity LinKed debt Securities
- EYES: Enhanced Yield Equity Securities
- PERQS: Performance Equity-linked Redemption Quarterly-pay Securities
- YEELDS: Yield Enhanced Equity Linked Debt Securities

(For a more complete list of convertible products, see Table 2.6.)

2.6   PRIDES: EQUITY FOR INCOME LOVERS

PRIDES, Preferred Redeemable Increased Dividend Equity Securities, are preferred shares which mandatorily convert into common shares at maturity. They offer significant yield advantage over the underlying common in exchange for limited upside participation. Because PRIDES offer no real downside protection, they are among the most equity sensitive convertible structures. As their brief performance history has proven, PRIDES are designed to move almost in tandem with their underlying equities.

2.6.1 Introduction

Since the first issue by MascoTech in July of 1993, the outstanding value of PRIDES[4] and other PRIDES-like structures has grown to $15.1 billion, nearly 13% of the US convertible market.

Initially viewed as an oddity and priced somewhat erratically, PRIDES have now found a niche amongst mainly Equity-Income funds for whom the need for yield and appreciation potential is paramount. PRIDES have found some support within the dedicated convertible fund community, but largely on a "story-specific" basis.

Many traditional convertible buyers have been wary of boosting PRIDES exposure because of their higher than average stock sensitivity in both up and down markets. Ironically for these managers, PRIDES outperformed more traditional structures by a

---

[4] Throughout this report we use the term PRIDES to refer to the family of convertible securities which also includes DECS and ACES.

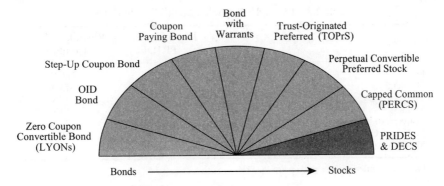

Figure 2.18   The convertible spectrum

wide margin in the first three years of their existence. In 1994, because of their minimal interest rate sensitivity, PRIDES suffered less than other convertibles when the bond market tanked. Then, from 1995 to 1997, when stocks soared to record levels, PRIDES reaped the benefit of their high equity sensitivity. For the four year period, PRIDES recorded an annualized total return of 19.37% compared to a 12.90% return for the ML All Convertibles Index. Perhaps more interesting is the fact that PRIDES nearly equaled the performance of their own underlying common stocks, which had a 19.41% annualized return. We would expect PRIDES to under perform other convertibles in periods of weak stock but strong bond market returns, however.

2.6.2   Security Description

PRIDES are convertibles which are exchangeable at a premium anytime (at the holder's option) into common shares, but mandatorily convert at maturity to common stock.

Typically they have the following terms:

- Three or four year maturity at which time PRIDES mandatorily convert to common stock
- Three years of call protection
- Conversion premiums of 20 to 25%
- Income advantage of 5–6 percentage points over their underlying common stock, and 2–3 percentage points over comparable convertible preferred stock
- Issue price same as common shares
- Quarterly income payment, usually on same payment date as common dividend

The easiest way to understand PRIDES is by working through an example. For illustration we'll use the Reynolds Metals 7% PRIDES.

As Figure 2.19 shows, there are three possibilities for the value of the PRIDES at maturity:

Table 2.3 Example: Reynolds Metals 7% PRIDES

	Reynolds Metals PRIDES	Reynolds Metals Common
Price	$47.25	$47.25
Dividend	$3.31	$1.00
Conversion Price	$57.62	N/A
Yield	7.0%	2.1%
Conversion Premium	22.0%	N/A
Minimum Conversion Ratio	0.82	N/A
Maximum Conversion Ratio	1.00	N/A

Prices reflect offering terms on January 18, 1994

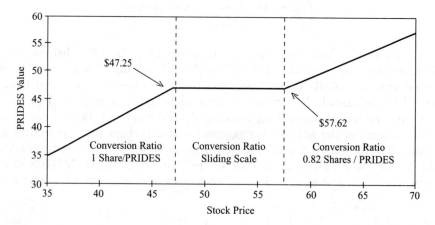

Figure 2.19 Reynolds Metals PRIDES value at maturity vs. Reynolds stock price

1. The common closes below the initial price. The PRIDES converts into one share of common.

2. The common closes between the initial price and the conversion price. The PRIDES converts into common according to a sliding scale designed to give the PRIDES holder common shares exactly equal in value to the initial price of $47.25. So if the common were at $50, the PRIDES would convert into 47.25/50 = 0.945 shares.

3. The common price exceeds the conversion price at maturity. The PRIDES converts into 0.82 shares of common, the minimum (or optional) conversion ratio.[5]

In the meantime, of course, the PRIDES holder enjoys a significantly enhanced dividend relative to the common, and, for that matter, relative to a comparable standard convertible preferred. PRIDES, since they are convertible into common stock at a premium, can be said to behave like convertible preferred with a higher dividend on the upside. And since they mandatorily convert into common at maturity, they will perform like common with a higher dividend on the downside.

---

[5] The minimum conversion ratio is simply 1 / (1 + Initial Conversion Premium).

2.6.3 Early Conversion and Redemption

PRIDES are generally convertible at any time prior to maturity at a premium. The holder has the option of exchanging the PRIDES for the minimum conversion ratio number of shares—0.82 in the case of Reynolds. (Exchangeable issues are generally not convertible at holder's option.) Of course, it is unlikely that a holder would exercise this option unless the common stock's dividend had grown so fast that the yield on 0.82 shares of the common exceeded that on the PRIDES.

An additional consideration is the possibility of early conversion being forced at the option of the issuer. (Exchangeable issues generally are not callable before the mandatory conversion date.) In the case of Reynolds, starting after three years the company can call the PRIDES at pre-specified premiums to the issue price plus accrued dividends (the call premium starts at $0.827 or one quarter's dividend, and amortizes to zero over the fourth year). The PRIDES converts into common shares equal in value to the call price, or into 0.82 shares, whichever is greater. Table 2.4 illustrates how this would work with the common at different prices (assuming no accrued dividends).

As Table 2.4 shows, if the common has declined in price after the first three years the company has very little incentive to redeem early. To do so effectively gives a put to the investor, since the issuer must grant the PRIDES holder the number of shares needed to recoup his initial investment. This type of early redemption therefore causes the issuer greater dilution than would occur at maturity, when each PRIDES would convert into only one share.

However, if the common has done well in the first three years, the probability of early redemption is higher. On the one hand, if the issuer redeems early it will save the incremental dividend on the PRIDES over the time left to maturity. On the other, if the company delays redemption the ultimate dilution will be reduced if the stock goes even higher. Of course, once it is more or less certain that the ultimate conversion ratio will be 0.82 (the minimum), the company has little incentive to delay redemption any further.

Case in point: Reynolds Metals PRIDES was called a year early on 12/31/96, forcing holders to convert. At the time the redemption was announced, RLM common was hovering around $60, high enough to insure the minimum ratio.

2.6.4 Valuation

Merrill Lynch has developed a valuation model for PRIDES consistent with our other convertible securities valuation models. The model combines the volatility of the stock,

Table 2.4 Reynolds Metals PRIDES—early redemption scenarios

Stock price	Shares received per PRIDES	Value
$35.00	1.35	$47.25
$40.00	1.18	$47.25
$45.00	1.05	$47.25
$47.25	1.00	$47.25
$50.00	0.95	$47.25
$55.00	0.86	$47.25
$57.62	0.82	$47.25
$60.00	0.82	$49.20
$65.00	0.82	$53.30

the appropriate spreads for the issuer's credit, and the early call features of the PRIDES to derive a value for the security. The model also calculates the PRIDES' sensitivity to changes in: the issuer's stock price and volatility; Treasury yields; and credit spreads.

A more simplistic but nonetheless useful approach is to treat the PRIDES as a combination of the following three securities:

1. A long position in one share of the issuer's common stock;
2. A short position in a four year, at-the-money call option on one share of the issuer's common stock;
3. A long position in 0.82 (in the case of Reynolds) of a three year call option[6] on the issuer's common stock struck at the conversion price (i.e. 22% out-of-the-money).

This combination would cost less to assemble than the current stock price because the premium for the at-the-money option sold is greater than the cost of the out-of-the-money option position bought. The difference could be invested in fixed income securities of the same credit as the issuer to generate yield. This additional yield should be equal to the yield advantage of the PRIDES over the common. A major issue with this approach is deciding how likely it is that the incremental yield will be earned for three years versus four.

2.6.5 Return Profile

Above we have shown PRIDES value at maturity for different potential common stock prices. Given the early redemption feature of the PRIDES, it is important to consider how they might be valued at times prior to maturity, however. Figure 2.20 shows how we would expect a PRIDES to perform against common stock after three years, when the early redemption feature first kicks in.

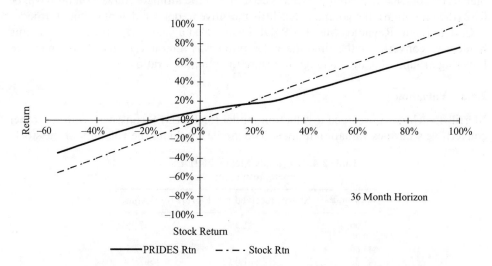

Figure 2.20 PRIDES vs. stock annualized total return after three years

---

[6] We conservatively assume a three-year life for the long option because the PRIDES becomes callable after three years. If the stock has advanced and the embedded long option is in the money we would expect the issue to be called. Again, this is irrelevant for exchangeable issues.

As Figure 2.20 shows, the PRIDES should provide a similar return profile to the common: under performing slightly on the upside; but outperforming on the downside by virtue of their enhanced yield.

2.6.6 Comparison to Traditional Convertible Preferred

PRIDES invite comparison with conventional convertible preferreds. However there are important differences:

- Yield advantage only lasts three to four years unlike conventional convertible preferreds.
- Mandatory conversion into common stock means PRIDES have more downside risk.
- In return for accepting more risk, PRIDES holders receive a higher yield, usually 2–3 percentage points.
- Upside participation in underlying common stock gains over the life of the security is slightly higher with PRIDES than with conventional convertible preferreds.

Because of these differences, a PRIDES' risk profile is more similar to that of common stock than to traditional convertible preferreds. To compensate for this, PRIDES pay a higher current yield than do convertible preferreds.

2.6.7 Alphabet Soup?

PRIDES is Merrill Lynch's acronym for these convertible securities.

However, various Wall Street firms have each spawned their own names for these securities:

- ACES: Automatically Convertible Equity Securities
- DECS: Debt Exchangeable for Common Stock and Dividend Enhanced Convertible Stock
- MARCS: Mandatory Adjustable Redeemable Convertible Securities
- PRIDES: Preferred Redeemable Increased Dividend Equity Securities
- PEPS: Preferred Equity Participation Securities
- SAILS: Stock Appreciation Income Linked Securities

(For a more complete list of convertible products, see Table 2.6.)

2.7 VARIATIONS ON A THEME: PRODUCT INNOVATIONS ABOUND

These days, the announcement of a new convertible structure leaves no one shocked. The popularity of convertible products tailored to specific market conditions and issuer needs has left us with a few "hard to categorize" mandatory structures. These newer products are not as confusing as they may first appear, however, because they can be easily explained using the terminology of their more familiar predecessors. Below are descriptions of the handful of unusual variations currently outstanding: Flex-Caps, Reset-PRIDES, Feline PRIDES, Enhanced PRIDES, and STRYPES.

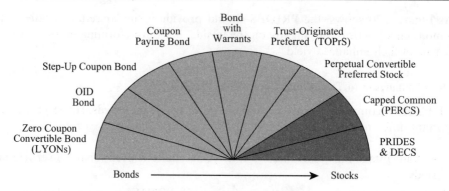

Figure 2.21 The convertible spectrum

2.7.1 Flex-Caps: Variation on PERCS

Flex-Caps are preferred shares which mandatorily convert into at most one share of common stock at maturity. A Flex-Cap participates in 100% of the stock's rise up to the partial cap, then 50% of any additional appreciation. So far SunAmerica has been the only issuer of Flex-Caps, though other transactions may follow.

Like other mandatory conversion preferreds, the downside protection Flex-Caps provide is solely due to their yield advantage over the underlying common stock. The essence of the Flex-Caps structure is that the investor gives up part of the stock's appreciation in exchange for a higher level of current income. Flex-Caps offer a current yield, which is comparable with that of a traditional convertible preferred but offer greater common stock participation in most cases.

Description

Basically, Flex-Caps holders exchange some potential appreciation for up-front income.

Flex-Caps have the following features:

- Approximately three year maturity at which time they convert into common stock.
- Issued at the same price as the common stock.
- Income advantage of 3–4 percentage points over the common stock yield.
- Quarterly dividend payment, usually on the same payment date as the common stock.
- Full stock participation up to 120% of the issue price, then share in 50% of the further appreciation.
- Callable at the option of the issuer, at a declining price payable in shares.

Valuation

Flex-Caps can be thought of as a combination of long one share of stock and short 0.50 calls struck 20% out-of-the-money.

The most intuitive way to analyze a Flex-Caps is to compare it to an option buy-write strategy. It is basically a combination of:

1. Long one share of common stock.

2. Short 0.50 of a call struck 20% out-of-the-money.

The enhanced yield the Flex-Caps offers over the common stock is essentially the money gained by selling the out-of-the-money call option. Unlike a straight buy-write option strategy, however, the premium is not received in an initial lump sum but is instead paid out in quarterly allotments. Thus the present value of the income stream should equal the value of the call option.

Return Profile

For moderate stock returns, Flex-Caps outperform common stock. In this example the crossover point, for a 36 month horizon, comes at a compounded annual stock return of roughly 14%. Figure 2.22 compares the return through maturity of a Flex-Cap, a traditional convertible preferred, and the stock. Generally Flex-Caps offer more immediate participation with the common, and do not begin to lag traditional preferreds, on the upside, until the stock rises substantially.

2.7.2 Reset-PRIDES: PRIDES with Downside Support

Reset-PRIDES are preferred shares which mandatorily convert into common stock at maturity. Unlike other members of the PRIDES family, Reset-PRIDES may convert into more than one share at maturity, up to some pre-specified maximum number of shares. This allows an issuer of Reset-PRIDES to offer investors more downside protection. In exchange for this enhanced downside support, Reset-PRIDES have lower current yield than regular PRIDES. The first Reset-PRIDES issue was AJL Trust convertible into Amway Japan ADSs, issued in late 1995. Only a few have yet been issued. One significant feature is that issuers must recognize the full potential

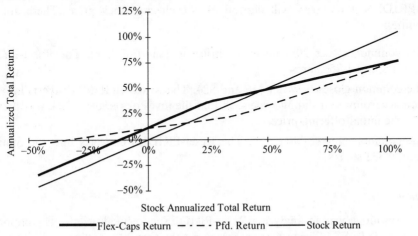

Figure 2.22   Flex-Caps return profile: three year horizon

This figure assumes the following: Stock Yield 1.35%, Volatility 25%, Credit Spread 80 Bps, Flex-Cap Yield 5%, Flex-Cap "Partial Cap" 20%, Preferred Yield 5%, Preferred Premium 24%

dilution (i.e. 1.25 shares per Reset-PRIDES) immediately. This may limit further issues to exchangeables, where Reset-PRIDES present a way for a holder of an illiquid stock to exit in an orderly and tax efficient manner.

Unlike other mandatory conversion preferreds, the downside protection Reset-PRIDES provide is partly due to their yield advantage over the underlying common stock, and partly due to the fact that the conversion ratio increases as the underlying stock price at maturity drops below the issue price. However, the increase in conversion ratio is bounded by a maximum. So in effect the investor is sheltered from the first 20% (for example) decline in the underlying stock, but shares in the risk of declines greater than this. A Reset-PRIDES can be thought of as a bridge between regular PRIDES and more traditional convertible structures. Its yield is closer to that of a traditional convert, and it has more downside support than a regular PRIDES, but it still converts mandatorily into common at the end of its life.

Description

Reset-PRIDES have the following features:

- Approximately three year maturity at which time they convert into common stock.
- Issued at the same price as the common stock.
- Income advantage of 3–4 percentage points over the common stock yield.
- Quarterly dividend payment, usually on the same payment date as the common stock.
- Conversion ratio between 1.25 and 0.833 shares depending on stock price at maturity.

The easiest way to understand a Reset-PRIDES is to work through a simple example. Consider an issue with the initial stock price at $20, where the Reset-PRIDES provides protection against the first 20% decline. The conversion ratio of the Reset-PRIDES at maturity will depend on the closing stock price. There are three possibilities:

1. The common closes 20% below its price at issue (i.e. $16). The Reset-PRIDES converts into 1.25 shares.
2. The common closes between $16 and $24. The Reset-PRIDES converts into common according to a sliding scale such that the investor receives stock worth exactly $20, the initial offering price.
3. The common closes above $24. The Reset-PRIDES converts into the minimum ratio, 0.833 shares.

Valuation

The most intuitive way to analyze a Reset-PRIDES is to break it into its components. For a Reset-PRIDES offering protection against the first 20% decline in the underlying stock, and roughly 80% participation in gains over 20%, the security is basically a combination of:

1. Long one share of common stock.

2. Long one at-the-money put.
3. Short 1.25 (100%/80%, or the lower strike level) puts struck at 80% of the initial stock price (i.e. 20% out-of-the-money).
4. Short one at-the-money call.
5. Long 0.833 call struck 20% out-of-the-money.

The enhanced yield the Reset-PRIDES offers over the common stock is essentially the net premium from writing and buying the various options embedded in the security. However, the premium is not received in an initial lump sum but is instead paid out in quarterly allotments. Thus the present value of the incremental income offered by a Reset-PRIDES over the stock should equal the net option premium.

An alternative (and slightly simpler) decomposition of a Reset-PRIDES is:

1. Long a zero coupon bond with a maturity value equal to the initial stock price.
2. Short 1.25 puts struck at 80% of the initial stock price.
3. Long 0.833 call struck 20% out-of-the-money.

In this case, the difference between the cost of this package and the initial stock price should equal the present value of the Reset-PRIDES dividend stream.

Return Profile

For moderate stock returns Reset-PRIDES outperform common stock. In our example the crossover point, for a 36-month horizon, comes at a compounded annual stock return of roughly 12%. Figure 2.23 compares the return of a Reset-PRIDES and its underlying stock. Generally Reset-PRIDES offer less upside participation with the common than standard PRIDES but do provide more downside support.

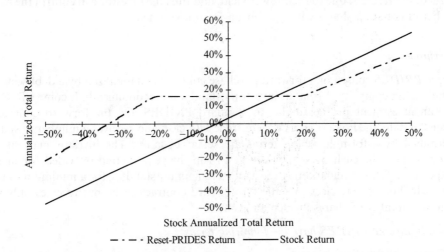

Figure 2.23   Reset-PRIDES vs. stock return at maturity

This figure assumes the following: Stock Yield 1%, Volatility 20%, Reset-PRIDES Premium 20%, Reset-PRIDES Downside Protection 20%, Credit Spread 80 Bps

2.7.3 Feline PRIDES: The Sum of Their Parts

Feline PRIDES were first issued by MCN in March 1997. Feline PRIDES consist of a purchase contract collateralized by a debt security. From a holder's perspective they have an investment profile similar to standard PRIDES. Specifically, Feline PRIDES incorporate a purchase contract that requires the holder to accept common stock at the end of a fixed period, and offer a significant yield advantage over the underlying shares in exchange for modestly limited upside appreciation.

Unlike PRIDES, Feline PRIDES can be held as component securities, namely Income PRIDES, Growth PRIDES and TOPrS. The TOPrS typically have a five year maturity and will remain outstanding after the three year purchase contract is settled. This structure allows investors ever more tailored investment options, and also imparts important tax and dilution benefits to the issuer.

Introduction

Feline PRIDES can be broken down into several components. The basic unit of these securities is called an Income PRIDES. From the investor's perspective, Income PRIDES are similar to standard PRIDES in many ways except they can be split into Growth PRIDES and TOPrS at the holder's option. The Growth PRIDES security contains a stock purchase contract identical to the one in the Income PRIDES, however, the forward contract is combined with a Treasury security, not the company's own debt.

All three components are generally offered to investors in the initial offering. Income PRIDES holders may also create Growth PRIDES in the secondary market by substituting a pre-specified Treasury security for the company debt (usually a TOPrS) which is sold in the open market. Similarly, Growth PRIDES holders can also purchase the corporate debt security and recombine it with the forward contract to create an Income PRIDES. The Growth PRIDES are issued at a lower nominal price than the Income PRIDES, due to their lower yield, and thus the investor can control the same number of common shares with a lesser up-front investment.

Description

Income PRIDES consist of a forward purchase contract collateralized by a debt security of the issuing company. From an investor's standpoint, economically Income PRIDES have an investment profile similar to standard PRIDES. On the forward contract's settlement date, the holder settles the contract with cash and receives a number of shares determined by a formula whose terms are set at issuance. The investor may, at his option, obtain the cash by selling the TOPrS in the remarketing provided for in the prospectus. After the remarketing the TOPrS remain outstanding for a minimum of two years. The holder may elect to settle the forward contract early, but receives only the minimum number of shares in such an event.

Typically Income PRIDES have the following terms:

* Three year forward contract
* Three years of call protection
* Premiums of 20–25%

- Income advantage of 5–6 percentage points over their underlying common stock's dividend
- Quarterly income payments, usually aligned with Treasury zero cycle
- Five year TOPrS with a liquidation value equal to the forward contract's settlement amount

The easiest way to understand an Income PRIDES is by working through an example. For illustration we will use the Ingersoll-Rand issue (Table 2.5).

As Figure 2.24 shows, there are three possibilities for the value of the Income PRIDES at the forward contract's settlement date:

1. The common stock closes[7] below the reference price. The Income PRIDES holder receives the maximum share ratio.
2. The common close is between the reference price and the threshold price. In this case the Income PRIDES holder receives common shares according to a sliding scale designed to give the holder shares equal in value to the Income PRIDES offering price. The number of shares received will be an amount between the maximum and minimum number of shares.
3. The common exceeds the threshold price at maturity. The Income PRIDES holder will receive the minimum share ratio.

Under each of these scenarios the investor will have to deliver cash equal to the TOPrS par value to satisfy his obligation under the forward contract. The TOPrS do not mature until year five so at year three, the forward contract expiration, the Income PRIDES holder has two options:

1. Cash settle the forward contract for $25 and retain a TOPrS whose interest rate has been reset, or
2. Cash settle the forward contract by allowing the TOPrS to be included in the remarketing process and use those proceeds.

Table 2.5   Example: Ingersoll-Rand Feline PRIDES

	Ingersoll-Rand Income PRIDES	Ingersoll-Rand Growth PRIDES	Ingersoll-Rand common stock
Issue Price	$25.00	$21.13	$48.25
Reference Stock Price	$48.25	$48.25	N/A
Threshold Stock Price	$58.384	$58.384	N/A
Contract Adjustment Payment Yield	0.53%	0.78%	N/A
TOPrS (Capital Securities) Yield	6.22%	N/A	N/A
Total Yield**	6.75%	0.78%	1.24%
Premium	21.0%	2.3%	N/A
Minimum Purchase Contract Ratio	0.4282	0.4282	N/A
Maximum Purchase Contract Ratio	0.5181	0.5181	N/A
Purchase Contract Settlement Date	5/16/2001	5/16/2001	N/A

** Represents only cash yield. Mutual fund accounting allows a higher declarable Growth PRIDES yield equal to the Contract Adjustment Payment yield *plus* accretion on the collateral Treasury Securities.

---

[7] There is a 20-day averaging period during which the common stock is valued under this formula.

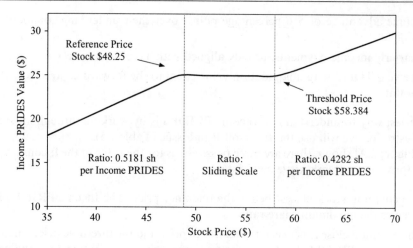

Figure 2.24   Ingersoll-Rand Income PRIDES value at maturity vs. Ingersoll-Rand stock
price

Income PRIDES investors who fail to elect option 1 will automatically be included in the remarketing (option 2).

Holders of TOPrS securities which are separate and not a component of Income PRIDES have the following options at the end of year three:

1. Continue to hold the reset TOPrS, or;
2. Deliver the TOPrS to the custodial agent to be included in the remarketing process.

At the forward contract's settlement, the interest rate on the TOPrS is reset such that the TOPrS are expected to trade at 100.5% of par. By participating in the remarketing, Income PRIDES and TOPrS holders incur a remarketing fee and may forego the ability to realize some, or all, of this excess value. Thus, it is theoretically advantageous to settle the forward contract with cash.

During the three year life of the forward contract, the Income PRIDES holder enjoys a significantly enhanced yield relative to the common stock. This enhanced yield to some extent lessens the risk of Income PRIDES relative to the common stock.

Income PRIDES can be held as their component pieces—forward purchase contracts and TOPrS. Income PRIDES consist of:

1. A purchase contract which is linked to a specific contract adjustment payment.
2. A $25 obligation from the investor to the issuer due at the end of year three.
3. A quarterly income stream from the TOPrS.
4. A $25 obligation from the issuer to the investor, due at the end of year five with remarketing available at the end of year three.

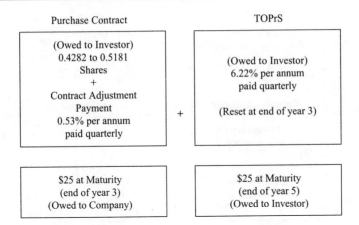

Purchase Contract

(Owed to Investor)
0.4282 to 0.5181
Shares
+
Contract Adjustment
Payment
0.53% per annum
paid quarterly

+

TOPrS

(Owed to Investor)
6.22% per annum
paid quarterly

(Reset at end of year 3)

$25 at Maturity
(end of year 3)
(Owed to Company)

$25 at Maturity
(end of year 5)
(Owed to Investor)

Figure 2.25   Ingersoll-Rand Income PRIDES schematic

Figure 2.25 shows these components and their cash flows for the Ingersoll-Rand Income PRIDES.

The $25 cash obligation the investor owes the company is offset by the value of the TOPrS, which should be worth slightly more than $25 in year three as a result of the remarketing. As a result, Income PRIDES have a similar economic profile to that of a standard PRIDES, which was described in an earlier section of this report.

Growth PRIDES and *TOPrS* may be purchased during the offering, or may result when an Income PRIDES holder sells off the TOPrS security and posts a Treasury security[8] to secure his obligation under the forward contract. The forward contract itself is unchanged, so Growth PRIDES and Income PRIDES represent the same number of common shares. However, the contract adjustment payment of the Growth PRIDES forward contract may be higher than the contract adjustment payment for the Income PRIDES, generally by 0 to 50 basis points.

If a Growth PRIDES investor wants to reverse back into the Income PRIDES, he can do so by purchasing the TOPrS in the open market and posting it with the collateral agent, who will then release the investor's Treasury security. Because Treasury securities have a $1000 par value and the TOPrS only a $25 par value, conversions must involve a minimum of 40 Growth PRIDES for the math to work out.

Figure 2.26 shows the components and their cash flows for the Ingersoll-Rand Growth PRIDES.

Although the forward contracts for Income PRIDES and Growth PRIDES are identical, there is an important distinction with respect to the collateral in the event of bankruptcy or default. We refer to this feature as the "default put". The terms of the Income PRIDES and Growth PRIDES contracts stipulate that in the event of default, the forward contract is voided and the underlying collateral is returned to the investor. In other words, the Growth PRIDES holder receives back his Treasury security which is unaffected by the issuer's credit problems, while the Income PRIDES holder receives

---

[8] The treasury security referred to here is specific for each issue and identified in the prospectus so that the maturity of the treasury coincides with the settlement date of the forward contract.

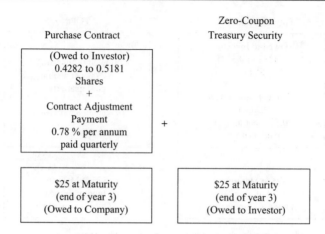

Figure 2.26 Ingersoll-Rand Growth PRIDES schematic

back his TOPrS, whose value is likely to be severely impaired. The exact terms of default are detailed in each issue's prospectus, but generally involve the following:

- Failure to pay interest for a certain period of time;
- Failure to repay principal at the forward contract's maturity; or
- Other events of insolvency, bankruptcy or reorganization.

Valuation

Merrill Lynch has developed a model for Feline PRIDES and their individual components, consistent with our other convertible models. The model combines the stock's volatility and the issuer's appropriate credit spread, with the security's income, forward contract, and call features to derive a value for the security.

Essentially an *Income PRIDES* can be treated as a combination of securities:

1. A forward purchase contract of the issuer that is upon the event of default. The forward purchase contract can be further modeled as

    (a) A short position in a three year at-the-money put option for 1 share that is void if the issuer defaults;

    (b) A long position in a three year out-of-the-money call option for a fraction of a share; and

    (c) The present value of the sum of contract adjustment payments made by the issuer.

2. A capital security or debt instrument of the issuer.

Growth PRIDES can be valued as a combination of:

1. The forward contract detailed above; and

2. A zero coupon Treasury strip whose maturity matches that of the forward purchase contact.

The strike and the exact fractional option proportions vary from issue to issue, but in general, the forward purchase contract can be valued as detailed above. The contract adjustment payments for Growth PRIDES and Income PRIDES need not be identical, and in fact the payments for Growth PRIDES are generally slightly higher.

Return Profiles

Figures 2.27 and 2.28 show the return profiles of Income PRIDES and Growth PRIDES relative to their underlying stock. The first graph depicts a 12-month horizon and the second a 36-month horizon (i.e. the entire forward contract life). Both securities provide

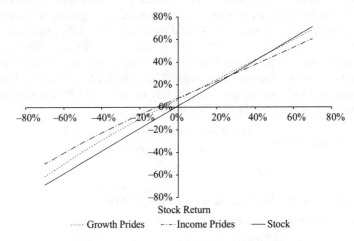

Stock Return

····· Growth Prides   ---- Income Prides   —— Stock

Figure 2.27   One year total return horizon

Source: Merrill Lynch Global Convertible Research

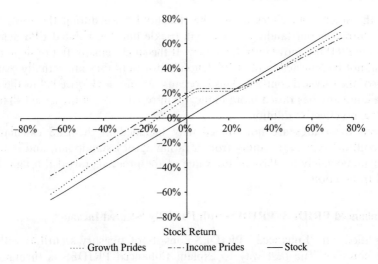

Stock Return

····· Growth Prides   ---- Income Prides   —— Stock

Figure 2.28   Three year total return horizon

Source: Merrill Lynch Global Convertible Research

a return close to that of the common stock; underperforming slightly on the upside; but outperforming on the downside by virtue of their enhanced yield. Growth PRIDES, which represent the same number of common shares, but are issued at a discount to Income PRIDES because of their lower yield, outperform the Income PRIDES as the stock return rises. Similarly, they underperform Income PRIDES as the stock return falls. The pivot point for the Growth PRIDES outperformance relative to Income PRIDES tends to fall at roughly a 10% compounded annualized stock return.

Accounting Implications

Feline PRIDES, because they consist of separate debt and forward equity purchase contracts, receive the same accounting treatment as equity options. This is primarily of importance to the issuer, but investors should understand the EPS calculation dynamics.

The TOPrS are classified as a Minority Interest on the issuer's balance sheet. The TOPrS distributions are tax deductible to the issuer, and are reported as Minority Interest Expense on the income statement. The shares are accounted for under the Treasury Stock method and are not immediately included in EPS calculations.

The dilution calculation formula is as follows:

$$AdditionalShr = \frac{MinRatio^*NumIssued^*(Price - ThreshPrice)}{Price}$$

where:

AdditionalShr = # of additional shares for Diluted EPS

MinRatio = minimum contract ratio

NumIssued = # of Feline PRIDES issued

Price = current stock price

ThreshPrice = threshold stock price

Thus, if the stock appreciates above the threshold price during the three years the forward contract is outstanding, shares will trickle into the Diluted EPS denominator as the Feline PRIDES move into the money. If the stock remains flat or depreciates, the shares will not be reflected in the EPS denominator until they are actually issued under the terms of the forward contract. This is because at any stock price below the threshold price, the company has raised more money than repurchase of the issued shares would cost, hence, no effective dilution.

Although the shares are not immediately included in the EPS calculations, the forward contract represents equity from a rating agency standpoint, and is credited to the issuer immediately for 90% of the value of the proceeds raised through the Feline PRIDES transaction.

2.7.4 Enhanced PRIDES: PRIDES with Partially Secured Income

Oversimplified, an "Enhanced" PRIDES consists of treasury securities with a stock purchase contract. The best way to explain Enhanced PRIDES is through a quick example: MCN Corp. 8.75% PRIDES pay semiannually, and the payments consist of interest on US Treasury Notes at 6.5%, plus unsecured, subordinated "*Yield Enhance-*

ment Payments" by the company (i.e. MCN) at 2.25%. The Yield Enhancement Payments are deferrable at the company's option. On the "*Final Settlement Date,*" (mandatory conversion date) the "Stated Amount," (purchase price) will automatically be applied to the purchase of between 0.833 and 1 share of the common stock depending on the stock's market price.

Sound like a standard 8.75% PRIDES? From an investor's viewpoint it is, with a few small exceptions. In the event of bankruptcy or reorganization, the purchase contract and Yield Enhancement Payments automatically terminate, while the Treasury securities are distributed to holders. Therefore, enhanced PRIDES do eliminate some credit risk. However, the mandatory conversion feature still makes the securities' equity sensitivity high. The return horizon scenario for Enhanced PRIDES is essentially the same as that of a standard PRIDES. (For graphic return scenario, see Figure 2.20.)

From an issuer's perspective an Enhanced PRIDES differs from a standard PRIDES in that it raises no current proceeds. However, the issuer does receive equity credit from the rating agencies equal to the maturity value of the Treasury collateral.

2.7.5 STRYPES: A Wrapper to Fit Around any Structure

STRYPES—STRuctured Yield Products Exchangeable for Stock—are basically a financing wrapper that can be used to facilitate a convertible issue. What separates STRYPES from other types of convertibles is not their payoff profile, but rather the presence of a third party issuer (a brokerage firm or trust) in the middle of the transaction. The essence of a STRYPES security is that the selling company engages in a forward sale of the underlying stock either to a brokerage firm or a 1940 Act Trust. The broker or the Trust then sells the STRYPES security to the public. If the STRYPES is issued by a brokerage firm the buyer accepts that broker's counter-party risk. If the

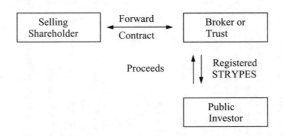

Figure 2.29   STRYPES at issuance

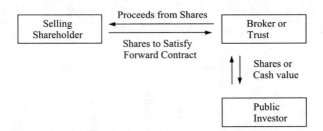

Figure 2.30   STRYPES at maturity

Table 2.6 Convertible product brand names

Product	Stands For	Performs Like[1]	Generic Description	Underwriter
ACES	Automatically Convertible Equity Securities	PRIDES	Mandatory conversion preferred with ratio determined by stock price at maturity	Goldman Sachs
CHIPS	Common-linked Higher Income Participating debt Securities	PERCS	Mandatory conversion preferred with limited upside participation	Bear Stearns
CRESTS	Convertible Redeemable Equity Structured Trust Securities	Traditional Preferred	Trust preferred, convertible at holder's option	NB-Montgomery
DECS	Debt Exchangeable for Common Stock *or* Dividend Enhanced Convertible Stock	PRIDES	Mandatory conversion preferred with ratio determined by stock price at maturity	Salomon
ELKS	Equity Linked Debt Securities	PERCS	Mandatory conversion preferred with limited upside participation, exchangeable into stock other than that of issuer (synthetic)	Salomon
ENHANCED PRIDES		PRIDES	PRIDES-type pfd consisting of Treasury securities plus a stock purchase contract	Merrill Lynch
EYES	Enhanced Yield Equity Securities	PERCS	Mandatory conversion preferred with limited upside participation	Merrill Lynch
EXCAPS	Exchangeable Capital Units	Traditional Preferred	Unit consisting of perpetual capital security and a stock purchase contract. Issued by a capital subsidiary of the company	Merrill Lynch
Feline PRIDES		PRIDES	PRIDES-type pfd consisting of TOPrS securities plus a stock purchase contract	Merrill Lynch
LYONs	Liquid Yield Option Notes	LYONs	Zero coupon convertible bond with put options	Merrill Lynch
MARCS	Mandatory Adjustable Redeemable Convertible Securities	PRIDES	Mandatory conversion preferred with ratio determined by stock price at maturity	UBS Securities
MCPDPS	Mandatory Conversion Premium Dividend Preferred Stock	PERCS	Mandatory conversion preferred with limited upside participation	Merrill Lynch
MIPS	Monthly Income Pay Securities	Traditional Preferred[2]	Preferred with monthly dividend payments, formed under a limited partnership	Goldman Sachs
PEPS	Preferred Equity Participation Securities	PRIDES	Mandatory conversion preferred with ratio determined by stock price at maturity; exchangeable into stock other than that of issuer (synthetic)	Morgan Stanley
PERCS	Preferred Equity Redemption Cumulative Stock	PERCS	Mandatory conversion preferred with limited upside participation	Morgan Stanley
PERQS	Performance Equity-linked Redemption Quarterly-pay Securities	PERCS	Mandatory conversion preferred with limited upside participation; exchangeable into stock other than that of issuer (synthetic)	Morgan Stanley
PIERS	Preferred Income Equity Redeemable Stock	Traditional Preferred	Trust preferred, convertible at holder's option	Lehman Bros.
PIES	Premium Income Equity Securities	PRIDES	Mandatory conversion preferred with ratio determined by stock price at maturity	Lehman Bros.

			Description	Issuer
PRIDES	Preferred Redeemable Increased Dividend Equity Securities *or* Provisionally Redeemable Income Debt Exchangeable for Stock	PRIDES	Mandatory conversion preferred with ratio determined by stock price at maturity	Merrill Lynch
QUIPS	Quarterly Income Preferred Securities	Traditional Preferred	Trust preferred, convertible at holder's option	Goldman Sachs
RECONS	Return Enhanced Convertible Securities	PERCS	Mandatory conversion preferred with limited upside participation	
SAILS	Stock Appreciation Income Linked Securities	PRIDES	Mandatory conversion preferred with ratio determined by stock price at maturity	CS First Boston
SPURS	Shared Preference Redeemable Securities	Traditional Preferred	Trust preferred, convertible at holder's option	Warburg, Dillon, Reed
STRYPES	Structured Yield Product Exchangeable for Stock	PRIDES or PERCS	Trust preferred with mandatory conversion, backed by Treasury securities	Merrill Lynch
TAPS	Threshold Appreciation Price Securities	PRIDES	Trust preferred with mandatory conversion, backed by Treasury securities	Smith Barney
TARGETS	Targeted Growth Enhanced Term Securities	PERCS	Mandatory conversion preferred with limited upside participation	Sun Co.
TECONS	Term Convertible Securities	Traditional Pfd (25–30 yr. mty)	Trust preferred, convertible at holder's option	JP Morgan
TIDES	Term Income Deferrable Equity Securities	Traditional Pfd (25–30 yr. mty)	Trust preferred, convertible at holder's option	CS First Boston
TIMES	Trust Issued Mandatory Exchange Securities	PRIDES	Trust preferred with mandatory conversion	Bear Stearns
TIPS	Trust Issued Preferred Securities	Traditional Preferred	Trust preferred, convertible at holder's option	Bear Stearns
TOPrS	Trust Originated Preferred Securities	Traditional Pfd (25–30 yr. mty)	Trust preferred, convertible at holder's option	Merrill Lynch
TrENDS	Trust Enhanced Dividend Securities	PRIDES	Trust preferred with mandatory conversion, backed by Treasury securities	DLJ
TRACES	Trust Automatic Common Exchange Securities	PRIDES	Trust preferred with mandatory conversion, backed by Treasury securities	Goldman Sachs
YEELDS	Yield Enhanced Equity Linked Debt Securities	PERCS	Mandatory conversion preferred with limited upside participation, exchangeable into stock other than that of issuer (synthetic)	Lehman Bros.
YES	Yield Enhanced Stock	PERCS	Mandatory conversion preferred with limited upside participation	Goldman Sachs

[1] See horizon analysis for graphical representation of projected performance.
[2] Investors will receive an IRS schedule K-1.

STRYPES is issued through a trust then the proceeds needed to pay the security's yield are posted in advance using US Treasury notes as collateral.

In the case of IMC Global 6.25% STRYPES, for example, the common shares are held by Merrill Lynch & Co. In the case of Nextel 7.25% STRYPES, the common shares are held by Nextel Trust, a subsidiary company. In each case, the entity holding the common shares is the STRYPES issuer, and the underlying common shares are called the "*Reference Property.*" The original seller has the option to satisfy the forward contract at maturity with common shares or cash of equal value.

To date most STRYPES transactions have been structured to have a basic PRIDES payoff profile (see Figure 2.20), however, the payoff profile is flexible and dependent upon the seller's goals. Issuers are attracted to STRYPES transactions for the following reasons:

- Ability to attain a tax deferred hedge on an equity stake
- Receipt of current proceeds
- Option to settle the forward contract with cash and therefore further postpone any potential capital gain
- Minimal price impact on shares monetized
- Facilitation of registered equity sale for a non-sec registrant

2.7.6 Acronyms Abound: Where's the Scorecard?

Over the last ten or so years, expansion of the convertible market has spawned a need for product innovations tailored to issuer and investor needs. These product innovations have generated a plethora of brand names which can be confusing to even the seasoned convertible user. We believe that confusion surrounding brand names should not over-shadow the convertible products themselves, which are not that complicated. Table 2.6 can serve as a quick lookup guide to convertible products, their names, and their return profiles.

2.8   CONVERTIBLE GLOSSARY

2.8.1 Traditional Convertibles Glossary

Bond Delta: Also known as Rho, this is the correlation of movements between the convertible price and interest rates.

Calls and Call Protection: Most bond issuers retain the right to redeem their bonds before the maturity date. This is known as a call. However, most bonds have call protection for a period of time. This call protection enhances the convertible's attract-iveness because it insures that the income advantage the convertible offers over the common stock may be enjoyed for a definite period of time.

Issuers usually redeem convertibles in order to force conversion into their underlying stock. For this to occur, parity must be well above the call price. If the underlying stock advances rapidly, and the issue is immediately callable, a convertible may be called before its income advantage has kicked in. Issuers also call convertibles when they have an opportunity to refinance at a lower interest cost.

Call protection usually takes one of two forms: (1) unconditional call protection where the issue cannot be called prior to a certain date and (2) conditional call protection where an issue cannot be called before a certain date unless certain conditions have been met, usually the underlying stock must trade at a premium for a specified period. Generally this is 130% (or some multiple) of the conversion price. The period of unconditional call protection is also known as the "Hard No Call" period.

Conversion Premium: The excess of the convertible's price above parity, usually expressed as a percentage.

$$Conversion\ Premium = \frac{Convertible\ Price - Conversion\ Parity}{Conversion\ Parity}$$

where Parity = Conversion Ratio × Current Stock Price

Conversion Price: Set at issue, the conversion price may be calculated as follows:

$$Conversion\ Price = \frac{Par\ Value}{Conversion\ Ratio}$$

Conversion Ratio: Also set at issue, the number of shares into which each bond may be converted.

Convertible Price: Recent price of the convertible security. Usually the offer price for convertibles that traded on the day of the data capture. For illiquid issues or issues with large bid/offer spreads, a mid-price is used.

Current Yield: The annual convertible bond coupon divided by the current price.

Equity Delta: The correlation between movements in the stock price and the convertible bond price.

Investment Value %: Also known as the bond floor, the level at which a straight bond with the same maturity and credit risk would trade. Investment value effectively provides a "floor" for the price of the convertible if it loses all its equity content and trades as a fixed income instrument.

Investment Value Premium: The premium of the convertible price above investment value, expressed as a percentage.

Issue: Convertible bonds are known by the name of the issuer, the coupon and the maturity date, e.g. Hanson 9.5% 31/1/2006. Issuers may have a number of different issues outstanding.

Issuer: The company name under which the security trades. As some bonds can be exchanged into shares of different entities, the issuer name is not always the same as the underlying security name.

Moody's/S&P: These are the latest available credit ratings for Moody's Investors Service and Standard and Poor's Corporation.

Parity: Also known as Conversion Value

$$Parity = Conversion\ Ratio\ \times\ Current\ Stock\ Price$$

Payback: The number of years it takes for the convertible's income advantage to offset the premium paid. In other words, payback is the premium recovery period. Although payback calculations give no credit to the time value of money, payback is still commonly used as a valuation benchmark. There are two methods of calculation:

(1)

$$Traditional\ Payback = \frac{\dfrac{\%\ \mathrm{Premium}}{1 + \%\ \mathrm{Premium}}}{Cvt\,Current\,Yield - \underline{StockDivYield}}$$
$$1 + \%\ Premium$$

where % premium is expressed in decimal form.

(2)

$$Dollar\ for\ Dollar\ Payback = \frac{\dfrac{\%\ \mathrm{Premium}}{1 + \%\ \mathrm{Premium}}}{Cvt\ Current\ Yield - Stock\ Div\ Yield}$$

We use the dollar for dollar method in all our research reports.

Share Price: Bid price of the underlying security into which the convertible is exchangeable.

Stock Dividend Yield: The annual yield on the common stock, i.e. the annual gross dividend / stock price.

Yields to Put and Call: The gross redemption yields that are calculated to the date of the earliest put or call.

Yield to Maturity %: YTM for bonds. This is calculated on an ISMA basis of 30/360 days unless otherwise specified and is an annual gross redemption yield to the final maturity. Where any other basis is used, this is specified.

2.8.2 PRIDES Glossary

Conversion Premium: The percentage difference between the PRIDES price and Conversion Value.

$$Conversion\ Premium = \frac{PRIDES\ Price}{(Stock\ price \times Minimum\ conversion\ ratio)} - 1$$

Conversion Value:

$$Conversion\ Value = Stock\ price \times Minimum\ conversion\ ratio$$

It is important to note that this value calculation uses the lowest conversion ratio (usually in the range 0.80–0.85). The actual conversion ratio could be as high as 1 depending on the common stock price at maturity.

Conversion Price: PRIDES are convertible into common stock at a premium price. The conversion premium can be calculated as follows:

$$Conversion\ Price = \frac{Stock\ price\ at\ Issue}{Minimum\ conversion\ ratio}$$

Early Redemption: After three years the company can call the PRIDES at pre-specified premiums to the issue price, plus accrued dividends (the call premium starts at one quarter's dividend, and amortizes to zero over the fourth year). The PRIDES will convert into common shares equal in value to the call price, or the optional conversion ratio of shares, whichever is greater.

Mandatory Conversion Ratio: At maturity the PRIDES mandatorily converts into common stock. The number of shares received per PRIDES is determined by the stock price on the conversion date. There are three possibilities for the value of the PRIDES at maturity:

1. *The common closes below the initial price.* The PRIDES converts into one share of common.

2. *The common closes between the initial price and the conversion price.* The PRIDES converts into common according to a sliding scale designed to give the PRIDES holder common shares exactly equal in value to the initial issue price. The exact ratio is laid out in the prospectus, but will be between 1 and the minimum ratio.

3. *The common price exceeds the conversion price at maturity.* The PRIDES converts into the optional conversion number of common shares.

Optional Conversion Ratio: The PRIDES holder has the right to convert into common stock at any time prior to the mandatory conversion date. A holder who converts early will receive the optional conversion ratio number of shares for each PRIDES share.

$$Optional\ Conversion\ Ratio = \frac{1}{(1 + Initial\ Conversion\ Premium)}$$

* 144A. This security may only be offered or sold to persons in the US who are Qualified Institutional Buyers ("QIB's") within the meaning of Rule 144A under the Securities Act of 1933, as amended.

Opinion Key [X-a-b-c]: Investment Risk Rating (X): A-Low, B-Average, C-Above Average, D-High. Appreciation Potential Rating (a: Int. Term-0-12 mo.; b: Long Term -> 1 yr.): 1-Buy, 2-Accumulate, 3-Neutral, 4-Reduce, 5-Sell, 6-No Rating, Income Rating(c): 7-Same/Higher, 8-Same/Lower, 9-No Cash Dividend.

Copyright 1999 Merrill Lynch, Pierce, Fenner & Smith Incorporated (MLPF&S). This report has been issued and approved for publication in the United Kingdom by Merrill Lynch, Pierce, Fenner & Smith Limited, which is regulated by SFA, and has been considered and issued in Australia by Merrill Lynch Equities (Australia) Limited (ACN 006 276 795), a licensed securities dealer under the Australian Corporations Law. The information herein was obtained from various sources; we do not guarantee its accuracy or completeness. Additional information available.

Neither the information nor any opinion expressed constitutes an offer, or an invitation to make an offer, to buy or sell any securities or any options, futures or other derivatives related to such securities ("related investments"). MLPF&S and its affiliates may trade for their own accounts as odd-lot dealer, market maker, block positioner, specialist and/or arbitrageur in any securities of this issuer(s) or in related investments, and may be on the opposite side of public orders. MLPF&S, its affiliates, directors, officers, employees and employee benefit programs may have a long or short position in any securities of this issuer(s) or in related investments. MLPF&S or its affiliates may from time to time perform investment banking or other services for, or solicit investment banking or other business from, any entity mentioned in this report.

This research report is prepared for general circulation and is circulated for general information only. It does not have regard to the specific investment objectives, financial situation and the particular needs of any specific person who may receive this report. Investors should seek financial advice regarding the appropriateness of investing in any securities or investment strategies discussed or recommended in this report and should understand that statements regarding future prospects may not be realized. Investors should note that income from such securities, if any, may fluctuate and that each security's price or value may rise or fall. Accordingly, investors may receive back less than originally invested. Past performance is not necessarily a guide to future performance.

Foreign currency rates of exchange may adversely affect the value, price or income of any security or related investment mentioned in this report. In addition, investors in securities such as ADRs, whose values are influenced by the currency of the underlying security, effectively assume currency risk.

Convertible bonds are traded over-the-counter. Retail sales and/or distribution of this report may be made only in states where these securities are exempt from registration or have been qualified for sale. MLPF&S may make a market in the convertible bonds of this company. To calculate theoretical values and return profiles, Merrill Lynch uses a proprietary arbitrage model to value the convertible as a combination of embedded options. The model is sensitive to, amongst other factors, the following inputs: stock volatility dividend yield, interest rate levels, and credit spread, all of which we hold constant. Further, we assume a similar discount/premium persists over the entire investment horizon. Our theoretical valuation in no way constitutes a fundamental opinion, nor does a theoretical discount necessarily constitute a recommendation.

3

The Life Cycle of Convertibles and Warrants

WILLIAM T. MOORE

The life cycle of a hybrid security such as a convertible or warrant begins with the issuance of the security, either through a public offer or a private placement. The cycle ends with expiration, redemption before expiration, or conversion (or exercise in the case of warrants). In this chapter several aspects of the life cycle are examined. Since most warrants and convertibles are issued publicly, and since many are called prior to maturity, resulting in conversion or exercise, these aspects of the life cycle will be examined in detail. In particular, we shall focus on three questions. First, does public issuance of convertibles and warrants have an effect on firm value? We will see that it does, and will then ask by how much an investor may expect stock prices to change as a result of issuance. Second, we will recognize that firms may call most convertibles and many warrants for redemption. What then are the effects on firms' stock values of calls of warrants and convertibles? Finally, how should the call provision be treated in valuing these securities? In other words, how should investors assess the value of the call provision in determining an appropriate value for a callable convertible or callable warrant? A related question has to do with deferred call provisions whereby callability is delayed for several years after issuance. What is the effect of such a deferral on the appropriate value of a callable convertible or warrant? How should the deferral be counted in determining the security's market value?

Several economic theories have been set forth to explain why issuance of hybrid securities may affect the market value of the issuing firm. These will be outlined before turning to the evidence. Economic theory also has something to say about the policy firms should adopt in calling convertibles and warrants. We shall examine firms' call decisions to judge whether they are in line with theory. Finally, we shall review some of the theoretical pricing models that have been applied to convertibles and warrants and will pay special attention to the treatment of the call provision in these models.

3.1 ISSUANCE OF WARRANTS AND CONVERTIBLES

US corporations issue convertible debt and convertible preferred stock, as well as warrants to purchase common stock, in amounts that vary substantially from year to year. For example, convertible debt issues made up nearly 40% of publicly issued debt in 1929, but were virtually absent from the financial landscape in the depths of

Handbook of Hybrid Instruments. Edited by Izzy Nelken. © 2000 William Moore. Published 2000 by John Wiley & Sons Ltd.

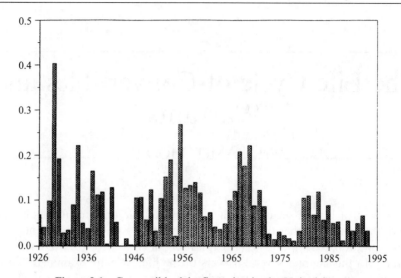

Figure 3.1   Convertible debt financing in the United States
The height of each bar represents the proportion of bonds issued in the US with conversion
features each year from 1926 through 1994
Source: US Securities and Exchange Commission

World War II, as seen in Figure 3.1. No convincing explanation of this pattern has been
reported, although we have some evidence that the popularity of convertibles appears to
be linked to rising equity markets and high interest rates.[1] Convertibles appear to be
more prominent sources of debt when equity market values have risen and when interest
rates are relatively high.

In the capital markets that are perfect or "frictionless" (no taxes, no transaction costs
and no information problems), then the well-known theorem of Nobelists Franco
Modigliani and Merton Miller (1958) shows that the firm's method of financing should
be a matter of indifference. Debt would offer no special advantage (or disadvantage)
compared to equity financing, and this would extend to hybrids such as warrant-debt
units, convertible bonds and convertible preferred stocks. But several widely examined
theories of corporate finance relax one or more of the perfect markets' assumptions
resulting in important implications for the choice of financing method in general and the
use of convertibles and warrants in particular. This means that a firm's decision to
finance investment with a convertible bond as opposed to a straight bond may affect its
market value, and therefore may not be a matter of indifference.

The theories that have had the most to say about valuation effects of convertible and
warrant issuance decisions are those based on information problems, specifically "information asymmetries" between firms' managers and outside investors. By asymmetric
information we mean that managers and other insiders know more about the firm's true
financial health than outside investors, clearly an uncontroversial assumption. Suppose
management knows that the firm's equity is overvalued in the market. This is an ideal

---

[1] Mikkelson (1980) identifies the pattern and is the first to consider explanations; Mann, Moore and Ramanlal (1999)
report evidence on the linkage to equity values and interest rates; compare their findings to Alexander, Stover and Kuhnau
(1979).

time to issue more of it, since it is in the interests of current stockholders. Conversely, if the stock is perceived to be undervalued, management might execute a share repurchase for the same reason, promotion of the interests of current shareholders. If the market is aware of these incentives, then an issuance of equity will be met by a negative share price reaction; i.e., firm value will suffer as investors infer that management is revealing a pessimistic assessment. This is the essence of an influential and widely supported argument made by Myers and Majluf (1984), and it extends readily to convertibles and warrants since they are tied directly to equity.

A related theory is due to Miller and Rock (1985) in which the firm's decision to issue *any* security conveys negative information. The setting is the same as in Myers and Majluf (1984) in that management is assumed to know more about the firm's earnings than outside investors. If management realizes that the firm will suffer a cash shortfall due to low earnings, a natural inclination is to raise external capital to compensate. However, the act of raising external capital reveals to the market that the firm has experienced a shortfall, hence its earnings are below expectations, and the stock price falls.

Another less exotic reason for a negative stock price reaction to a convertible or warrant financing decision is the possibility that the demand schedule for the firm's shares is downward sloping.[2] If such is the case, the firm can issue new shares, which will be the case upon conversion or warrant exercise, only by reducing the price to attract sufficient demand and thus reducing firm value. Whether or not the resulting devaluation will be permanent depends on whether the downward sloping feature applies to short-run demand, long-run demand or both.

In careful analysis of stock market data, we have come to know that the decision to issue convertible debt is met by a negative stock price response on average. Employing a method known as the "event study," pioneered by Fama, Fisher, Jensen and Roll (1969), economic researchers have been able to measure the price reaction due to convertible debt financing announcements. The event study method adjusts for market movements in stock prices and seeks to isolate the effect of the announcement. Dann and Mikkelson (1984), Eckbo (1986) and Mikkelson and Partch (1986) report stock price reactions to convertible debt issuance announcements that average about −2%. These estimates are statistically reliable and, though 2% may not sound like much, consider that this reaction is measured in a very short period, usually two trading days.

The decision to issue convertible preferred stock should also result in a negative common stock price reaction according to the information-based theories as well as downward sloping demand. Linn and Pinegar (1988) report event study results that are in line with this prediction. They find that common stock prices fall on average over 1.4% for industrial firms upon announcement of convertible preferred financing.

Similar analysis has been done of firms' decisions to issue debt with attached warrants. Phelps, Moore and Roenfeldt (1991) document a negative common stock price reaction of about 1.3% during the announcement period, roughly in line with the magnitude of reactions to convertible debt and preferred issuance announcements. However, Billingsley, Lamy and Smith (1990) find mixed evidence. On the announcement day they find a negative price reaction on average, but it is not statistically reliable. The differences in the findings appear to be due to sampling method and the manner of defining the announcement period.

---

[2] See Harris and Gurel (1986).

The negative price reactions to financing decisions documented in the scientific studies are largely confined to issues containing equity; i.e., convertibles, warrants and common stock. For instance, issuance of straight bonds and straight preferred stock result in average stock price reactions that are barely perceptible.[3] On the other hand, when firms issue new common stock the average price reaction is around −3%.[4] Thus, while issuance announcements of hybrids such as convertibles and warrant-debt units have a negative average effect on firm value, the magnitude of the devaluation is even more severe when pure equity is issued. These results are consistent with the Myers and Majluf (1984) information story, whereby the demand curve for the firm's shares shifts downward. The results are also consistent with a stationary but downward sloping demand curve; i.e., equilibrium price per share must be lowered due to an increase in supply.

What does all this mean for managers and investors? Managers should be aware that the costs of issuance of new securities include not only direct flotation costs such as underwriter expenses and fees charged by the Securities and Exchange Commission, but also losses in equity value resulting from information conveyed by the decision. As shown in Figure 3.2, convertible bonds have flotation costs averaging about 2% for large issues (over $500 million) to nearly 9% for small issues (under $10 million). Compare this to straight debt issues in Figure 3.2. Direct flotation costs average under 2% for large

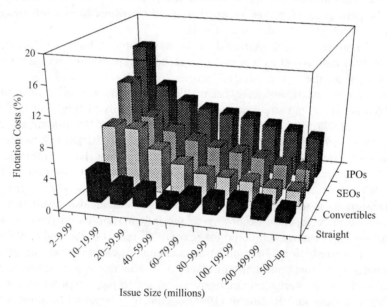

Figure 3.2   Direct flotation costs for new security issues

Bar heights represent direct flotation costs as a percentage of the amount issued for straight debt (straight), convertible bonds (convertibles), seasoned equity offerings (SEOs), and initial public offerings of equity (IPOs)

Source: Reproduced by permission from "The Cost of Rising Capital," by J. Lee, S. Lochhead, J. Ritter and Q. Zhao, *Journal of Financial Research*, Spring 1996

---

[3] See Linn and Pinegar (1988), Mikkelson and Partch (1986), Dann and Mikkelson (1984), and Eckbo (1986).
[4] See, for example, Mikkelson and Partch (1986), and the excellent survey article by Smith (1986).

issues and a little over 4% for small issues. When the negative stock price reactions to the decisions are taken into account, the total costs of issuance of convertibles further exceed those for straight bonds.

Firms' stated motives for issuance of hybrids have long included "delayed equity financing" and "debt sweetening."[5] By issuing convertibles or warrant-debt units as temporary or bridge financing, firms must endure increased leverage only until their stock prices have increased and investors have converted their bonds or preferreds, or exercised their warrants (see Stein 1992 for a formal development of "backdoor equity" financing; see also Mayers 1998).

By adding conversion features or warrants, firms may ameliorate costly conflict among different classes of investors. For instance, stockholders and creditors have good reason to disagree on investment policy where risk is concerned. Creditors, by the nature of their fixed claims, naturally prefer a conservative policy. After all, if the firm gambles and does well, creditors do not receive anything more, and if the gamble fails, they suffer. Conversely, stockholders prefer for the firm to take calculated risks due to the call option feature inherent in equity claims. If the firm does well stockholders gain, and if it does poorly they are insulated by limited liability from losses exceeding 100% of their investment. By adding warrants or conversion features to debt (or preferred stock), firms may secure lower borrowing rates or relaxed covenants. The reason is that convertibles and warrants make creditors more like stockholders; i.e., their economic interests are more nearly aligned with stockholders' interests than would be the case for straight debt.[6] Consequently, convertible investors may demand less compensation (lower coupon or dividend rate), or require fewer restrictions, due to improved alignment of their interests with those of common stockholders.

Brennan and Schwartz (1988) suggest that convertibles may solve problems arising from differences in opinion as to the firm's risk. Creditors naturally focus on the firm's default risk and price bonds down to compensate. But the flip side of a convertible bond is that volatility (which is directly linked to default risk) influences conversion value upward. If investors overestimate the firm's risk, straight debt will be penalized more than convertibles or warrant-debt because of the offsetting overvaluation of the equity option. Thus hybrids may be useful in overcoming such disagreements.

Several academic studies have investigated why firms issue hybrids in order to shed light on some of the theories.[7] But investors should know that once firms announce intentions to issue securities that have equity components, regardless of their underlying motives, stock values will decline on average. The available evidence suggests that the devaluations appear to be permanent. Thus while convertibles and warrants may present certain advantages to the firm, such as reduced restrictions in the covenant structure, or perhaps lower coupon or dividend rates, it is clear from the evidence developed to date that they pay for these advantages to some extent in the form of higher flotation costs and equity value reductions. There is no free lunch.

---

[5] See Pilcher (1955) for an early survey; also Hoffmeister (1977), Brigham (1966), and Billingsley and Smith (1996).

[6] For extensive analysis of the conflicts among different security classes see Jensen and Meckling (1976); see Mikkelson's 1980 dissertation for detailed analysis of the role of warrants and convertibles in resolving the conflict, followed by Moore (1982) and Green (1984).

[7] See Billingsley, Lamy and Thompson (1988), Jen, Choi and Lee (1997), and Lewis, Rogalski and Seward (1998), for example.

3.2 CALLING CONVERTIBLES AND WARRANTS

Most convertible bonds and preferred stocks have call provisions, enabling firms essentially to *force* conversion (see Crabbe and Helwege 1994 for a discussion of the call provision and how it can help manage the conflict between bondholders and stockholders). Firms usually call convertibles, both bonds and preferred stocks, when they are "in the money." To see what this means, define *conversion value* as the number of shares into which an issue may be converted multiplied by the current price per share of the common stock. This gives the value the issue would command if it were converted immediately. Now define the *effective call price* as the sum of the nominal call price (usually given in a schedule in the contract) and accrued interest (on bonds) or dividends (on preferreds). This is what the investor would receive if the convertible were surrendered for redemption in response to a call. Exhibit 3.1 is an excerpt from the description in *Moody's Industrial Manual* of a callable convertible preferred stock issued by Anheuser-Busch in 1983. Notice that the issue may be redeemed for $40 per share, plus accrued dividends.

In general, if the conversion value exceeds the effective call price when an issue is called, the investor should choose to convert rather than surrender the security for redemption. When conversion value exceeds call price, the issue is said to be "in-the-money," and a call while in the money is often referred to as a "conversion-forcing call" because it pushes investors to convert.

Note also in Exhibit 3.1 that Anheuser-Busch must give 30 to 60 days notice to investors. This is known as the call notice period and represents a lower bound on the

---

1. Anheuser-Busch Companies, Inc. convertible redeemable preferred; par $1:
AUTH—All series, 40,000,000 shs.; outstg., this series, Dec. 31, 1984, 7,500,766 shs.; par $1.
DIVIDEND RIGHTS—Entitled to cumulative cash dividends at an annual rate of $3.60 per share, payable quarterly.
DIVIDEND RECORD—Initial dividend of $1.26 paid Mar. 10, 1983. Regular quarterly dividends paid thereafter.
VOTING RIGHTS—Holders are entitled to 0.645 of one vote for each share of such stock held of record with the same rights as holders of common shares. Such voting rights shall be subject to adjustment from time to time consistent with the adjustments to the conversion rate referred to below. Holders of the preferred Shares are also entitled to the special voting rights described below.
   If the equivalent of six or more full quarterly dividends payable on any series of preferred stock are in arrears, the number of directors will be increased by two, and the holders of the preferred shares and any other series of preferred stock so entitled to vote (voting as a single class) shall have the right to elect such two directors until all dividends in arrears have been paid or declared and set apart for payment (at which time the number of directors will be reduced by two, and two directors so elected by the holders of the preferred stock will cease to be directors).
LIQUIDATION RIGHTS—In liquidation, entitled to $40 per sh.
CONVERSION RIGHTS—Into common at any time at the rate of 0.645 com. shs. for each preferred sh., subject to adjustments under certain conditions. Conv. privilege protected against dilution.
REDEMPTION PROVISIONS—On and after the fifth anniversary of the Effective Date, Co. may, upon not less than 30 nor more than 60 days notice, redeem the Anheuser-Busch Preferred Shares in whole or from time to time in part, at a redemption price of $40 per share together with accrued dividends to the date of redemption. If less than all of the Series A Convertible Preferred Stock is redeemed, the particular shares to be redeemed shall be allocated among the holders of Series A Convertible Preferred Stock pro rata or by lot, as the Board of Directors of Co. may determine.

Exhibit 3.1 Anheuser-Busch Convertible Preferred Stock

Source: *Moody's Industrial Manual*, 1983, p. 1030. Reproduced by permission of Moody's Investors Service

life expectancy of the conversion option. That is, if Anheuser-Busch announces a call, investors still have at least 30 days to convert; i.e., the option is not extinguished immediately upon call announcement.

Finally, the Anheuser-Busch preferred issue was not callable until five years had lapsed from the date of issuance. This illustrates deferred callability and most convertibles have deferred call provisions requiring waiting periods of three to five years.

Before the early 1980s most warrants issued in the US were not callable, but that began to change in this period and recently about one-third of newly issued warrants have either explicit call provisions or they stipulate that the firms may accelerate expiration of the warrants. Either way, exercise may be forced and warrant contracts often specify that calls cannot be executed (or expiration may not be accelerated) unless the firm's common stock exceeds the exercise price by a specified amount. Thus calling a warrant or accelerating its expiration date will usually result in immediate exercise of the issue. Exhibit 3.2 is an excerpt from *Moody's Industrial Manual* describing the call provision of Storer Communications in its warrant issue. Notice that the warrant was callable commencing in 1986, and that the stock price must be 1.5 times the amount of the exercise price for at least 20 days in order for the firm to call, hence a call of this issue will almost certainly result in forced exercise. Exhibit 3.3 is an excerpt for Geothermal Resources International, also from *Moody's Industrial Manual*. This firm may accelerate the expiration date of its warrant issue, and as in the case of the explicit call provision of Storer Communications, the stock must satisfy certain minimum price requirements in order for expiration to be accelerated.

Wts. are callable, at option of Co., in whole or in part on or after May 15, 1986 at $10 per warrant, subject to adjustment, in event that closing price of Co.'s common stock has been in excess of 150% of the then effective exercise price of warrants on any 20 trading days within a period of 30 consecutive trading days.

Exhibit 3.2   Storer Communications' warrants

Source: Excerpt from *Moody's Industrial Manual*, p. 5999, 1984. Reproduced by permission of Moody's Investors Service

---

Co. may accelerate date to as early as November 15, 1987 if common stock has a closing price of not less than 150% of current exercise price for 30 consecutive days.

Exhibit 3.3   Geothermal Resources international warrants

Source: Excerpt from *Moody's Industrial Manual*, p. 2968, 1989. Reproduced by permission of Moody's Investors Service

3.3   WHEN SHOULD WARRANTS AND CONVERTIBLES BE CALLED?

What *should* happen to the firm's common stock value when a conversion-forcing call is executed, or when a warrant is called or has its expiration shortened? What *does* happen when these events occur?

To appreciate the answers to these questions, we first need a policy prescription for calling convertibles and warrants. Such a prescription was provided by Ingersoll (1977a) and Brennan and Schwartz (1977) in a perfect markets setting. Recall that Modigliani and Miller show that, in such a market, the firm's value will be independent of its capital structure. This means the firm can call and force conversion from bonds or preferreds to common, and as long as no change in investment policy is made, the firm's total market value will remain the same.

Why then would a firm's management execute a call? While total firm value will remain unchanged, the value apportioned to various security holders will not be invariant to the change. In particular, the convertible holders or warrant holders have call options on the firm's common stock. As long as the options are "alive" they will have value. In the case of convertibles, this means the bond or preferred should be valued at least as high as the greater of its conversion value or its straight value. That is, even if the conversion value is low, the issue still has a minimum or floor value as a straight security. As conversion value grows, this establishes a new (higher) floor.[8] As soon as the firm calls, assuming for the moment that there is no minimum call notice period, this option value goes to zero. Thus the convertible bond or preferred should decline in value, and assuming the Modigliani–Miller (1958) result holds, as it will in a perfect market, the lost option value will revert to the equity holders.

Thus we have a wealth expropriation possibility and Ingersoll (1977a) and Brennan and Schwartz (1977) go on to develop the policy which will maximize the expropriation. They show that it is optimal to call and force conversion as soon as the conversion value rises to the effective call price. If the firm delays calling beyond this point it leaves a valuable option in the hands of the convertible holders, thus ignoring an opportunity to improve shareholder wealth. If the firm calls before this point, it ends up paying more (the nominal redemption price plus accrued coupon interest or dividends) for the convertible issue than it is worth (conversion value). Hence the policy that maximizes shareholder wealth is to call as soon as conversion value exceeds the call price.

No sooner was this policy developed than researchers reported that it did not describe firms' decisions in practice. What's worse, the deviations from the policy were so dramatic that they forced some theoreticians to reconsider the underlying assumptions. Ingersoll (1977b) found that firms "delayed" calling convertible bonds until their conversion values exceeded call price by 83.5% on average (median 43.9%). The story with convertible preferreds was not much better—these calls were delayed until conversion value was 69.9% above call price on average (median 38.5%). Hence a new "anomaly" was born; i.e., firms call convertibles "too late."

Ingersoll (1977b) modified his theory to allow for a minimum call notice period, averaging about 30 days in practice. This change actually suggested that the firm should call *before* conversion value reached the call price, further deepening the gap between theory and practice! He then reconsidered the call policy by relaxing the perfect markets assumptions. In order to avoid a cash shortage, firms might wait until the conversion value exceeds call price by a safety margin sufficient to insure that the issue does not drift "out of the money" during the period from the call announcement to the effective date of redemption; i.e., during the call notice period. This presumed that costs of raising the necessary cash to redeem the issue, should that become necessary, were significant. The problem was that in simulations of Ingersoll's convertible pricing model, it became apparent that such a safety margin could stand to be far less than that observed, often put at 20% above call price. Jaffee and Shleifer (1990) set forth an argument based on costly financial distress. If the costs of raising cash in the event of an unintended

---

[8] See Brigham (1966) for early discussion.

redemption were very high, and the firm would suffer costly financial distress, even bankruptcy, if the cash were not raised, then such a safety margin might be feasible.

Constantinides and Grundy (1987) argued that it may make sense for firms to delay calling when there is a yield difference between the called issue and the common stock into which it is convertible. If the yield on the firm's common stock exceeds that on the convertible, investors should voluntarily convert. If the yield on the convertible bond or preferred is lower than the yield on the common, then it would be prudent for the firm to delay. The reason is that if a call imposes some costs on the firm it is better to wait for investors to convert voluntarily to capture the higher yield. This is analogous to the idea that a call option on a zero dividend common stock should not be exercised prior to expiration, but a call on a dividend paying stock may rationally be exercised "early" because of the dividend payment. Thus Constantinides and Grundy argue that a firm should be indifferent between voluntary and forced conversion, but if forcing conversion generates some costs, it may be better to wait for voluntary conversion.

Campbell, Ederington and Vankudre (1991) examine the argument of Constantinides and Grundy on a sample of convertible bonds. They adjust the coupon yield on the bonds by the corporate tax rate to make the dividend yield on the common and the coupon yield on the debt comparable on an after-tax basis (following Constantinides and Grundy). They find that the stock market reaction to call announcements is conditioned on the relative yields of the convertible and the common, supporting the reasoning of Constantinides and Grundy. Firms with a "yield disadvantage," a common stock dividend yield exceeding the tax-adjusted convertible bond yield, experience a significant negative price reaction to call announcements. This suggests that after-tax cash flow commitments to convertible holders will rise as a result of conversion. For their sample of low yield stocks, where the firm enjoys a "yield advantage" as a result of conversion, the stock price reaction is negligible.

Another perfect markets assumption is relaxed by Harris and Raviv (1985). They allow for asymmetric distribution of information between the firm's management and outside investors. Their story is essentially that firms should call and force conversion if they believe their stock prices will soon fall. By forcing conversion when the price is high, current stockholders are helped at the expense of the convertible holders. If the firm waits until the bad news has been reflected in the stock value, it is too late from the point of view of the current stockholders. If the future looks bright, on the other hand, management should delay calling, assuming that there are some costs associated with executing a call. Thus according to this argument, firms will reveal bad news by calling and good news by delaying.

Ofer and Natarajan (1987) report that firms' earnings decline following conversion-forcing calls of bonds. This lends support to the prediction of Harris and Raviv, however, Campbell et al. (1991) challenge this finding with meticulous analysis of earnings relative to industry levels.

The Harris and Raviv story was constructed to explain *two* puzzles, the observation that firms call "late" and the finding that call announcements result in negative stock price reactions (more on this later). Let's now consider the evidence on delayed calls. Asquith and Mullins (1991) and Asquith (1995) examine convertible debt calls and find that the 20% safety margin explains most call behavior. This finding is challenged however by Ederington, Caton and Campbell (1997) who find a significant number of exceptions; i.e., instances where call was delayed to the point where conversion value well exceeded the 20% margin over call price. Byrd, Mann, Moore and Ramanlal (1998) find numerous exceptions for their sample of convertible preferred stock calls. Dunn and Eades (1989) consider the difference in yields between convertible preferreds and common stocks and show that, once the yield differential is taken into account, most but not all issues are called or voluntarily converted in a timely manner.

Warrants that may be called or whose expiration may be accelerated are found to be extinguished in a "timely" fashion. That is, beyond the point where call is contractually delayed, warrant calls are executed quickly.[9] This could be because the cash outlay required to call a warrant issue is usually very small, hence no significant distress costs arise in the event a redemption is required by a retreating stock price.

Byrd et al. (1998) argue that there is a more fundamental condition that is key in determining whether calls are indeed "late." They refer to the original perfect markets call policy to call and force conversion as soon as conversion value exceeds call price. Remember that the underlying reason for executing a call at this point is to transfer the value of the conversion option from senior securities to common stock. If we assume symmetric rationality; i.e., both investors and firms' managers act rationally, then why would investors in convertible securities impound an option premium once the call condition has been met? In other words, why would investors pay a premium for an option that may be extinguished at any moment (once conversion value exceeds call price)? This question is even more compelling when we consider that the very act of impounding a positive option premium under these conditions should *provoke* a conversion-forcing call! If investors do not impound such a premium once the issues become conversion-forceable, there is no wealth transfer motive to call and we may expect calls to occur at arbitrary times during the life of the securities. In other words, calls would be executed for reasons other than transfer of wealth to common stockholders, hence there is no delay in the sense intended by Ingersoll (1977a).

Constantinides and Grundy (1984) performed an early study of this question but their findings have remained unpublished. They examined convertible bonds and found support for this argument; i.e., convertible bond investors typically do not pay an option premium for bonds that are conversion-forceable. Byrd et al. (1998) examine daily prices of a sample of convertible preferred stocks and find that those that had positive option premia (market price exceeding conversion value) were called quickly. Figure 3.3 is from their study and it shows the median option premium per share (vertical axis) as a function of the longest period (in months) during which each issue in their study was callable and in-the-money; i.e., conversion could have been forced. Those with positive premia were left outstanding only a few months, while those with zero or negative premia were left uncalled for periods up to 240 months. They argue that there is therefore no "anomaly" to explain; i.e., firms have not systematically violated the optimal call policy set forth in the most elementary conditions by Ingersoll (1977a) and Brennan and Schwartz (1977). This recent evidence, as well as the earlier evidence of Constantinides and Grundy (1984), suggests that firms have not called convertibles "late."

Further evidence is being developed on convertible bond calls paralleling that of Byrd et al. Regardless of how the final answers evolve, it appears that firms do not systematically make call decisions that are deleterious to their shareholders. If a valuable

---

[9] See Schultz (1993).

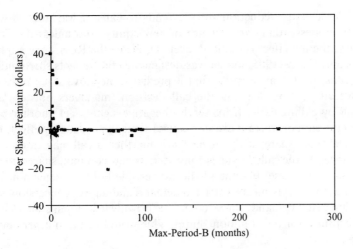

Figure 3.3   Conversion option premium versus maximum length of time in which conversion may be found

Median conversion option premium per share is plotted on the vertical axis, and the maximum period of time (in months) each convertible preferred was callable and in-the-money is on the horizontal axis

Source: Reproduced by permission from "Rational Timing of Calls of Convertible Preferred Stocks," by A. Byrd, S. Mann, W. T. Moore, and P. Ramanlal, *Journal of Financial Research*, **21**, 1998

option exists that may be transferred to common, managers appear to exploit it as soon as it is practical to do so. This has implications for the specification of valuation models of hybrids, which will be taken up as our last topic.

3.4   WHAT HAPPENS TO FIRM VALUE WHEN FIRMS FORCE CONVERSION OR EXERCISE?

Remember there are *two* puzzles associated with firms' call decisions. The first is the notion of "late" calls, which seems to have been put to rest. The second is the finding that stock values decline on average when firms announce conversion-forcing calls of convertible bonds (Mikkelson 1981) and preferred stocks (Mais, Moore and Rogers 1989). On average, calling firms' shares drop by about 1.5 to 2% almost immediately when calls are announced. When firms call warrants their share prices drop even more dramatically, averaging 4% or more (Schultz 1993, and Fields and Moore 1995).

Why? As Smith (1986) has pointed out, capital structure decisions that reduce financial leverage almost always result in negative effects on equity values, and the decision to force conversion of a bond or preferred results in lower leverage. The reason for a negative reaction could be lost debt tax shields (for convertible bonds only), or adverse information (see Mikkelson 1985 for evidence on lost tax shields as an explanation). Ross (1977) sets forth a theory that implies managers signal bad news by deleveraging. This is the flip side of Ross' argument that leverage reveals confidence in the firm's abilities to meet fixed obligations in the future. By extinguishing such obligations by forcing conversion to common equity, managers may convey a pessimistic outlook to the market. The leverage reduction story extends to calls of warrants as well. Forced warrant exercise is essentially an issuance of new equity, and unless the firm borrows simultaneously, the net effect is reduced leverage, hence the Ross story applies.

The Harris and Raviv (1985) model was designed to fit the facts surrounding conversion-forcing calls, so it is no surprise that it predicts a negative stock price reaction to such calls. Recall that by delaying the call decision, managers bolster the market's optimism, and by calling early, firms send a negative signal. Yet another possibility is that forced conversion or warrant exercise causes some type of supply effect. If the short-run demand curve for shares is downward sloping, then a call may cause a short-term reduction in price. As the called issue is converted to new common shares, the number of outstanding shares will rise. If some of the convertible holders prefer not holding new shares, then the new supply meets restricted demand and a price concession is needed for sellers. The long-run demand curve could be downward sloping as well, owing to imperfect substitutes for the common shares. This would result in a permanent decline in share price.

What is the evidence? Researchers were guided initially by the presumption that the price reduction upon conversion-forcing calls was permanent. Mikkelson (1985) found support for lost tax shields as an explanation of the value decline, and this represents a permanent loss. Of course, this explanation did not extend to forced conversion of preferred stocks which were later shown by Mais et al. (1989) to exhibit a similar negative valuation effect. The Ross (1977) signaling model supports a negative valuation effect of either type of call and extends to warrant calls as well. Harris and Raviv's (1985) model predicts a negative effect of a call of a convertible bond, but their model does not readily extend to preferred stocks. The reason is that their model depends on the presence of a fixed maturity date by which the bonds either will be converted to common or redeemed for cash. In the case of most preferred stocks, no fixed maturity date exists due to their perpetual nature.

Mazzeo and Moore (1992) and Byrd and Moore (1994, 1996) revisit the issue and question whether the price reduction is permanent. They argue that the effect could be short-run due to selling pressure during the conversion period, usually lasting about 30 days. Mazzeo and Moore (1992) find that the two-day price reduction at the call announcement is erased by the end of this period. On average stock prices rise to a level exceeding their pre-call levels by the end of the conversion period. This makes explanations such as lost tax shields and negative information signaling untenable. Mazzeo and Moore also find that stock prices that fall the most also recover the most following convertible bond calls, but they do not find this effect for preferred calls. Such rebounding would be expected if the short-term selling pressure explanation holds. However, Kadapakkam and Tang (1996) later re-examine the question and, using a larger sample and carefully controlling for other information effects, they show that the rebounding effect is exhibited for convertible preferred calls as well.

Byrd and Moore (1996) investigate the issue further by comparing analysts' earnings forecasts before and after call announcements. If the information stories are controlling, as supported earlier by Ofer and Natarajan (1987), analysts should revise estimates downward in response to calls. The researchers find just the opposite—analysts revise short-term and long-term profit forecasts *upward* following conversion-forcing calls. Shastri and Shastri (1996) report similar findings. Recall that Campbell et al. (1991) failed to find support for earnings deterioration following calls. Instead they found that firms experienced *above* average growth in earnings *before* mounting conversion-forcing calls, and this may be what led Ofer and Natarajan (1987) to conclude that such calls precede bad news.

An extension in the spirit of Harris and Raviv's model is set forth and examined by Singh, Cowan and Nayar (1991) and Cowan, Nayar and Singh (1992). They suggest that firms with bad earnings projections call convertibles through underwriters. This gives them insurance that the calls will be successful. In the event the stock price falls during the call notice period, and the issue goes "out of the money," the underwriter will be responsible for redeeming the issue. The authors find evidence consistent with the argument; i.e., underwritten calls produce the strongest negative average price reactions. But Byrd and Moore (1998) report evidence that the decision to engage an underwriter may be due simply to the size of the issue to be called. Larger issues should result in more selling pressure, hence negative price reactions. They find that the price reaction is short-lived for *both* types of calls, underwritten and nonunderwritten, and that once size is taken into account, the presence of an underwriter has negligible effect on the stock price reaction.

The message for managers and investors at this point seems to be that a short-term price reduction of the firm's common stock is to be expected when firms call and force conversion of bonds and preferred stocks. The effect should not last beyond the conversion period, so this might be borne in mind in making portfolio decisions. For exercise-forcing calls of warrants, the results are less persuasive. While stock prices return to pre-call levels on average in a few weeks following call announcements, no published study as yet has shown the rebounding effect. That is, it is not the case that those that decline the most recover the most.

3.5   ASSESSING THE VALUE OF THE CALL PROVISION IN THEORETICAL MODELS

A call provision in a convertible or warrant represents a short call to the investor, hence the value of the option should be subtracted from the value the security would command if it were not callable. Some early valuation models for convertibles such as that by Ingersoll (1977a) took this feature into account and resulted in closed form solutions; i.e., mathematical models that could be calculated directly given appropriate parameters. No further manipulations such as integration were needed. Brennan and Schwartz (1980) illustrate valuing a convertible bond by numerical solution of the fundamental differential equation developed by Merton (1974) and applied by Ingersoll (1977a) and Brennan and Schwartz (1977). Merton (1974) shows that any security (with value F) issued by a firm with value V can be viewed as a function of V and time (t). The firm's value is assumed to follow Wiener–Bachelier dynamics as described by:

$$dV = (\alpha V - C)dt + \sigma V d\bar{z}. \qquad (3.1)$$

In (3.1), α is the rate of growth expected for V and C is the cash flow rate for all securities issued by the firm (dividends and interest payments). The term $\sigma V d\bar{z}$ is the product of an instantaneous standard deviation (σ) and a Wiener–Bachelier variate ($d\bar{z}$).

A given security issued by the firm has price dynamics assumed as follows:

$$dF = (\alpha_F F - c)dt + \sigma_F F d\tilde{z}.$$ (3.2)

In (3.2), α_F is the expected rate of growth in the security's value, and c is the cash flow rate for that security. In obvious notation, the term $\sigma_F F d\tilde{z}$ describes the Wiener–Bachelier dynamics.

By application of Ito's lemma, dF in (3.2) is expressed in terms of the first and second derivatives of F with respect to V, denoted by F_V and F_{VV}, respectively. Then by applying arbitrage arguments, Merton shows that the market value of the security (F) must satisfy the partial differential equation:

$$\frac{1}{2}\sigma^2 V^2 F_{VV} + (rV - C)F_V - rF + c + F_t = 0.$$ (3.3)

In (3.3), r denotes the instantaneous risk-free rate of interest. The equation (3.3) may be solved by adding boundary conditions. For instance, in the simplest version (Model 1), tested by Ramanlal, Mann and Moore (1998), the lower boundary is $F(V = 0) = 0$, reflecting limited liability, and the upper boundary is $F(V = \infty) = c/r$, a riskless perpetuity.

Ramanlal et al. (1998) report extensive tests of the pricing method using a sample of daily prices of 24 callable convertible preferred stock issues. Their Model 1 ignores callability and convertibility and values each issue as a straight preferred. The model's theoretical prices are below actual market prices by over 35% on average. Model 2 includes a boundary condition for the conversion feature but ignores callability. As expected, this version overstates market prices by nearly 13% on average. These models can be solved simply, but the resulting prices are intolerably different from market prices.

Ingersoll (1977a) develops an analytical solution to (3.3) allowing for callability at price K and convertibility into the proportion γ of the firm's equity value. Model 3 of Ramanlal et al. is that developed by Ingersoll (1977a) modified to allow for dividend payments on the common stock. It is expected to underprice on average and this is the case in their study. The mean pricing error is -3.17%. Emanuel (1983a) derives a model that allows for payment of dividends in arrears on the preferred and nonconstant dividends on the common stock. This is Model 4 and, like the Ingersoll (1977a) version, it does not allow for deferred callability, hence it is expected to underprice. The mean pricing error is -6.88%.

Ramanlal et al. (1998) then test the extended version (Model 5) which allows for callability, convertibility and the deferred call provision. This method requires extensive computer programming but the additional burden seems to be worthwhile. The mean pricing error is $-.18\%$, within the bid-ask spread on most convertible preferreds. In Figure 3.4 the frequency distributions of percentage pricing errors for all five versions are shown for comparison.

Ramanlal, Mann and Moore (1996) develop an approximation for the value of a callable convertible preferred issue with deferred call. Their method avoids the need for programming and solving a partial differential equation and can be solved on many handheld calculators. Their model follows from the same price dynamics as in equations (3.1) and (3.2). If the conversion value (γV) exceeds the call price (K) on a preferred that is callable anytime, the issue's price should be its conversion value. If αV is less than K, the issue is out of the money and its value, following Ingersoll (1977a) should be:

$$\frac{\gamma - [(c/C)(\gamma/K)F(K/\gamma)]V - (c/C - \gamma)F(V)}{[1 - (\gamma/K)F(K/\gamma)]} \tag{3.4}$$

The expression $F(K/\gamma)$ in (3.4) is:

$$F(K/\gamma) = \frac{C}{r}[1 - P(a, ad) + P(a+1, ad)/d], \tag{3.5}$$

where $a = 2r/\sigma^2$, $d = C/r/(K/\gamma)$, and $P(a, ad)$ and $P(a+1, ad)$ = the gamma ratio with parameters $\{a, ad\}$ and $\{a+1, ad\}$, respectively. The expression for $F(V)$ in (3.4) is the same as (3.5) but with $d = C/r/(K/\gamma)$.

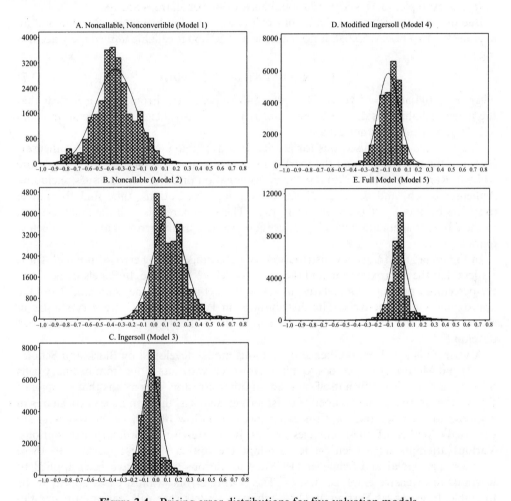

Figure 3.4   Pricing error distributions for five valuation models

Each panel depicts the distribution of pricing errors (model price–market price) for daily observations on 24 callable, convertible preferred stock issues

Source: "Convertible Preferred Stock Valuation: Tests of Alternative Models," by P. Ramanlal, S. Mann and W. T. Moore, *Review of Quantitative Finance and Accounting*, **10**, 1998, 303–319

Suppose a firm has a callable convertible preferred issue callable at $K = \$300$ million. The firm's total equity value (V) is $2.5 billion. Annual dividends on the preferred (c) total $27 million, whereas dividends on the preferred and common combined total $71.4 million. The conversion ratio (γ) is .0911, the risk-free rate is .104 and the volatility of the firm's equity (σ) is .2522. The value of the issue from solving (3.5) is about $37.60 per share based on 7.5 million preferred shares outstanding. If this issue were *not* callable, its value would be γV if preferred dividends (c) exceeded dividends on converted shares (γC), because investors would convert. If, on the other hand, $c < \gamma C$, as is the case here, the issue would be worth:

$$\gamma V + [c/C - \gamma]F(V) \tag{3.6}$$

In this example, (3.6) is $396\,590\,000$, hence value per share is $52.88.

But suppose the issue *is* callable, but call is deferred for five years. Ramanlal et al. average the two prices, $52.88 if not callable and $37.60 if callable immediately according to:

$$(1 - e^{-rt})(52.88) + e^{-rt}(37.60), \tag{3.7}$$

where $r = .104$ and $t = 5$ years. This gives $43.80 per share. From (3.7), it is clear that the longer callability is deferred, the closer is $1 - e^{-rT}$ to 1, hence the value approaches $52.88, the price if it is not callable.

The example we just used was for a callable convertible preferred issue of Anheuser-Busch in the early 1980s and the market price at the time was $44 per share (compare $43.80). Ramanlal et al. (1996) test the approximation on 24 preferred issues, including Anheuser-Busch, and for over $27\,000$ daily price observations, they find the model misprices by about $.40 per share on average. They compare this with the exact solution of the differential equation which produces an average pricing error of about $.20 below market price.

In Figure 3.5 are frequency distributions of percentage pricing errors. In Panel A it is evident that the approximation and the exact model are very close. In Panels B and C are the percentage pricing errors relative to actual market prices for the exact model and the approximation, respectively. The distributions in Panels B and C are very similar in shape, hence little value appears to be lost in using the approximation formula they develop.

A warrant is a call option, hence the famous model developed by Black and Scholes (1973) and Merton (1973) comes to mind. However, warrants differ from ordinary calls in that the writer is the firm itself, and not another investor. This means that exercise of the warrant increases the number of outstanding shares as the firm issues new shares in response to exercise, and the firm experiences an inflow of cash as the warrants are exercised. Neither of these changes results from exercise of ordinary call options. Various attempts have been made to adapt the option pricing apparatus to these realities; e.g., Galai and Schneller (1978). And various models have been applied to warrants in extensive empirical tests.[10] The pricing errors in most cases appear to be tolerable, however, as Ferri et al. (1988) show, warrants with call features are significantly mispriced by the Black–Scholes method.

---

[10] See Chen (1975), Schwartz (1977), Noreen and Wolfson (1981), Sinkey and Miles (1982), Ferri, Moore and Schirm (1988), Lauterbach and Schultz (1990), and Kremer and Roenfeldt (1993).

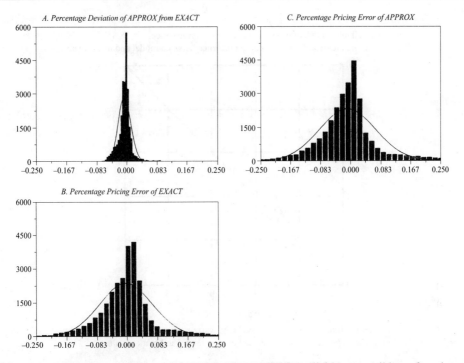

Figure 3.5   Pricing errors of approximate valuation model for callable convertible preferred stock

The exact model (EXACT) is the differential equation of Merton (1974), and the approximate model (APPROX) is the closed form solution of Ramanlal, Mann and Moore (1996)

Source: Reproduced by permission from "A Simple Approximation of the Value of Callable Convertible Preferred Stock," by P. Ramanlal, S. Mann, and W. T. Moore, *Financial Management*, **25** 1996, 74–85. © Financial Management Association International, University of South Florida, College of Business Administration -#3331, Tampa, FL 33620–5500, Tel. (813)974 2084

Merton (1973) derives a model value for a callable warrant, but his solution is restricted to a perpetual warrant and deferred callability is not taken into account. Burney and Moore (1997) develop and test a warrant valuation model that takes callability into account, but their model does not allow for deferred callability. They test the model on warrants for which the deferred call period has lapsed, hence their sample fits their model's assumptions. Their model produces an average pricing error of −3.31%, whereas the Black–Scholes model (ignoring callability) overprices actual warrants on average by 12.51%. Pricing errors for the Black–Scholes model and the Burney–Moore model are shown in Figure 3.6.

Where does this leave us? No simple model of warrant value with deferred callability has been set forth. And the approximation method developed by Ramanlal et al. (1996) is applicable to preferred stocks but not bonds. The most prominent method now used in practice for valuing option embedded bonds and preferreds, as well as warrants, involves binary or quadranary trees (Nelken 1997) following from the binomial option pricing framework set forth by Cox, Ross and Rubinstein (1979). This approach holds much promise, it is easy to understand, and computer programs are now available to make it useable. For instance, *ConvB* developed by Supercomputing Consultants, Inc., takes

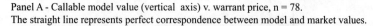

Panel A - Callable model value (vertical axis) v. warrant price, n = 78.
The straight line represents perfect correspondence between model and market values.

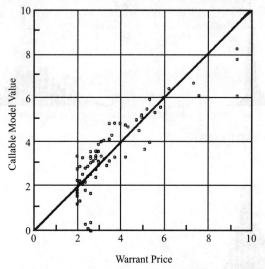

Panel B - Black–Scholes model value v. warrant price, n = 78. The straight line
represents perfect correspondence between model and marked values.

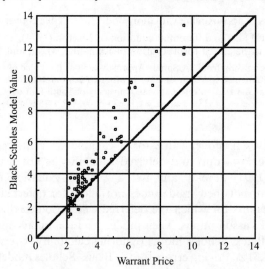

Figure 3.6   Predicted warrant values

Source: Reproduced by permission from "Valuation of Callable Warrants: Theory and Evidence," by R.
Burney and W. T. Moore, *Review of Quantitative Finance and Accounting*, **8** 1997, 5–18.

explicitly into account the deferred nature of the call provision as well as a host of other
realistic features. No large-scale studies of the pricing accuracy of this method have been
reported at this time, but anecdotal evidence suggests that the model will give reliable
prices.

3.6 REFERENCES

Alexander, Gordon J., Roger D. Stover and David B. Kuhnau (1979). "Market Timing Strategies in Convertible Debt Financing," *Journal of Finance* **34**, 143–155.

Asquith, Paul (1995). "Convertible Bonds Are Not Called Late," *Journal of Finance* **50**, 1275–1289.

Asquith, Paul and David W. Mullins, Jr. (1991). "Convertible Debt: Corporate Call Policy and Voluntary Conversion," *Journal of Finance* **46**, 1273–1290.

Billingsley, Randall S., Robert E. Lamy and G. Rodney Thompson (1988). "The Choice Among Debt, Equity, and Convertible Bonds," *Journal of Financial Research* **11**, 43–56.

Billingsley, Randall S., Robert E. Lamy and David M. Smith (1990). "Units of Debt with Warrants: Evidence of the 'Penalty-Free' Issuance of an Equity-Like Security," *Journal of Financial Research* **13**, 187–200.

Billingsley, Randall S. and David M. Smith (1996). "Why Do Firms Issue Convertible Debt?" *Financial Management* **25**, 93–99.

Black, Fischer and Myron Scholes (1973). "The Pricing of Options and Corporate Liabilities," *Journal of Political Economy* **81**, 637–654.

Brennan, M.J. and E.S. Schwartz (1977). "Convertible Bonds: Valuation and Optimal Strategies for Call and Conversion," *Journal of Finance* **32**, 1699–1715.

Brennan, Michael J. and Eduardo S. Schwartz (1980). "Analyzing Convertible Bonds", *Journal of Financial and Quantitative Analysis* **15**, 907–929.

Brennan, Michael J. and Eduardo S. Schwartz (1988). "The Case for Convertibles," *Journal of Applied Corporate Finance* **1**, 55–64.

Brigham, Eugene F (1966). "An Analysis of Convertible Debentures: Theory and Some Empirical Evidence," *Journal of Finance* **21**, 35–54.

Burney, Robert B. and William T. Moore (1997). "Valuation of Callable Warrants: Theory and Evidence," *Review of Quantitative Finance and Accounting* **8**, 5–18.

Byrd, Anthony K. and William T. Moore (1994). "Valuation Effects of Convertible Security Calls," *Quarterly Journal of Business and Economics* **33**, 26–40.

Byrd, Anthony K. and William T. Moore (1996). "On the Information Content of Calls of Convertible Securities," *Journal of Business* **69**, 89–101.

Byrd, Anthony K. and William T. Moore (1998). "Re-examining the Stock Price Response to Underwritten Calls of Convertible Securities," University of South Carolina working paper.

Byrd, Anthony K., S. Mann, W.T. Moore, and P. Ramanlal (1998). "Rational Timing of Calls of Convertible Preferred Stocks," *Journal of Financial Research* **21**, 293–313.

Campbell, Cynthia J., Louis H. Ederington and Prashant Vankudre (1991). "Tax Shields, Sample-Selection Bias, and the Information Content of Conversion-Forcing Bond Calls," *Journal of Finance* **46**, 1291–1324.

Chen, Andrew (1975). "A Model of Warrant Pricing in a Dynamic Market," *Journal of Finance* **25**, 1041–1060.

Constantinides, George and Bruce Grundy (1984). "Are Convertibles Called Late?" University of Chicago working paper.

Constantinides, George and Bruce Grundy (1987). "Call and Conversion of Convertible Corporate Bonds: Theory and Evidence," University of Chicago working paper.

Cowan, Arnold R., Nandkumar Nayar and Ajai K. Singh (1992). "Underwriting Calls of Convertible Securities: A Note," *Journal of Financial Economics* **31**, 269–278.

Cox, John C., Stephen A. Ross, and Mark Rubinstein (1979). "Option Pricing: A Simplified Approach," *Journal of Financial Economics* **7**, 229–264.

Crabbe, Leland E. and Jean Helwege (1994). "Alternative Tests of Agency Theories of Callable Corporate Bonds," *Financial Management* **23**, 3–20.

Dann, Larry Y. and Wayne H. Mikkelson (1984). "Convertible Debt Issuance, Capital Structure Change and Financing-Related Information: Some New Evidence," *Journal of Financial Economics* **13**, 157–186.

Dunn, Kenneth B. and Kenneth M. Eades (1989). "Voluntary Conversion of Convertible Securities and the Optimal Call Strategy," *Journal of Financial Economics* **23**, 273–302.

Eckbo, B. Espen (1986). "Valuation Effects of Corporate Debt Offerings," *Journal of Financial Economics* **15**, 119–152.

Ederington, Louis H., Gary L. Caton and Cynthia J. Campbell (1997). "To Call Or Not To Call Convertible Debt," *Financial Management* **26**, 22–31.

Emanuel, David (1983a). "A Theoretical Model For Valuing Preferred Stock," *Journal of Finance* **38**, 1133–1155.

Emanuel, David C. (1983b). "Warrant Valuation and Exercise Strategy," *Journal of Financial Economics* **12**, 211–235.

Fama, Eugene F., Lawrence Fisher, Michael C. Jensen and Richard Roll (1969). "The Adjustment of Stock Prices to New Information," *International Economic Review* **10**, 1–21.

Ferri, Michael G., Scott B. Moore and David C. Schirm (1988). "Investor Expectations about Callable Warrants," *Journal of Portfolio Management* **14**, 84–86.

Fields, L. Page and William T. Moore (1995). "Equity Valuation Effects of Forced Warrant Exercise," *Journal of Financial Research* **18**, 157–170.

Galai, Dan and Meir I. Schneller (1978). "Pricing of Warrants and the Value of the Firm," *Journal of Finance* **33**, 1333–1342.

Green, Richard C. (1984). "Investment Incentives, Debt, and Warrants," *Journal of Financial Economics* **13**, 115–136.

Harris, Milton and Artur Raviv (1985). "A Sequential Signaling Model of Convertible Debt Call Policy," *Journal of Finance* **40**, 1263–1281.

Harris, Lawrence and Eitan Gurel (1986). "Price and Volume Effects Associated with Changes in the S&P 500: New Evidence for the Existence of Price Pressures," *Journal of Finance* **41**, 815–830.

Hoffmeister, J. Ronald (1977). "Use of Convertible Debt in the Early 1970s: A Reevaluation of Corporate Motives," *Quarterly Review of Economics and Business* **17**, 23–32.

Ingersoll, Jonathan E., Jr. (1997a). "A Contingent-Claims Valuation of Convertible Securities," *Journal of Financial Economics* **4**, 289–321.

Ingersoll, Jonathan (1977b). "An Examination of Corporate Call Policies on Convertible Securities," *Journal of Finance* **32**, 463–478.

Jaffee, Dwight and Andrei Shleifer (1990). "Costs of Financial Distress, Delayed Calls of Convertible Bonds, and the Role of Investment Banks," *Journal of Business* **63**, S107–S124.

Jen, Frank C., Dosoung Choi and Seong-Hyo Lee (1997). "Some New Evidence On Why Companies Use Convertible Bonds," *Journal of Applied Corporate Finance* **10**, 44–53.

Jensen, Michael C. and William H. Meckling (1976). "Theory of the Firm: Managerial Behavior, Agency Costs and Ownership Structure," *Journal of Financial Economics* **3**, 305–360.

Kadapakkam, Palani R. and Alex P. Tang (1996). "Stock Reaction to Dividend Savings of Convertible Preferred Calls: Free Cash Flow or Price Pressure Effects?" *Journal of Banking and Finance* **20**, 1759–1773.

Kremer, Joseph W. and Rodney L. Roenfeldt (1993). "Warrant Pricing: Jump-Diffusion vs. Black–Scholes," *Journal of Financial and Quantitative Analysis* **28**, 255–272.

Lauterbach, Beni and Paul Schultz (1990). "Pricing Warrants: An Empirical Study of the Black–Scholes Model and its Alternatives," *Journal of Finance* **45**, 1181–1209.

Lewis, Craig M., Richard J. Rogalski and James K. Seward (1998). "Understanding the Design of Convertible Debt," *Journal of Applied Corporate Finance* **11**, 45–53.

Linn, Scott C. and J. Michael Pinegar (1988). "The Effect of Issuing Preferred Stock on Common and Preferred Stockholder Wealth," *Journal of Financial Economics* **22**, 155–184.

Mais, Eric L., William T. Moore and Ronald C. Rogers (1989). "A Re-Examination of Shareholder Wealth Effects of Calls of Convertible Preferred Stock," *Journal of Finance* **44**, 1401–1410.

Mann, S., William T. Moore and P. Ramanlal (1999). "Timing of Convertible Debt Issues," *Journal of Business Research*, **95**, 100–105.

Mayers, David (1998). "Why Firms Issue Convertible Bonds: the Matching of Financial and Real Investment Options," *Journal of Financial Economics* **47**, 83–102.

Mazzeo, Michael A. and William T. Moore (1992). "Liquidity Costs and Stock Price Response to Convertible Security Calls," *Journal of Business* **65**, 353–370.

Merton, R.C. (1973). "The Theory of Rational Option Pricing," *Bell Journal of Economics* **4**, 141–183.

Merton, Robert C. (1974). "On the Pricing of Corporate Debt: the Risk Structure of Interest Rates," *Journal of Finance* **29**, 449–470.

Mikkelson, Wayne H. (1980). "Convertible Debt and Warrant Financing: A Study of the Agency Cost Motivation and the Wealth Effects of Calls of Convertible Securities," unpublished Ph.D. thesis, University of Rochester.

Mikkelson, Wayne H. (1981). "Convertible Calls and Security Returns," *Journal of Financial Economics* **9**, 237–264.

Mikkelson, Wayne H. (1985). "Capital Structure Changes and Decreases in Stockholders' Wealth: A Cross-Sectional Study of Convertible Security Calls," *Corporate Capital Structure in the United States*, ed. B.M. Friedman, Chicago: University of Chicago Press.

Mikkelson, Wayne H. and M. Megan Partch (1986). "Valuation Effects of Security Offerings and the Issuance Process," *Journal of Financial Economics* **15**, 31–60.

Miller, Merton H. and Kevin Rock (1985). "Dividend Policy Under Asymmetric Information," *Journal of Finance* **40**, 1031–1051.

Modigliani, Franco and M.H. Miller (1958). "The Cost of Capital, Corporation Finance and the Theory of Investment," *American Economic Review* **48**, 261–297.

Moore, William T. (1982). "Agency Theory: A Model of Investor Equilibrium and a Test of the Agency Cost Rationale for Convertible Bond Financing," unpublished Ph.D. thesis, Virginia Polytechnic Institute.

Myers, Stewart C. and Nicholas S. Majluf (1984). "Corporate Financing and Investment Decisions When Firms Have Information That Investors Do Not Have," *Journal of Financial Economics* **13**, 187–221.

Noreen, Eric and Mark Wolfson (1981). "Equilibrium Warrant Pricing Models and Accounting for Executive Stock Options," *Journal of Accounting Research* **19**, 384–398.

Nelken, Israel (Ed.) (1997). *Option Embedded Bonds*. Chicago: Irwin.

Ofer, Aharon R. and Ashok Natarajan (1987). "Convertible Call Policies: An Empirical Analysis of an Information-Signaling Hypothesis," *Journal of Financial Economics* **19**, 91–108.

Phelps, Katherine L., William T. Moore and Rodney L. Roenfeldt (1991). "Equity Valuation Effects of Warrant-Debt Financing," *Journal of Financial Research* **14**, 93–104.

Pilcher, C. James (1955). "Raising Capital With Convertible Securities," *Michigan Business Studies* (Ann Arbor: University of Michigan, Bureau of Business Research) **21**.

Ramanlal, Pradipkumar, Steven V. Mann and William T. Moore (1996). "A Simple Approximation of the Value of Callable Convertible Preferred Stock," *Financial Management* **25**, 74–85.

Ramanlal, Pradipkumar, Steven V. Mann and William T. Moore (1998). "Convertible Preferred Stock Valuation: Tests of Alternative Models," *Review of Quantitative Finance and Accounting* **10**, 303–319.

Ross, S.A. (1977). "The Determination of Financial Structure: the Incentive-Signaling Approach," *Bell Journal of Economics* **8**, 23–40.

Schultz, Paul (1993). "Calls of Warrants: Timing and Market Reaction," *Journal of Finance* **48**, 681–696.

Schwartz, Eduardo S. (1977). "The Valuation of Warrants: Implementing a New Approach," *Journal of Financial Economics* **4**, 79–93.

Shastri, Karen A. and Kuldeep Shastri (1996). "The Information Content Calls of Convertible Preferreds: the Evidence from Earnings Forecasts," *Journal of Accounting, Auditing and Finance* **11**, 607–622.

Singh, Ajai K., Arnold R. Cowan and Nandkumar Nayar (1991). "Underwritten Calls of Convertible Bonds," *Journal of Financial Economics* **29**, 173–196.

Sinkey, Joseph F., Jr. and James A. Miles (1982). "The Use of Warrants in the Bail Out of First Pennsylvania Bank: An Application of Option Pricing," *Financial Management* **11**, 27–32.

Smith, Clifford W., Jr. (1986). "Investment Banking and the Capital Acquisition Process," *Journal of Financial Economics* **15**, 3–29.

Stein, Jeremy C. (1992). "Convertible Bonds as Backdoor Equity Financing," *Journal of Financial Economics* **32**, 3–22.

4

Derivative Data

JOHN POIGNAND

4.1 INTRODUCTION

This chapter provides the reader with a detailed overview of the data required to understand a derivative investment issue. The data includes the attributes of the derivative and the investment instrument into which it converts. Derivative issues are inherently more complex than "straight" bonds or simple stocks. Yet to the diligent investor, who has invested the time to understand the issue and its related issues, derivatives can provide investment opportunities. There is of course a wide range of derivatives. This chapter focuses on the information requirements of Convertible Bonds and Convertible Preferreds and provides a guide to the information vendors who provide this information. The first section, entitled "The Convertible Bond and Convertible Preferred", provides a guide to the information necessary to analyze the issue as a bond only. The second section, entitled "Conversion and Related Data" provides a guide to the data on the issue into which the derivative security is based, and the third section describes items which can be derived from data readily available from most vendors and which are required to understand fully a particular convertible bond or its underlying security.

4.2 SECTION ONE: THE CONVERTIBLE BOND AND CONVERTIBLE PREFERRED

One can initially consider these two instruments as standard bonds. The exception being that in addition to having interest payments these bonds may convert to another instrument. Therefore in attempting to understand such bonds the investor needs first to have information about the bond. Once the bond has been understood conversion information is needed. Conversion information is discussed in the section entitled "Conversion and Related Data".

4.2.1 Identification Numbering Systems

All US investment issues are issued a nine-digit CUSIP number. This unique number assigned by the American Bankers Association provides a secure means of identifying an issue and is used in most trading systems, portfolio and master file systems. It contains

Handbook of Hybrid Instruments. Edited by Izzy Nelken. © 2000 John Poignand. Published 2000 by John Wiley & Sons Ltd.

three parts. The first six digits represent the issuer, the next two the specific issue, while the last is a check digit which is used as a means of validating the preceding eight numbers. Due to the large number of CUSIPs issued the seventh and eighth numbers of bonds are often letters.

Boston Chicken's issuer number is 100578. The convertible issue of 4.5% with a maturity of 2004 was assigned the issue extension of AA. The check digit of 1 is automatically assigned to complete the number as shown here: 100578AA1.

It should be noted that very large corporations may have multiple issue numbers due to the large number of issues that such corporations have. Examples include Chrysler Corp. and Chase Manhattan Bank.

A full description of CUSIPs rules is available from the American Bankers Association. However it is useful at this time to note that CUSIP assigns the numbers 10 and 20 in the seventh and eighth fields to common and preferred stocks respectively. The numbers 11 through 19 are generally reserved for warrants and rights. Therefore Boston Chicken's common stock CUSIP number is 100578103.

In the recent past and in an attempt to make identification numbering codes global the ISIN number has been introduced. This number contains a two-digit country code, a one-digit exchange identifier, eight digits for the local official identifier, which in the case of a US security is the CUSIP number, followed by a check digit.

4.2.2 Issue Related Data

Issuer Name

All issues have an issuer name that enables the user to equate a security to its organization. Databases for the convenience of storing such names often abbreviate parts of the issuer name. The abbreviations are not always consistent, occasionally making the use of a name difficult. Examples include the words international, communications, or even bank, which are abbreviated in multiple ways: e.g. Bank, Bnk, or Bk.

Issue Description

Generally the issue description provides a quick idea of the security and contains in a single reference the type of issue and, if relevant, the coupon and maturity date. This information is generally provided in text form. An example is SBNT 4%04. In this case the issue description states that this is a subordinated note paying 4% and maturing in the year 2004.

Maturity Date

Maturity date is the date at which the issuer agrees to pay the investor any outstanding principal. In general, dates provided by most computer services are maintained in Julian calendar form which simplifies making calculations which require dates. Most programs such as Microsoft's Excel or Lotus's 123 provide a ready means for converting dates from Julian form to easily recognized date forms. Maturity date is not provided for convertible preferred bonds. In the example below the Julian number 36453 is converted by simply formatting the cell with the desired Excel date format.

    36453   20-Oct-99
                   10/20/99
             October-99
        10/20/99 12:00 AM

Note 1:   The use of Julian numbers provides a method of assigning date values that are fully compliant with year 2000, permitting the ready calculation of time periods between such dates as 20 Oct. 99 and 20 Oct. 00.

Note 2:   Early versions of Microsoft's Excel prior to version 7.0 did not permit the conversion of Julian dates larger than September 2000. This has been corrected in all later versions and now permits dates 10 000 years into the future.

Coupon

This is the interest percentage provided by the issue. It is generally expressed as a decimal, however data suppliers may provide the value as a whole number with the expectation that the user will make the adjustment prior to using the information in any calculation. Recently the market has introduced issues whose securities pay a variable rate coupon requiring vendors to provide users with a coupon schedule containing the start date and the coupon rate.

Issue Amount

This is the face value of the amount raised at issue date. This is usually expressed in millions of dollars.

Issue Date

The date the security was issued for purchase.

Rating

Ratings by the ratings agencies such as Moody's Investor Services, Standard and Poors, Fitch, and Duff and Phelps provide the investor with an indication of the quality of the issuer. These agencies review the financials of the issuer, interview its management and review the plans of the organization and arrive at a subjective rating of the organization. Issuers rating favorably are able to raise money at issue date at a smaller premium or spread over the risk free rate of the related Treasury bond. A lowering of the rating has the effect of lowering the price of the issue in the market to compensate buyers for the perceived increased risk. A rating by Moody's Investor Services of Aaa is the highest rating whereas a C is the lowest. Most bonds wishing to attract institutional investors acquire a rating from the leading ratings agencies.

Payment Frequency

Most bonds in the US pay twice a year, however this is not always the case. Bonds can pay one a year, semi-annually, quarterly and even monthly. Bonds can also pay in arrears or accrue the interest until a final payment. Obviously payment frequency is important in evaluating yield.

First Interest Payment Date

This is the date from which the calculation of interest due the investor starts to accrue. This date also permits the calculation of subsequent payment dates such as last or prior pay date, next pay date. Vendors usually indicate NA in this field for zero coupon bonds.

Puts and Calls

Puts and calls provide investors in the case of puts and the issuer in the case of calls with the ability to either demand payment or call in the bond at a prescribed amount and date. This information is important to the investor since it affects the expected duration of the security and therefore its yield. For example: A bond issued a maturity of 2004, a call provision in 1999. The issuer discovers it has sufficient profits to call the issue or a better credit condition such as a lower interest rate or a better credit rating; one might expect the issue to be called at this early date. In the event that the investor was hoping to hold the security to conversion date or maturity, then the call right could impact the investor and the value of the conversion option. One of the difficulties of processing put and call data is the fact that there is usually no ready means to identify how many records are in a particular call or put record. Securities can contain almost any number of call records varying anywhere from none to 30. There also exists the rule associated with calls the data of which has elapsed during the prior year. Such a bond is callable with 30 days notice up to 30 days of the next call data. Therefore in processing yield to call, one needs to evaluate both past and future calls.

Sinking Funds: Mandatory and Optional

These represent scheduled reductions of the bond amount outstanding at prescribed amounts. This scheduled data is usually expressed in a record containing identifier, date, price, and amount where amount is the amount of the bonds outstanding that are being redeemed.

Price

Bonds are usually sold in units of $1000. However prices are generally expressed in terms of $100. If the bond is listed on an exchange then trade data such as bid, ask, high, low and close are available from the exchange upon which the issue trades. A bond does not necessarily trade each day with some closely held bonds rarely trading. Additionally many bonds are not traded on an exchange. Vendors who provide prices generally acquire prices directly from institutions that make a market in such issues. Several vendors supplement such price lists with "modeled prices" which use trader provided data as a benchmark to set the spread above the Treasury bond price for similar rated bonds. These modeled prices vary in sophistication and generally do not provide for user input.

144a

Bonds are often issued at a discount at initial offering to financial institutions only. In such cases the issue number is assigned and the issue is called a 114a issue or an issue issued under the SEC rules of 144a. When the issue is subsequently offered in the normal fashion it receives a new CUSIP number. Both issues can remain active with the two registration numbers and will price in an identical fashion. Most vendors provide a yes/no flag for this item.

Lead & Co Manager

In general this data is available in coded fashion with the vendor providing the ability to convert the code to text.

Currency & Country Codes

Most US convertible issues are issued and pay in US Dollars. The underlying issue into which the issue converts is usually a US stock and, if paying dividends, pays these in US Dollars. In these cases the currency and country code etc. are all US or the US ISO code. Convertibles are issued by many companies located around the world and in some cases the convertible bond will be issued in one country and convert to an issue of another. For this reason, in developing programs for managing convertible bond data one needs to create the capability to hold currency codes for both the bond interest payments and the dividend and country codes for both the original bond and its related underlying issue. In addition, if the reader intends to monitor global securities it needs a source of currency exchange rates.

4.3   SECTION TWO: CONVERSION AND RELATED DATA

Having reviewed the information requirements for convertible bond and convertible preferred as a standard bond, it is now reasonable to review conversion data. Often conversion data is provided as record data. Conversion records are likely to contain the information pertaining to identifying the underlying security into which the bond converts, number of shares provided for each bond, the price that the stock has to reach before conversion takes place and a conversion date.

Underlying Issue

This is the CUSIP number of the issue into which the convertible converts. As stated under CUSIPs, issues with "10" in the seventh and eighth field of the CUSIP number are common stock and preferred stock respectively.

The number of shares is sometimes referred to as the conversion ratio. It should be noted that the number of shares must be adjusted in the event of share splits or changes in the securities adjustment factor.

Adjustment Factor

An adjustment factor is provided as a means by which pricing data, earnings per share, dividends information and more gets adjusted to reflect changes in the number of shares outstanding as affected by such corporate action as splits. Some vendors automatically adjust data to reflect splits while others, including the stock exchanges, tend to ignore splits and record unadjusted data. It therefore behooves the investor to validate how each vendor treats splits. (See section 4.4 below.)

Special Provisions

Certain convertible bonds contain special provisions upon which the convertible bond will automatically convert. An example of this is found in Boston Chicken's Convertible. In this case the bond automatically converts if the price of the under-lying stock trades above a prescribed value for 20 days during a 30 day period. Data such as this is generally provided in a record form. Another example is conversion at a simple percentage of the price at which the stock was trading at the time of offer of the convertible bond. Examples include 150%. Again this information is often provided as a record which includes the identifier, the percentage and the duration.

Pricing Issues

Having identified the issues into which a convertible bond converts and the number of the underlying securities that will be delivered upon conversion, the stock, its price movement and its volatility become important. The usual reason for purchasing a convertible bond is to gain the payments due for the bond while retaining the principal. Of equal importance is the right to be rewarded with any capital gains achieved by the underlying issue. However it is also important to note that the holder of a convertible bond is not entitled to any dividend payments made prior to conversion. The convertible bond is really an option to purchase a number of shares at a future price while being paid interest for the load of principal. The issuer or borrower is able to acquire the loan at a lower interest payment in return for the right for the lender to realize anticipated capital gains. Therefore in addition to the acquisition of the price of the underlying issue, the investor also needs history prices so that he or she can calculate volatility and the value and frequency of the dividend.

Underlying Issue Price

The price of a security is readily available from the exchanges. It is the practice to use the bid price as the basis for any calculation of the value of the bond. History is available from the exchanges but is generally in an unadjusted form which means that in the event of a stock split the investor would need to adjust the history to reflect this change. Most vendors provide both adjusted and unadjusted price data. In addition real time informa-tion is available. Most pricing services use a close of market or near close of market price to value the bond.

Volatility

Volatility is either provided by the vendor or must be calculated from historical prices. The steps for deriving volatility are shown in Exhibit 4.A at the end of the chapter. The data required are typically the latest 60 days of prices. It should be noted that during such periods holidays may result in the vendor providing an NA or "not available," or under some vendors NE, "not expected." In these cases decisions with regard to the processing of NA or NEs need to be addressed. Methods include assigning the security price of the previous day to the dates with an NA or removing the dates containing the NA. Arguments pro and con each method appear equally valid. In removing the NAs by either method one has to recognize that occasionally more than one consecutive date in a sequence may need to be addressed. Unadjusted Prices subject to splits and other share adjustments require adjusting. For instance a security with a two for one simple split requires price data prior to the split being divided by two. It should also be noted that the number of shares provided by conversion of the convertible bond need to be adjusted to reflect the split.

Announcement Data

Announcement data provides important information about both the bond and the underlying issue. Announcement data advises of court actions by or against the issuer, any impending capital actions such as splits, bankruptcy proceedings and company meetings. In general this information helps the investor keep in touch with events that may have a direct bearing on the value of the asset. This information is gathered by Xcitek and provided to most data vendors.

Status

Generally this is coded information that provides information as to whether or not a particular issue has stopped trading, is in bankruptcy, matured, and more. Vendors usually provide both coded data and the decoded text. In general the vendor updates this data at the end of each day.

4.4   SECTION THREE: CALCULATED DATA

Many of the data items required to understand fully a particular convertible bond or its underlying security are not provided by the vendor. However this data may be calculated. Below is a list of items derived from data readily available from most vendors.

Bond Trading Premium (Points)
Bond Trading Premium (Percentage)
Yrs to Next Call or Mat.
% Bond Above Call Price
Duration
Convexity
Underlying Issue's Beta

Underlying Issue's Volatility
Yield to Maturity
Yield to Next Call
Convertible Bond 13d Report Level
Spread Over Treasury Issue
Spread Attributed to Credit Rating

4.4.1   Sources of Fundamental Data

Fundamental data is annual and quarterly report information. It provides the companies' balance and income sheets and flow of fund information. The most recent company information is now fairly readily available from each company's web site. In addition vendors such as Compustat, Value Line or Datastream provide fairly substantial amounts of history of this data with Compustat providing "normalized" data. Normalized data provides information that has been adjusted for restatements and structured in a manner that provides for inter-company comparability. Compustat and Value Line provide coverage of US Corporations while Datastream provides data on a large number of non-US companies.

4.4.2   News

As with fundamental data, news is often available through companies' web sites. Those with access to Bloomberg and other real time news providers can access news items. Such organizations provide facility to screen for recent news items on a particular company.

4.4.3   History

For most persons analyzing a convertible bond history has little value. However, to calculate volatility one needs history. It is also useful following a period of time after the issue date to view how the bond has behaved in the market.

Calculating Volatility

Step One: Normalize the price data in cells B5 through B65 by replacing any #N/As with the prior value. This step can be performed by placing the following formula in cell B5: " = if (ISNA(B5) = true,B6,B5)". Then copy equation down to C65. The reason for doing that is that in most programs #N/As propagate and defeat further calculations.

Step Two: Calculate the absolute value of the Log of the change between C5 and C6. This can be performed with the equation:" = if (C5 = C6, 0, LN (ABS(C5/C6))). Copy down as in step one.

Step Three: Calculate the Square Root of the Standard Deviation of the data held in D7 through D67 and multiply the results by the Square Root of 60. This can be done with the equation: = STDEV (D7:D67)*SQRT (60).

3COM COl Best Price

08-Dec-97	37.5	37.5	0.028742	34.32%
05-Dec-97	36.4375	36.4375	0.072921	
04-Dec-97	33.875	33.875	−0.030883	
03-Dec-97	34.9375	34.9375	−0.010676	
02-Dec-97	35.3125	35.3125	−0.083169	
01-Dec-97	38.375	38.375	0.056967	
28-Nov-97	36.25	36.25	0.045863	
27-Nov-97	#N/A	34.625	0	
26-Nov-97	34.625	34.625	−0.007194	
25-Nov-97	34.875	34.875	0.038361	
24-Nov-97	33.5625	33.5625	−0.041939	
21-Nov-97	35	35	0.018019	
20-Nov-97	34.375	34.375	0.031397	
19-Nov-97	33.3125	33.3125	−0.005613	
18-Nov-97	33.5	33.5	−0.018485	
17-Nov-97	34.125	34.125	0.11847	
14-Nov-97	30.3125	30.3125	−0.00206	
13-Nov-97	30.375	30.375	−0.016327	
12-Nov-97	30.875	30.875	−0.128966	
11-Nov-97	35.125	35.125	−0.02634	
10-Nov-97	36.0625	36.0625	−0.055617	
07-Nov-97	38.125	38.125	−0.071176	
06-Nov-97	40.9375	40.9375	−0.059277	
05-Nov-97	43.4375	43.4375	−0.004307	
04-Nov-97	43.625	43.625	0.004307	
03-Nov-97	43.4375	43.4375	0.047137	
31-Oct-97	41.4375	41.4375	0.029076	
30-Oct-97	40.25	40.25	−0.071887	
29-Oct-97	43.25	43.25	−0.038275	
28-Oct-97	44.9375	44.9375	0.087126	
27-Oct-97	41.188	41.188	−0.10641	
24-Oct-97	45.8125	45.8125	−0.02426	
23-Oct-97	46.9375	46.9375	−0.037888	
22-Oct-97	48.75	48.75	0.007722	
21-Oct-97	48.375	48.375	−0.03927	
20-Oct-97	50.3125	50.3125	0.011243	
17-Oct-97	49.75	49.75	−0.02604	
16-Oct-97	51.0625	51.0625	−0.044292	
15-Oct-97	53.375	53.375	0.002345	
14-Oct-97	53.25	53.25	−0.036871	
13-Oct-97	55.25	55.25	−0.006764	
10-Oct-97	55.625	55.625	0.005634	
09-Oct-97	55.3125	55.3125	−0.007318	
08-Oct-97	55.71875	55.71875	0.012984	
07-Oct-97	55	55	0.01373	

06-Oct-97	54.25	54.25	0.060553
03-Oct-97	51.0625	51.0625	0.008605
02-Oct-97	50.625	50.625	0.002472
01-Oct-97	50.5	50.5	−0.014742
30-Sep-97	51.25	51.25	−0.009709
29-Sep-97	51.75	51.75	0.013374
26-Sep-97	51.0625	51.0625	0.01604
25-Sep-97	50.25	50.25	−0.044992
24-Sep-97	52.5625	52.5625	0.010759
23-Sep-97	52	52	0.031749
22-Sep-97	50.375	50.375	0.052208
19-Sep-97	47.8125	47.8125	0.023811
18-Sep-97	46.6875	46.6875	0.004024
17-Sep-97	46.5	46.5	−0.03305
16-Sep-97	48.0625	48.0625	−0.018042
15-Sep-97	48.9375	48.9375	

5

The Value Line Experience with Convertibles

LAWRENCE CAVANAGH

Convertible securities and warrants have been around since the early part of this century. Value Line started offering evaluations of convertible bonds, preferreds and warrants in the 1970s, using models that had been developed in-house. Today, *The Value Line Convertibles Survey* offers weekly evaluations of more than 600 convertibles[1] and 120 warrants both in print and online. These evaluations include the Value Line Convertibles model's estimation of whether the security is underpriced, overpriced or fairly priced. In addition, if the stock is ranked by *The Value Line Investment Survey*, then the convertible is also ranked based on a combination of the underlying common stock rank and the pricing and risk characteristics of the convertible itself.[2]

This chapter is in two parts. The first part reviews the various *Value Line Convertible Indexes* that have been compiled by the company since the early 1980s. The performance of these indexes will be compared to the performance of some standard stock and bond market indicators. As an asset class, convertibles can be shown to have performed very well, especially on a total-return risk-adjusted basis. We also review the more in-depth *Convertible Market Profile* data that provide a more descriptive "snapshot" of the US convertible market and its characteristics.

The second part of this chapter examines the performance of the highly ranked convertibles and warrants that *The Value Line Convertible Survey* has recommended for buying and holding. These results suggest that, while underlying stock selection plays a significant part in a convertible portfolio's performance, selections that are based on favorable mis-pricings can also play a significant role in creating a portfolio with the desired risk/reward characteristics.

5.1 VALUE LINE'S CONVERTIBLE INDEXES AND MARKET PROFILES

There exist a plethora of published financial market indexes, some are broad-based, and some are devoted to a particular instrument, industry or level of market capitalization. Many of the major stock market indexes, such as the S&P 500, are "capitalization weighted" by the dollar value of each company's outstanding shares. By way of contrast,

Handbook of Hybrid Instruments. Edited by Izzy Nelken. © 2000 Lawrence Cavanagh. Published 2000 by John Wiley & Sons Ltd.

the broad-based Value Line Composite stock indexes are unweighted, with all shares counting equally in the average performance.[3]

Starting in March 1982, Value Line began publishing the *Value Line Convertibles Indexes*. These indexes, which are updated weekly, are based on all the convertible bonds and preferreds—and warrants—listed in *The Value Line Convertibles Survey*. (As of May 3 1999, there were 421 convertible bonds and 180 convertible preferreds in the publication with respective market values of $91.6 billion and $46.5 billion. On this same date, there were 120 warrants listed with a total market value of $2.3 billion.)

Designed as they are to evaluate the performance of the US dollar denominated convertible and warrant markets, these indexes measure:

1. All Convertibles Price Index;
2. All Convertibles Total Return Index (includes coupon and dividend accruals);
3. Convertibles Ranked 1 Price Index;
4. Convertibles Ranked 1 Total Return Index (includes coupon and dividend accruals); and
5. All Warrants Price Index.

Items 1 & 2 are also published each week in *Barron's* and are widely used by the securities industry as benchmarks. The Convertibles Ranked 1 Indexes (items 3 & 4) are based on the convertibles to which *The Value Line Convertible Survey* has assigned a convertible rank of 1. As of May 3 1999 there were 98 such issues listed in the publication, most of which were based on stocks with Value Line Common Stock ranks of 1,2 or 3.

As with the Value Line Composite stock indexes, the Value Line Convertibles Indexes are not capitalization-weighted. Rather, equal weights are given to each security's weekly advance or decline. The advance or decline in the index is then calculated from the geometric average of these weekly changes in the individual securities. This type of weighting and averaging is employed to provide as realistic as possible an indication of how an investor's portfolio is likely to have performed, assuming approximately equal holdings of each issue. If the index were "cap-weighted," then a relatively small sample of the issues would drive the index, since the 100 largest capitalization convertibles (16% of the issues in the service) would have more than 60% of the weighting. Starting in mid-1998, to augment the analysis of these indexes, Value Line has published weekly indexes of the price performance of the All Convertibles and Warrants Indexes' underlying stocks.

5.1.1 Index Performance

How have these indexes performed over the years? Graph 5.1 shows the performance of the All Convertibles Total Return Index since early 1995. For comparison purposes, we have added the Russell 2000 Index of lower capitalization stocks and the Salomon Brothers Corporate Bond Total Return Index to this graph. To examine how the All Convertibles Total Return Index relates to the straight equity and bond markets, we have added a regression line using the All Convertibles Total Return Index as the

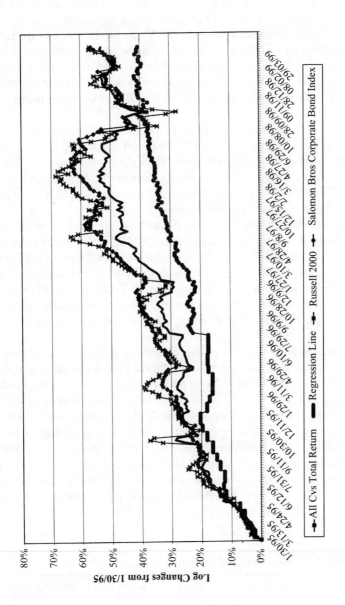

Graph 5.1 Value Line All Convertibles Index versus Stock and Bond Indexes

dependent variable and the Russell 2000 and Salomon Brothers corporate bond indexes as the independent variables.

Notice that over the 46-month period, the Value Line Convertibles Total Return Index and the Russell 2000 tracked very closely, although the Convertibles Index was easily the less volatile of the two. The linear regression showed an R2 of 0.96 and strongly positive coefficients for each of the independent variables.

Graph 5.2 shows the relative performance of the Value Line Rank 1 Convertibles total return and again the Russell 2000 and the Salomon Brothers Corporate Bond Index (total return). Notice the Rank 1 Convertibles strongly outperformed the Russell 2000 by a wide margin. Also the fit between the indexes was not as close as with the All Convertibles Index, although with an R2 squared of 0.96, the relationship was still a strong one.

Table 5.1 shows statistical analysis of these two convertible indexes as well as of the other two benchmarks. It appears that the dividend and coupon yield of these convertible indexes, which ranged between 6.00% and 7.00% p.a. over the period, did much to reduce their statistical volatility. Consequently, both the All Convertibles Total Return Index and the Rank 1 Convertibles scored very well on risk adjusted basis, with Sharpe Ratio scores well above those for the stock index alone.[4]

Our Convertible Market Profile, which is printed on the back page of the Part 2 Convertibles Evaluation Section, provides important additional information about the convertibles market. Looking at Table 5.2 notice that we show the averages (and in some cases the median values) from the convertible data listed in our service. Convertible bonds and convertible preferreds are differentiated with total market values for each. In addition to price and yield data, we also show the median conversion and investment value premiums as well as the average leverage numbers for a 25% up and a 25% down move in the underlying stock.

In Graph 5.3, we plot the median convertible price against their conversion and investment values. The data in the Convertible Market Profile can provide some insight about how the convertible market is likely to perform given a move in the stock market. Notice that when conversion value is well above investment value, convertibles as a group tend to be in-the-money and sensitive to stock market movements. Usually, when conversion value goes below investment value (i.e. when the conversion value premium exceeds the investment value premium), the convertible price becomes relatively less sensitive to changes in conversion value. However, the recent experience has been somewhat different, with both conversion value and investment value having fallen sharply in recent months and with both the conversion and investment value premiums approximately equal at low levels.

Table 5.1   Performance of the Value Line Convertible Indexes

	Value Line Convertibles	Rank1 Convertibles	Russell 2000	Salomon Bros. Corporate Bond Index
Per Annum Return	15.32%	40.30%	13.06%	11.54%
Standard Deviation	9.67%	11.43%	20.62%	6.18%
Relative Volatility	0.31	0.37	0.67	0.20
Sharpe Ratio	1.04	3.07	0.38	1.02

97

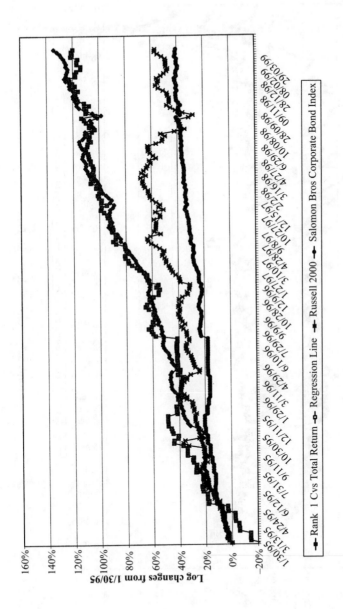

Graph 5.2 Value Line Rank 1 Convertibles versus Stock and Bond Indexes

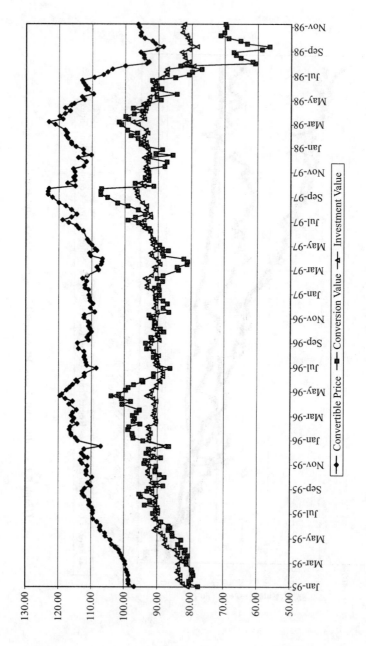

Graph 5.3 Convertible Profile Data

Table 5.2 Convertible and warrant market profiles as of May 10 1999

Convertible Bond Market Profile

Pricing date	Com price	Conv price	Com yield	Conv yield	Prem over Cv val	Prem over I.V. val	25.0%	−25.0%
29/03/99	$26.05	96.78	1.1%	6.2%	45%	20%	7.6%	−6.1%
05/04/99	$25.87	98.25	1.1%	6.3%	45%	21%	7.5%	−5.9%
12/04/99	$26.75	98.70	1.0%	6.1%	46%	19%	7.5%	−6.0%
26/04/99	$26.82	100.33	1.1%	6.0%	40%	20%	7.8%	−7.0%
03/05/99	$26.86	100.34	1.0%	6.0%	41%	21%	7.9%	−7.1%

Convertible Preferred Market Profile

Pricing date	Com price	Conv price	Com yield	Conv yield	Prem over Cv val	Prem over I.V. val	25.0%	−25.0%
29/03/99	$23.44	$50.05	4.6%	7.9%	26%	28%	11.2%	−9.4%
05/04/99	$23.62	$50.47	4.5%	7.8%	29%	32%	11.2%	−9.3%
12/04/99	$24.41	$52.20	4.3%	7.8%	29%	34%	11.3%	−9.3%
26/04/99	$26.36	$54.51	3.9%	7.4%	23%	36%	11.8%	−11.6%
03/05/99	$26.66	$56.28	4.2%	7.3%	20%	38%	12.3%	−11.8%

Warrant Market Profile

Pricing date	Com price	Warrant price	Com yield	Prem over tangible val	25.0%	−25.0%	Market val ($Bil)
29/03/99	$15.11	$3.65	0.5%	15.7%	70.7%	−39.3%	$1.9
05/04/99	$15.10	$3.61	0.6%	15.8%	77.2%	−39.2%	$2.0
12/04/99	$15.13	$3.64	0.5%	16.0%	72.5%	−40.7%	$2.0
26/04/99	$15.49	$3.55	0.5%	15.6%	87.2%	−29.9%	$1.9
03/05/99	$15.11	$3.55	0.6%	16.2%	71.4%	−39.2%	$1.8

5.2 THE PERFORMANCE OF VALUE LINE'S RECOMMENDED CONVERTIBLES

The classic "plain vanilla" convertible is a hybrid of a corporate fixed income security, bond or preferred stock (usually with a call provision) and a warrant to exchange this security for a fixed number of shares. Because convertibles are fairly complex instruments, they can become significantly underpriced or overpriced at different times under different market conditions.

Often when underpriced, convertibles can offer significant value in terms of reward versus risk. This is because the investor can enjoy both the upside of the stock and the returns and safety of the fixed income security. Unless they are very overpriced, almost all convertibles enjoy what is known as "positive curvature." That is, for equal moves up or down in the stock, they tend to gain more on a rise than they lose on a decline.

For over 20 years, Value Line has been ranking convertibles from 1 to 5 for expected future performance. These convertible ranks are based partly on the Value Line Common Stock Ranks and partly on the pricing and risk characteristics of the convertibles themselves.

While the ideal convertible, according to Value Line's convertible model, is one that is both underpriced and based on a highly ranked stock (i.e. rank 1 or 2), often a convertible can be ranked 1 when only one of these two criteria is met. For instance, it is entirely possible for the Value Line Convertibles model to give a convertible a rank of 1 based on the underlying common having a rank of 1 even if the security is calculated to be somewhat overpriced. Alternatively, our model can rank some convertibles as a 1 even if the underlying stock has a neutral rank of only 3. A general rule of thumb is that the more the convertible is like the stock (i.e. the lower its premium over conversion value), the greater will be the weighting given to the underlying common stock rank. The more the convertible is like a straight bond or a preferred (i.e. the higher its premium over conversion value and the lower its premium over investment value), the greater will be the weighting given to under- or overpricing.

5.2.1 Risk Groups for Recommended Convertibles

To help investors select convertibles that are likely to suit their investment objectives, Value Line Convertibles does a further screening of highly ranked convertibles, creating what is called its Especially Recommended List. For a convertible to be on this list, it must meet the following three criteria:

1. Its curvature must be positive;
2. It cannot have an undue amount of call risk;
3. It is not a likely candidate for a downgrade by one or more of the fixed income rating institutions.

The assumption is that convertibles are purchased when the convertible rank goes to a 1 "buy" and held as long as the rank is a 2 for "hold". When the convertible rank goes to a neutral 3, the convertible is treated as "sold" for purposes of the track record. Recommended convertibles are also treated as "sold" when they are called for redemption (using the better of the market price or the call price) or when the underlying common stock ceases to be ranked by Value Line. The average holding period for recommended convertibles using these criteria is about nine months, but actual holding periods can vary considerably. It is not that unusual for a convertible to switch ranks from a 1 to a 2 and back again several times over the course of its life as a recommended convertible.

In addition to compiling "buy" and "hold" lists, Value Line Convertibles assigns these Especially Recommended Convertibles into different risk groups, which are based on each security's "Relative Volatility." This latter term refers to measurement or risk that is based on: (1) each convertible's expected sensitivity to the underlying stock, (2) the volatility of the underlying stock itself, and (3) finally the convertible's inherent risk as a fixed income security (based on bond duration and credit quality).

This risk measure is then benchmarked to the volatility of the stock with the median historical volatility from among the 1700 stocks in the Value Line Investment Survey. As of the second quarter of 1999, this median stock had an historical volatility (or annualized standard deviation) of 32.2% a year based on five years of weekly measurement.

Almost always according to these measures, a convertible will prove to be less risky than its underlying stock. Typically, a convertible that is "at-the-money" (i.e. conversion value equal to investment value) will have a Relative Volatility that is about half its underlying stock's Relative Volatility.

Especially recommended convertible bonds and preferreds that have a Relative Volatility of 95 and above (versus the median stock benchmark of 100) go into the *Above Average Volatility Group*. These can be viewed as having about the same level of risk as a reasonably conservative stock market investment, even if their underlying stocks' risks are higher. Especially Recommended Convertibles with a Relative Volatility of 65 to 90 go into the *Modest Volatility Group*, while those with a Relative Volatility below that go into the *Low Volatility Group*.

Warrants, on the other hand, which are typically leveraged several times to the underlying stocks, are placed into a *High Volatility Group*, with risk that is typically several times that of the median stock.

How has Value Line's Especially Recommended Warrants and Convertibles *performed over the long haul?* Each quarter, *Value Line Convertibles* calculates the total return performance of all the Especially Recommended warrants and convertibles (bought, held and/or sold) and presents the average return of all the Especially Recommended Convertibles and also the average returns of the convertibles within each of the *Volatility Groups*.

Table 5.3 shows the track record from the first quarter of 1982 through the first quarter of 1999 (17 1/4 years). In addition to *All Especially Recommended Convertibles*, the table shows the average total return performance of three different securities benchmarks: (1) the *Value Line All Convertibles Index*; (2) the *Salomon Brothers Long-Term Corporate Bond Index*; and (3) of the S&P 500 Index.

To show reward versus risk, certain additional calculations have been performed. Volatility is expressed both as annualized Standard Deviation and as Relative Volatility. We also show each group's Sharpe Ratio and the Sharpe relative to that of the S&P 500 over the same period (i.e. benchmarked to that of the S&P 500).

Over the 17 1/4 year period, the *Especially Recommended Convertibles* scored a gain of 18.4% beating the S&P 500 which returned 17.3% over the same period. This higher return was achieved with a lower volatility than the market—i.e. 13.0% versus the market's 14.3%. Thus, on risk-adjusted basis, our Especially Recommended Convertibles beat the stock market by a wide margin with a relative Sharpe Ratio of 1.22.

The *High Risk Group* (i.e. Especially Recommended Warrants) scored a per annum gain of 47.6%, but it did this with volatility of 67.2%. As a result, on a risk-adjusted basis, these warrants did not perform so well, although our data suggests that a small investment in warrants can be an attractive addition to a convertible portfolio.

The *Above Average Risk Group* returned a spectacular 27.6% per annum with a volatility of 19.6%. On a risk-adjusted basis the performance was very positive, with Relative Sharpe Ratio of 1.40. This particular group was profitable in 78.3% of the quarters and it beat the S&P 500 59.4% of the time. This group also scored a gain of 35.4% in 1998, beating even the S&P 500 by a wide margin.

The *Modest Risk Group* returned 19.9% p.a., achieving this result with a volatility of 19.6%. On a risk-adjusted basis, this group matched the performance of the S&P 500.

The *Low Risk Group* returned 14.8% and had the lowest volatility of any of our risk groups—11.6%. On a risk-adjusted basis, this group slightly underperformed the S&P 500 with a relative Sharpe Ratio of 0.96. However, it was also the risk group with the lowest Beta or sensitivity to the stock market, garnering a large part of its profits from interest and dividends. On this basis, it compares very favorably with the Corporate Bond Index shown in the right hand column.

Table 5.3 Comparative performance—Especially Recommended Convertibles versus the benchmarks.

First Quarter 1982 through First Quarter 1999—Total Return

	Especially Recommended					Benchmarks		
	All. Esp Rec.	High risk warrants	Above average risk	Modest risk	Low risk	All Converts	S&P 500	Long-term corporate bonds
Return p.a.	18.4%	47.6%	27.6%	19.6%	14.8%	13.7%	17.3%	13.4%
Standard Deviation p.a.	13.0%	67.2%	19.9%	17.5%	11.5%	12.9%	14.3%	9.8%
Relative Volatility	42%	217%	64%	57%	37%	42%	46%	32%
Sharpe Ratio	0.93	0.61	1.06	0.76	0.73	0.56	0.76	0.72
Relative Sharpe Ratio	1.22	0.81	1.40	0.99	0.96	0.74	1.00	0.95
Beta	0.72	2.30	0.88	0.87	0.61	0.69	1.00	0.20
Alpha	0.07	0.50	0.13	0.10	0.06	0.07	–	0.08
% Quarters > 0%	79.7%	58.0%	78.3%	75.4%	72.5%	72.5%	79.7%	73.9%
% Quarters > S&P 500	58.0%	49.3%	59.4%	52.2%	43.5%	39.1%	0.0%	39.1%
Largest Loss	−14.2%	−67.9%	−21.6%	−23.2%	−14.2%	−22.4%	−25.7%	−6.3%

5.3 SUMMARY

The Value Line's experience longer-term track record certainly indicates that a well-chosen portfolio of convertibles can help the investor meet his or her objectives. Over the 17 1/4-year timeframe, our *Above Average Risk Group* strongly outperformed the S&P 500, achieving this result with a significantly better Sharpe Ratio. Our *Moderate Risk Group* also outperformed the benchmark, with a Sharpe Ratio that was very close to that of the market. Finally, while our *Low Risk Group* underperformed the S&P 500 on a risk-reward basis, its performance compared very favorably with the Long-Term Corporate Bond Index, producing both a higher return and a slightly higher Sharpe Ratio.

5.4 ENDNOTES

1. The Value Line Convertibles Survey covers "classic plain vanilla" US dollar denominated convertible bonds and preferreds, including Euro-convertibles, convertibles issued at discount and zero coupon convertibles. The publication does not cover mandatory conversion securities such as PERCS.
2. The Value Line Investment Survey ranks 1700 stocks for relative performance over the following six to twelve months. Generally, the top 100 receive a rank of 1, the next 300 a rank of 2, the next 900 a rank of 3, the next 300 a rank of 4 and the bottom 100 a rank of 5. A number of studies over the years have evaluated these common ranks, finding significant outperformance of the top ranks over the bottom ranks. See Black, Fischer (1973), "Yes, Virginia, There is Hope: Tests of the Value Line Ranking System," *Financial Analysts Journal*, 10–14.
3. On a daily basis, Value Line publishes two composite indexes of all the stocks in its 1700 stock universe, one calculated using geometric averages of the stock changes and the other calculated using arithmetic averaging. It is this latter "Arithmetic" index that is used as the basis of the Kansas City Board of Trade's Value Line Futures contract and for the Value Line Index options traded on the Philadelphia Stock Exchange.
4. The Sharpe Ratio, a commonly used measure of risk-adjusted return, is calculated by subtracting the risk-free rate from the total return of the asset (or portfolio) and then dividing this result by the standard deviation of the asset (or portfolio). Sharpe, William F., "Mutual Fund Performance", *Journal of Business* (January 1966), 119–138.

6

Hybrid Instruments: A Tax Planning Synopsis*

LINDA E. CARLISLE

6.1 FUNDAMENTAL ECONOMIC CHARACTERISTICS OF THE INSTRUMENTS

6.1.1 Overview

Various publicly traded financial instruments that go under various proprietary names (e.g., DECS, ACES, PEPS, ELKS, PRIDES, YEELDS, SAILS and TRACES[1]) have been devised to allow investors to speculate on the price of publicly traded stock and earn a current return that is expected to exceed the dividend yield from the stock. Issuers, including individuals, can use these instruments to hedge the value of portfolio stock holdings, retain a share of any future appreciation in such stock holdings, monetize the position without current recognition of gain, and claim a deduction for interest expense. Corporate issuers may also use these instruments to lock in a favorable issue price for their stock and obtain favorable non-tax treatment for issuing the securities. Individuals typically are not able to register securities, but can enter into private transactions with a corporation or investment banker that issues back-to-back securities to the public. Although there are numerous variations in the terms and structures of these instruments, they all share the following basic characteristics.

Issue Price

The issue price of the instrument is equal to the market price of a specified stock on the date the instrument is priced. Typically, the specified stock is the common stock of a subsidiary of the issuer or the common stock of a corporation in which the issuer has a portfolio investment. However, the specified stock also can be the common stock of the issuer or, in some cases, the stock of a corporation in which the issuer has no investment.

---

[1] Respectively, "Debt Exchangeable for Common Stock," "Automatic Common Exchange Securities," "Premium Exchangeable Participating Shares," "Equity Linked Securities," "Provisionally Redeemable Income Debt Exchangeable for Stock," "Yield Enhanced Equity Linked Debt Securities," "Stock Appreciation Income Linked Securities," and "TRust Automatic Common Exchange Securities."

* Editor's note: the following chapter relates to the US tax code only. Any references to "tax law"and "tax code"should be construed to mean "US Tax Law"and "US Tax Code"respectively. In any case, qualified, professional tax counsel should be retained before assessment of any specific tax liabilities may be attempted.

Handbook of Hybrid Instruments. Edited by Izzy Nelken. © 2000 Linda E. Carlisle. Published 2000 by John Wiley & Sons Ltd.

Payments

In return for an initial cash payment, the investor receives a current, fixed coupon during the term of the instrument (typically three to five years). Upon maturity of the instrument, the investor receives a variable number of shares of the specified stock, as determined under a formula, that gives the investor a portion of the downside risk and upside potential of owning the specified stock. Generally, such instruments can be settled in cash at the issuer's option.

Downside Risk

The formula for determining the amount of stock received by the investor on maturity typically gives the investor all of the downside risk with respect to the specified stock. Thus, if the price of the specified stock at maturity is equal to or less than the issue price of the instrument, the investor receives one share of the specified stock. See, e.g., the Estee Lauder TRACES (discussed below) in which an investor is entitled to a portion of any appreciation above a set price but has no downside protection. The instrument, however, can be structured to give the investor some downside protection. See, e.g., the Amway Japan Limited PEPS (discussed below) in which an investor is entitled to receive up to 1.25 shares of Amway Japan Limited if the price of the stock declines by as much as 20%.

Upside Potential

The instruments are structured so that the investor and the issuer share the upside potential with respect to the specified stock. The following examples demonstrate how such risk-sharing may be accomplished. Assume that the issue price of the instrument (and the initial market price of the specified stock) is $80 and that the investor receives one share of the specified stock if the price of the stock at maturity is $80 or less.

1. In one variation, if the price of the stock at maturity is between $80 and $100, the investor receives a fractional share of the specified stock that has a value of $80. If the maturity price of the stock exceeds $100, the investor receives 8/10ths of a share of the stock. Thus, the investor receives none of the benefit of any appreciation up to $100 but receives 80% of any appreciation above $100.

2. In another variation, if the price of the specified stock at maturity is between $80 and $100, the investor receives one share of stock. If the price of the specified stock exceeds $100, the investor receives a fractional share that has a value of $100. Thus, the investor receives the benefit of any appreciation up to $100, but does not benefit from any appreciation in excess of $100.

3. There are countless other ways for the investor and issuer to share the upside potential in the specified stock. In some cases, the investor nominally has the right to receive one share of the specified stock at maturity, but the issuer has the right to call the instrument at a variable discount immediately before maturity if the specified stock has appreciated in value, with the practical result that the benefit of any appreciation in the value of the specified stock is shared between the issuer and the investor.

Option Similarities

The payments that the investor receives during the term of the instrument may be the same as, more than, or less than the interest that the issuer would pay on straight debt, depending on how the downside risk and upside potential with respect to the specified stock is shared between the issuer and the investor. The investor's position with respect to the specified stock is like that of a person that sells a put and buys a call on the specified stock.

1. If the price for the put exactly matches the price for the call, the net consideration for selling the put and buying the call is zero and the coupon on the instrument should reflect a market rate of interest on straight debt.

2. If, however, the price that would be received for the put is less than the price that would be paid for the call, the investor must pay net consideration, which he pays by accepting a reduced coupon.

3. If the price for the put exceeds the price for the call, the investor should receive net consideration, which he receives in the form of an increased coupon.

6.2   THREE FORMS OF THE TRANSACTION

6.2.1   Portfolio Exchangeable Debt

1. The most common form in which these instruments are issued is that of a debt obligation of the issuer that is mandatorily exchangeable into stock of another corporation.

2. The instrument is issued in the form of an investment unit that consists of a noncontingent, interest bearing debt obligation of the issuer combined with a forward contract that obligates the investor to purchase a variable number of shares of the specified stock with the proceeds from the maturity of the debt instrument. The issuer and investor agree to allocate the entire issue price of the overall instrument to the debt component and allocate none of the issue price to the forward contract.

3. The issuer and investor treat the coupon paid to the investor as interest. The transfer of the specified stock to the investor upon maturity of the instrument is treated as a sale of the specified stock by the issuer to the investor for an amount equal to the issue price of the instrument.

4. Debt that is mandatorily exchangeable into the stock of the issuer or a related party may be treated as equity by the Internal Revenue Service. See Notice 94-47, 1994-1 C.B. 357. Moreover, under new section 163(l), which applies to instruments issued after June 8 1997, no deduction is allowed for interest on "disqualified debt," which includes debt that provides for the payment of interest or principal in the form of stock of the issuer (or a related corporation).

5. Accordingly, new structures (and acronyms) have evolved to replicate the economics of exchangeable debt.

6.2.2 ACES

1. ACES are exchangeable securities in which the investor receives stock of the issuer or stock of a corporation controlled by the issuer. If these securities were issued in the form of debt, the issuer's deduction for interest could be disallowed. See, Portfolio Exchange Debt discussed above.

2. To avoid, or minimize, the problem of the issuer paying a coupon for which no deduction is allowed, ACES are issued in the form of an investment unit that combines an interest in a pool of Treasury notes and a forward contract.

3. The entire issue price of the overall instrument is used to purchase Treasury notes that mature on the maturity date of the ACES instrument. The investor receives all of the interest income from the Treasury notes and is treated as the owner of the Treasury notes by both the issuer and the investor. The issuer may also pay the investor a nondeductible annual "fee" to bring the yield on the instrument up to the required market yield. Thus, although the issuer is not allowed any deduction for the coupon yield that the investor receives, the issuer does not include the interest from the Treasury notes in its income, which is economically equivalent to a deduction.

4. Upon maturity of the Treasury notes, the proceeds are used to fulfill the investor's obligation to purchase the specified stock.

5. ACES are not used to monetize an issuer's position in appreciated stock because the issue price of ACES must be used to purchase Treasury notes.

6.2.3 PEPS and TRACES

1. PEPS and TRACES are enhancements on portfolio exchangeable debt which allow the issuers to monetize their stock holdings without current recognition through prepaid forward contracts and provide the investors with tax free coupon payments. Investors in portfolio exchangeable debt and ACES must include the coupon yield in income. In the case of PEPS and TRACES, the investors receive cash flows that are equivalent to the cash flows from a normal portfolio exchangeable debt instrument, but the structure allows the investor to claim that most of the coupon is a tax-free return of capital.

2. In November 1995 Amway Japan Limited ("AJL") PEPS were issued by a newly organized, 3.25 year grantor trust. Each AJL PEPS is an investment unit consisting of an interest in stripped US Treasury securities and in a prepaid forward contract to purchase AJL stock from individuals who are major shareholders of AJL.

3. In May 1998, the Lauder family filed a disclosure statement with the SEC announcing the pending formation of a grantor trust that would issue Estee Lauder ("EL") TRACES. Each EL TRACES will similarly consist of an interest in stripped US Treasury securities and in a prepaid forward contract to purchase EL Class A common stock from Lauder family members.

4. The mechanics of both AJL PEPS and EL TRACES can be illustrated as follows.

    (a) Each trust uses a portion of the issue price (e.g., $20x) to purchase stripped Treasury securities. An investor's cash flow from the Treasury securities corresponds to the coupon yield that an investor would receive on a typical exchangeable debt instrument or ACES (i.e., if the normal coupon yield is 7%, an investor would receive $7x per year from the proceeds of the Treasury securities).

(b) Each trust pays the remainder of the issue price (e.g., $80x) to the shareholders as a prepayment on a forward contract to purchase a variable number of shares of the relevant stock for $100x.

(c) Since the trusts are "grantor trusts," the investors are treated and taxed as the owners of the stripped Treasury securities and each investor therefore includes in income the discount that accrues on the Treasury securities. Most of the cash flow from the Treasury securities, however, represents a tax-free return of the amount paid for the Treasury securities. Thus, the investor receives cash flows corresponding to the coupon yield from a typical exchangeable debt instrument or ACES, but includes only a small portion of the cash flow in income.

(d) Although the investor pays only $80x in satisfaction of his obligation to pay $100x for the relevant stock, the investor does not treat the $20x discount as income.

6.3 OBJECTIVES

6.3.1 Issuers

1. Corporations and individuals that issue portfolio exchangeable debt.

(a) Monetize the issuer's position in appreciated stock without triggering immediate gain.

(b) Hedge the appreciated value of portfolio stock investments and retain a share of future appreciation.

(c) Gain a deduction for the coupon yield paid to investors (or the economic equivalent).

2. Corporations that issue instruments exchangeable into the stock of the issuer.

(a) Realize the appreciated value of the issuer's stock before having to actually issue the stock.

(b) Reduce the cost of raising capital by issuing instruments that qualify as debt for tax purposes and as equity for financial, regulatory, and/or credit rating purposes.

6.3.2 Investors

1. Instruments exchangeable into common stock pay current coupon returns that exceed the dividend yield on the specified stock. The investor pays a price for the enhanced yield by giving up a specified portion of any appreciation in the price of the underlying stock.

2. Investors seek to treat any gains from appreciation in the price of the underlying stock as capital gains that are recognized when the investor sells the stock or receives cash from the issuer in settlement of the instrument.

6.4 OPEN ISSUES

6.4.1 Is the Issuance of an Exchangeable Instrument a Present Sale of the Underlying Stock?

1. The issuance of an exchangeable instrument should not be treated as a present sale of the underlying stock since the issuer typically has the right to sell or assign the underlying stock, retains the right to dividends on the underlying stock, and retains the right to vote the stock. In the AJL PEPS and EL TRACES, the shareholders pledge either EL or AJL stock as collateral for their obligation to deliver the stock upon maturity of the PEPS or TRACES, but the shareholders retain the right to dividends and the right to vote with respect to the pledged stock. The shareholders also have the right to substitute other collateral and thereby retain the right to sell or assign the underlying stock.

2. Section 1259 treats certain transactions relating to appreciated stock (including futures or forward contracts to deliver appreciated stock) as constructive sales of the stock. Assuming that an exchangeable security is treated as an investment unit that includes a forward contract to sell specified stock, there is an issue whether such forward contract should be treated as a constructive sale under section 1259.

    (a) A forward contract is defined in section 1259(d)(1) as a contract that provides for the delivery of a substantially fixed amount of stock at a substantially fixed price. The issuance of exchangeable debt should not be treated as entering into a forward contract within the meaning of section 1259 because the amount of stock to be delivered is not substantially fixed.

    (b) To the extent provided in prospective regulations, other transactions that eliminate substantially all of a taxpayer's risk of loss and opportunity for gain with respect to appreciated stock may be treated as constructive sales. Since the issuer of exchangeable securities typically retains a significant portion of any future appreciation in the price of the stock, regulations issued under section 1259(c)(1)(E) generally should not treat exchangeable securities as constructive sales. However, if an exchangeable security transfers to the investor both all of the downside risk and substantially all of the upside potential with respect to the specified stock, such a security could be treated as a constructive sale under regulations.

6.4.2 Is the Overall Instrument an Investment Unit that Consists of a Forward Contract and either a Debt Obligation of the Issuer or an Interest in Treasury Securities? Or is the Overall Instrument an Integrated Contingent Payment Debt Instrument?

1. Regulations relating to the taxation of contingent payment debt instruments clearly contemplate the existence of debt for which the return of principal is contingent.

2. Contingent payment debt issued on or after August 13, 1996, is subject to Reg. §
    1.1275-4. Debt convertible into the stock of the issuer or a related party is not
    treated as contingent payment debt. Reg. § 1.1275-4(a)(4). The Preamble to the
    regulations states that debt convertible into the stock of an unrelated party ("port-
    folio exchangeable debt") is contingent payment debt.

3. Contingent payment debt issued for money is subject to the non-contingent bond
    method in Reg. § 1.1275-4(b).

    (a) Generally, interest is accrued according to a schedule of the fixed payments
         under the instrument and the projected contingent payments under the in-
         strument that would produce an overall yield equal to the yield from
         the issuer's fixed rate straight debt with similar terms and conditions ("com-
         parable yield"). Adjustments to interest accruals are made if the actual amount
         of contingent payments are more or less than the projected contingent
         payments.

    (b) If the stated interest on an exchangeable debt instrument is equal to the
         comparable yield, the interest accruals on the instrument would equal the
         stated interest on the instrument. If the stated interest is less than the compar-
         able yield, the instrument would have OID. If the stated interest is more than
         the comparable yield, a portion of the stated interest would be treated as a
         return of capital.

    (c) If the amount paid to the investor upon maturity of the exchangeable debt,
         either in cash or in stock, differs from the projected amount, any positive
         difference is treated as additional interest income. Any negative difference
         first reduces interest accruals for the year of maturity, then is treated as an
         ordinary loss to the extent of interest accrued in prior years, and then is treated
         as a capital loss.

4. The issue as to whether an exchangeable security should be treated as a contingent
    payment debt instrument arises with respect to portfolio exchangeable debt and
    other securities, such as ACES, PEPS and TRACES, which do not purport to
    include debt of the issuer. If such securities are treated as contingent payment
    debt instruments, the coupon received by the investor would be treated as interest
    paid by the issuer and such interest (if paid by a corporation) could be subject to
    disallowance under section 163(l).

6.4.3 Is the Shareholder's Position with Respect to the Exchangeable Instrument and the Underlying Stock a "Straddle" to which the Straddle Rules of Sections 1092 Apply?

1. A straddle consists of "offsetting" positions in personal property. The shareholder's
    rights and obligations under an exchangeable instrument are an offsetting position
    with respect to the stock specified in the instrument. Therefore, if the shareholder
    owns the specified stock, the shareholder has a straddle.

2. The loss deferral rules and special holding period rules that apply to straddles,
    however, should not have any practical consequences for the issuance of exchange-
    able instruments.

(a) The loss deferral rule of section 1092(a), which disallows any loss incurred with respect to one leg of a straddle until the gain in the offsetting leg is realized, has no effect if the shareholder delivers the specified stock upon maturity of the instrument. If the shareholder elects to settle in cash, however, the loss deferral rule could come into play.

(b) The special holding period rules for straddles, Reg. § 1.1092(b)-2T, do not apply if the shareholder's holding period for the underlying stock satisfied the long-term capital gain holding period before the straddle was established.

6.4.4 In the Case of ACES, Who Owns the Treasury Notes?

1. The issuer is at risk that the issuer will be treated as receiving the issue price and buying Treasury notes to secure its obligation to pay the coupon return. In that event, the issuer must include in income the interest from the Treasury notes but it receives no deduction for paying the coupon to the investor.

2. It does no good to inquire who receives the economic benefits from the Treasury notes because the proceeds from the Treasury notes are dedicated to the purchase of stock from the issuer. The terms of ACES, however, provide that the investor receives the Treasury notes and has no obligation to purchase the stock from the issuer if the issuer goes bankrupt. In addition, the investor can accelerate the contract to purchase the stock for cash and receive the Treasury notes.

6.4.5 In the Case of the AJL PEPS and EL TRACES, Who Owns the Stripped Treasury Securities?

1. If the investor owns the Treasury securities, the investor has interest income from the Treasury securities, but the purchase price of the Treasury securities is recovered tax free.

2. If the shareholders own the Treasury securities, holding them as collateral for the payment of the coupon, the entire proceeds from the maturity of the Treasury securities is income to the investor, thereby eliminating the enhancement offered by the AJL PEPS and EL TRACES structure to the investor.

3. Upon the bankruptcy of the shareholders, the Treasury securities are transferred to the investors and the forward contract to purchase the AJL or EL stock is accelerated.

6.5 CONCLUSIONS

6.5.1 Evolution

Portfolio exchangeable debt securities were first issued in 1993. Since then, similar securities have been issued with variations and enhancements to achieve desired tax results.

6.5.2 Tax Law Responses

Two of the most important developments in the tax law since 1993 that relate to the treatment of exchangeable securities are the issuance of contingent payment debt regulations in 1996 and the enactment of the constructive sale rules in section 1259 in 1997.

1. The issue of whether exchangeable securities should be treated as contingent payment debt instruments is difficult to resolve since there is no guidance on the issue. For investors, this issue is very important because the gains from the equity "bet" would be treated as ordinary gain or loss if the instruments were treated as contingent payment debt instruments.

2. Exchangeable securities should not be treated as forward contracts within the meaning of section 1259 because the amount of stock to be delivered is not substantially fixed. Regulations under section 1259 should not treat most exchangeable securities as constructive sales because the issuer typically retains a significant share of future appreciation in the specified stock. Issuers should be cautious not to transfer too large a share of the upside potential in order to reduce the coupon on the security.

6.5.3 Current Status

Exchangeable securities may be structured to provide beneficial tax treatment to both issuers and investors.

7

Mandatory Convertible Reset Structures

COLUM McCOOLE

7.1 INTRODUCTION

Convertible reset bonds have been around for well over a decade, but arguably gained most notoriety and profile with the issuance of as many as ten jumbo Japanese bank bonds between 1995 and 1998. The pattern of trading of these issues presents as good a practical illustration of the product as any, and will form the basis of this overview.

Convertible bonds with "resettable" conversion prices are fairly common in the domestic Japanese convertible market and have more recently found limited application in the Asian convertible universe. Rather than having a fixed conversion price, as is the case for regular convertibles, these structures allow for an adjustment to that price, depending on the performance of the underlying stock. Among the domestic issues, reset features are typically offered in conjunction with a definable cash redemption value, which distinguishes them from the "bank reset" issues, where conversion into the underlying stock at maturity is mandatory.

The reset, in some cases, is both downward and upward, but most commonly downward only. In the event of share price weakness, and by implication downward pressure on a bond's parity,[1] the conversion price becomes reset downwards to that lower share price, typically annually. Given that the nominal value of the bond remains unchanged, the effect of the downward reset to the conversion price is to boost the conversion ratio—the number of shares received, per bond, upon conversion.

Since successive downward resets can increase the number of shares issuable upon conversion, thereby worsening the ultimate dilution effect of the bond, there is typically some pre-defined floor, beyond which there is no adjustment. A floor set at 80% of the original conversion price, for instance, will compensate bondholders for an initial 20% drop in the share price. The purpose of the reset, from the issuer's perspective, is to retain some degree of equity sensitivity in the instrument such that the probability of conversion remains high. Having a less common upward reset empowers the issuer to force conversion early in the event of a strong share price. Faced with the prospect of having the conversion price reset upwards and the conversion ratio reset downwards, investors are motivated to convert early.

---

[1] Parity refers to the value of shares underlying a convertible bond. It is the current share price times the fixed conversion ratio (share entitlement per bond). It enables one to express the share price in the same percentage-of-par basis as the bond.

Handbook of Hybrid Instruments. Edited by Izzy Nelken. © 2000 Colum McCoole. Published 2000 by John Wiley & Sons Ltd.

Mandatory structures have become commonplace in the convertibles universe during the 1990s. Motivated by a need for issuers to know with certainty that their bonds would eventually become equity, and therefore get favorable treatment from rating agencies, securities such as PEPS, DECS and PRIDES[2] began to emerge. Rather than paying a cash redemption amount at maturity, allowing for the calculation of a quantifiable bond floor, these instruments adjusted a pay-out ratio of shares based upon the share price at maturity. A higher ratio is payable for a share price below a predefined floor (usually 80%), a lower ratio for a share price above a predefined cap (usually 120%) and a sliding-scale ratio for a share price between those two points. As an added incentive, investors are typically offered high current yield in the form of large coupons. The mandatory convertible reset structures adopted by the Japanese banks owe their origins to these synthetics, but are refined to emphasize downward resets with much lower floors and upward resets are removed as are any initial triggers required for adjustment of conversion ratios given share price weakness.

7.2 ORIGINS OF THE JAPANESE BANK RESET MARKET

Faced with a worsening operating environment in the mid-1990s and deteriorating capital ratios, Japanese banks were obliged to recapitalize themselves. At the time, financing by way of a straight bond issuance wasn't particularly compelling and conditions in the equity market were not conducive to large secondary share offerings. Instead, the convertible market was considered a viable alternative, enabling issuers to tap into a broader investor base while delaying the inevitable stock dilution.

Mitsubishi Bank, prior to its merger with the Bank of Tokyo, was the first to issue a jumbo US$2 billion deal in September 1995. This issue was to differ significantly from successive deals in that it was redeemable for cash in the event that its share price at maturity was less than 50% of the original conversion price. This clause meant it got treated as lower tier two capital, under BIS capital ratio[3] calculations. All other subsequent bank reset issues excluded any cash redemption features and were accordingly treated as upper tier two capital, playing a key off-setting role to the treatment of Japanese banks' falling unrealized equity holding component, reflective of the depressed state of the Japanese equity market.

A combination of falling asset prices (both real estate and equity holdings), worsening profitability levels and the necessity to write off rising incidences of non-performing loans, seriously depleted capital at most Japanese banks by the mid-1990s. In seeking to maintain minimum defined BIS capital ratios, mandatory convertible reset instruments offered a viable solution and thus emerged as a key form of financing for Japanese banks from late 1995 up to early 1998.

---

[2] PEPS (Premium Exchangeable Preferred Shares), DECS (Debt Exchangeable Common Stock) and PRIDES (Preferred Redeemable Increased Dividend Securities) are trademark products of Morgan Stanley Dean Witter, Salomon Brothers and Merrill Lynch respectively.

[3] The Bank of International Settlements (BIS), in its role as overseer of risk in the global banking system, devised a framework to establish minimum levels of capital for internationally active banks. A bank's capital is defined in two tiers (tier 1 consisting of a bank's core equity capital and published reserves and tier 2, supplementary capital, consisting of, among other elements, undisclosed reserves, revaluation reserves, Hybrid debt capital instruments and subordinated term debt). A full explanation to the framework is contained in a report entitled the "Basle Committee on Banking Supervision: International Convergence of Capital Measurement and Capital Standards", Basle 1988. It is available on the internet at http://www.bis.org/publ/bcbs04a.pdf.

Table 7.1 Glossary of key issuance terms for selected Japanese Bank mandatory reset convertible issues

	BOT-Mitsubishi Bank 3% due 11/2002	Sumitomo Bank 0.75% due 2001	Sanwa Bank 1.25% due 2005
Fixed Issuance Terms			
Issue Price	100	100	100
Issue Premium	10.00%	10.00%	2.50%
Issue Date	Sep 95	May 96	Feb 98
Issue Size	US$2bn	¥ 100bn	¥ 150bn
Nominal Size	US$1,000	¥1,000,000	¥3,000,000
Lead Manager	Morgan Stanley	Goldman Sachs	Merrill Lynch
Coupon	3%	0.75% Non-Cumulative	1.25% Non-Cumulative Pref.
Coupon Freq./Dates	Semi-annual, 30 Nov/31 May	Semi-annual, 30 Nov/31 May	Semi-annual, 31 Mar/30 Sep
Maturity	30 Nov 02	31 May 01	31 Jul 05
Conversion Period	Apr 96 to Nov 02	1 Aug 96 to 25 May 01	1 Jul 98 to 31 Jul 05
Ticker	8315.T	8318.T	8320.T
Early Mandatory Conversion			
Beginning Date	30 Nov 1998	31 May 2000	1 Oct 2005 and 1 Oct 2006
Onwards Annually on	30 Nov	~	
Performance Criteria	ADS Equiv. Price* must be > 75% of original conv. price (i.e. 20.95 × 0.75 = 15.71)	Early Mand.conversion only permitted if Share price > 85% orig. conv. price on 31 Mar 2000	Average Market Price over 30 trading day period from t-45 is >75% of original conv. price
Call Fractions	20% of bonds can be Mandatorily converted annually (for each of 5 yrs). Those not called can accumulate to next mand.conv. date	Up to 50% of bonds (less those converted) can be Mandatorily converted 31 May 2001	30% of bonds then outstanding can be Mandatorily converted on 1 Aug 2003, then 50% of then outstanding 1 Aug 2004
Reset Features			
First Reset Date	30 Nov 1996	31 May 1997	1 Aug 1999
Annual Reset Date Thereafter	30 Nov	31 May	1 Aug
Final Reset Date	30 Nov 2002	May 2001	Aug 2004
Reset Calculation Period	20 bus. Day period, excluding holidays in Jap. or NY, ending 15 days before the Reset Date	20 business day period, excluding holidays in Japan, ending 15 trading days before the Reset Date	30 business day period, excluding holidays in Japan, commencing 45 days before the Reset Date
Calculation Type	Simple Avg. of ADS Equivalent Price over Calculation Period	Simple Average over Calculation Period	Arithmethic avg. as calculated by the AQR function on Bloomberg
Percentage Reset Trigger	In order for reset to take effect, new reset price must be >1% below prevailing conv. price. Adj. of <1% are carried forward	In order for reset to take effect, new reset price must be >¥1 below prevailing conv. price. Adj. of <¥1 are carried forward	In order for reset to take effect, new reset price must be >¥1 below prevailing conv. price. Adj. of < ¥1 are carried forward

Continued Overleaf

Table 7.1 *Continued*

	BOT-Mitsubishi Bank 3% due 11/2002	Sumitomo Bank 0.75% due 2001	Sanwa Bank 1.25% due 2005
Original Conversion Price	US$22 adjusted to US$20.95 on BOT merger	¥ 2,255	¥ 1,283
Current Conversion Price	US$13.61	¥ 1,239	¥ 1,283
Current Conversion Ratio	73.42	807.10	2338.27
Initial Reset Floor (% of orig. conv. price)	65%	50%	58%
Initial Reset Floor (Price)	US$13.61	¥ 1,128	¥750
Final Reset Floor (% of orig. conv. price)	50%	37%	58%
Final Reset Floor (Price)	US$10.47	¥ 850 (31 May 2001)	¥750
Cash Option	Yes, ADS Equiv. Price < 50% original conv. price (US$10.47)	No	No

Source: Issue Prospectuses, Morgan Stanley Dean Witter Research, data as at 1 May 1999.

More recently, Japan's Financial Crisis and Management Committee has begun to apply the newly established Recapitalization Law with a ¥7.5 trillion programme designed to further recapitalize 15 major Japanese banks. They have sought to implement this programme through the purchase (by way of private placement) of convertible preference reset shares issued by each bank. These preference shares are similar in many respects to their publicly tradeable counterparts that form the basis of this note.

For the purpose of illustration, the intention is to use three of the ten bank reset issues. Sumitomo Bank 0.75% due 2001 gives a good overall picture of how these instruments react to severe share price weakness, with successive annual resets downwards. The BOT-Mitsubishi Bank 3% due 2001, with its cash redemption clause and therefore definable bond floor, trades significantly differently in practice, as a result. To bring some sense of currency to this analysis, the most recently issued Sanwa Finance 1.25% due 2005, whose first reset approaches, is also considered. Terms for all three are detailed in Table 7.1. A timeline of these three securities appears in Figures 7.9, 7.10 and 7.11 respectively.

7.3 GLOSSARY OF KEY TERMS

As a means to explaining some of the key features of the issues illustrated in Table 7.1, it's worth highlighting some of the key differences in the structure of each.

7.3.1 Coupon and Premium Levels

The levels at which these terms are set is predominantly reflective of market conditions at the time of pricing of the relevant issue. In the case of Mitsubishi Bank issue, its pioneering nature and its denomination in US dollars, meant a relatively high coupon of 3% compared to issues that followed. The premium level of 10% had become standard practice for Japanese convertible issues in the euro-market. By 1998, investor appetite for the product had been arguably filled and sweeter terms on the Sanwa 1.25% issue (higher coupon and lower issue premium) are evidence of this.

7.3.2 Initial and Final Reset Floors

The extent to which floors were set below the original conversion price became key criteria for investors to assess the degree of defensiveness of different issues. In hindsight, the initial 65% floor established by the Mitsubishi Bank deal was to be the highest floor of all issues. Most ranged around the 50% level, while a few took the final floor as low as 35% (as was the case for Tokai Bank and Fuji Bank). Three of the ten bank reset issues built in initial, then lower final floors (generally in the final year) into their structures, but this practice became less common for later issues. Part of the reason for this was that bank share prices had all tended to lower by this point and often articles of association dictated against the overly-dilutive effect of setting floors significantly lower than already depressed stock prices.

Essentially, the lower the reset floor is set, the better it is for the bondholder, since the issuer bears the risk of underlying share-price weakness to a much lower level.

7.3.3 Cash Options at Maturity

What characterized most of these issues was their mandatory conversion into shares at maturity. The only two exceptions to this were the Mitsubishi Bank issue which allowed for cash redemption in the event that the share price at maturity fell below 50% of the original conversion price. The Toyo Trust & Banking issue is also unusual in that it reverts to an FRN paying Euro-yen Libor plus 250bp from September 2002.

7.3.4 Reset Calculation Periods

Key interest as to whether issues get reset downwards, in any given year, and to what extent, centers around the predefined reset calculation periods. There's no unique methodology to this process across issues though. All periods are set sufficiently long enough so as to prevent against any possible manipulation and more recent issues tend to centre their calculation periods in September to coincide with stock re-registering thereby limiting any impact of short-selling. Both Mitsubishi Bank and Sumitomo Bank deals (from Table 7.1) apply similar calculation methodologies—a simple average of closing stock prices over 20 trading days ending on the 15th business day prior to their respective reset dates. The Sanwa Bank issue opts for an arithmetic average over a longer 30 day period, beginning on the 45th business day prior to its reset date. The single cross-currency Mitsubishi Bank issue adds a further level of complexity in that an ADS Equivalent price is used (as against the potentially more thinly traded ADR) for the purposes of determining, if applicable, a new conversion price. Usually the newly calculated conversion price must be below the current conversion price by at least ¥1, otherwise any relevant adjustment is carried forward to the next reset period and the conversion price remains unchanged.

7.3.5 Early Mandatory Conversion Clauses

As with most convertible issues, the issuer retains a call option, given fulfillment of certain criteria, to force early conversion. The size and mandatory nature of these issues have necessitated the use of call fractions—whereby only a part of the issue can be called in any given year. This avoids forcing all bondholders into the shares at once, which may result in undue pressure on the stock. Since the whole issue isn't called at once, some form of lottery is used to establish those bonds affected. Where a call fraction isn't taken up by an issuer in a given year, it typically carries forward cumulatively to the next.

7.4 MECHANICS OF THE RESET

A convertible's reset feature typically becomes operational on the first anniversary after issuance and is resettable annually thereafter, usually until maturity. In some cases there is an initial reset floor, below which there are no adjustments made to the conversion price, and a final reset floor set at some lower level, which is activated in the final year before maturity.

In Figure 7.1, we assume a reset bond is issued on a stock, X, with a floor set at 65% of the original conversion price. We further assume that the price of stock X declines

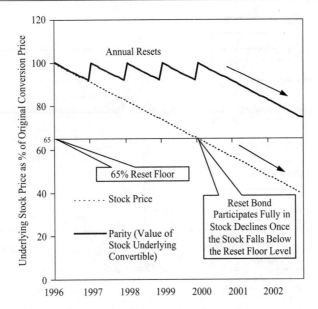

Figure 7.1 Hypothetical illustration of the reset mechanism
Source: Morgan Stanley Dean Witter Research

uniformly towards 40% of its original value over 7 years (the dashed line). In year 1, the stock declines by 7.95% and the bond's parity (heavy continuous line) falls to 92.05%.

Upon reset, the conversion price gets reset downwards, the conversion ratio is adjusted upwards and parity gets reset back to 100%. The process is repeated annually for share price falls below the prevailing conversion price but above 65% of the original conversion price. If the share price on any given reset anniversary happens to be at or above the current conversion price, then there would be no reset.

By practical illustration, let's take the case for the Sumitomo Bank 0.75% issue due 2001 (Figure 7.2). The original conversion price upon issuance in May 1996 was set at ¥2255. By early May 1997, on completion of the first reset calculation period, the newly calculated conversion price had fallen to ¥1493 (point A).

At issuance:

$$Conversion\ Ratio = \frac{Nom.Value}{Conv.Price} = \frac{1\,000\,000}{2255} = 443.45\ shares\ per\ bond$$

May 1997:

$$Conversion\ Ratio = \frac{Nom.Value}{Conv.Price} = \frac{1\,000\,000}{1493} = 669.8\ shares\ per\ bond$$

Even though the share price has clearly fallen during that period, one becomes entitled to a larger number of shares per bond (up from 443.45 to 669.8) upon conversion. The effect on parity is for it to get reset back towards 100% (at point B in Figure 7.2), offsetting losses on the shares. In May 1998, the conversion price got reset downwards further to ¥1239 with the conversion ratio rising to 807.1 (at point D in Figure 7.2).

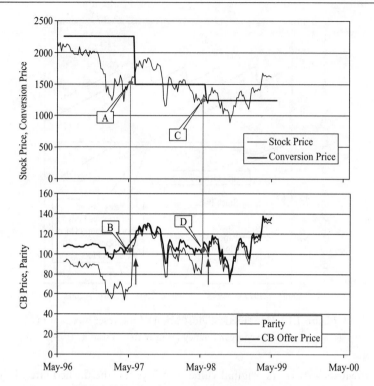

Figure 7.2   Sumitomo Bank 0.75% due 2001

The upper chart plots Sumitomo Bank's share price and overlays it with prevailing conversion
prices out to May 1999. The lower chart plots parity against empirical bond prices

Source: Morgan Stanley Dean Witter Research

The bond price should theoretically remain above 100 so long as the share price
remains above the given floor level, since parity is effectively guaranteed to be reset to
at least parity annually. This was largely the case for the Sumitomo Bank bonds, until
their most recent reset in May 1998.

The effect of this reset was to adjust the conversion price to within 10% of the floor
(1239/1128) transforming the bonds into a largely equity sensitive issue with high
correlation to the underlying shares both on the upside and the downside—hence the
close tracking of the two instruments from point D onwards in Figure 7.2. As the next
reset for Sumitomo approaches (in May 1999), stock price strength has meant the
probability of a further reset downwards to the conversion looks low.

7.5   VALUING MANDATORY CONVERTIBLE RESETS

The theoretical price profiles of Mandatory Convertibles with downward reset structures all follow a similar general pattern. As an investor, you are effectively long a call
option (with an adjustable strike price depending on where the present conversion price
has been reset to) and short a put option (with a strike price set at the relevant issue's
reset floor price level). A combination of both this long call and short put gives us the

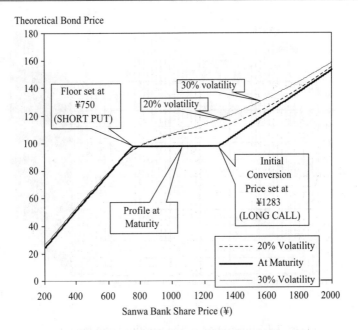

Figure 7.3 Sanwa Bank 1.25% due 2005
This bond retains its original conversion price of ¥1283 (effective strike on the long call), against a
floor of ¥750 (the effective strike on the short put)
Source: Morgan Stanley Dean Witter Research

familiar kinked curve (at issuance), offering a degree of defensiveness vis-à-vis the
underlying stock in a range either side of the prevailing conversion price (from Figure
7.3). At both lower and higher stock price levels, the bond's sensitivity to movements in
the underlying equity increases.

Several elements will influence how this theoretical price profile will change over time.
The degree of assumed volatility (in determining those option values) will influence the
steepness of the curve (higher volatility assumptions implying a steeper slope on both
long call and short put ends of the curve). Time to expiration will also play a factor in the
degree to which the curve diffusion reverses and becomes flatter as time value erodes.
The greatest influence on the curve, though, will be from changes to the bond's conversion price arising from downward resets. Following a reset downwards, the effective
strike on the long call position gets progressively lowered and an out-of-the-money
call gets shifted back to being an at-the-money one (as is the case in Figure 7.5, later on).

In modeling resettable bonds, we use a form of finite-difference equation to solve
for theoretical convertible bond values. The reset model is an extension of the
regular convertible bond model and can handle both resets upwards and downwards.

Intuitively, at least, our modeling makes use of a two-dimensional lattice structure
where each node corresponds to a value for a given time and stock price level (see Figure
7.4). The stock price at each node within the lattice is based on the assumed underlying
stock growth and volatility levels, with a broader structure for higher volatility stocks.
Possible final convertible values at maturity, on the right axis of the grid, can be

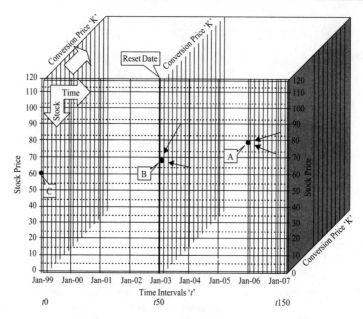

Figure 7.4   Illustration of the workings of a reset model
Source: Morgan Stanley Dean Witter Research

calculated as the normal pay-off equation: *max(redemption_value, parity)*, keeping in mind that in the case of mandatory resets, redemption value will be zero.

At each time interval, the convertible values are discounted back to give a range of possible values for a given stock price level at the current period $t = 0$. The process of moving across the lattice, from right to left, and the values passed from node to node will depend on several "boundary conditions" specific to that particular bond—including whether or not the bonds are convertible at time "t", if the issuer's call is active, whether the investor can put the bonds back to the issuer or not, or whether there is a resettable feature.

For resettable bonds, the level of complexity increases. Unlike a regular convertible that just requires a two-dimensional lattice structure, we use a three-dimensional grid due to the variability of the conversion price, which itself becomes contingent on the stock price level. From Figure 7.4, time to maturity for a given resettable bond is spliced into 150 periods. At maturity ($t150$), end values are determined. As with a regular convertible, one discounts back through each time period solving the finite difference equation (a derivation of Black–Scholes) applying the many boundary conditions that exist (point A). Additionally, at each node, a third dimension of all possible conversion prices needs to be considered in solving for the theoretical value to be passed to the next node. At point B ($t50$), a reset date, that third dimension of possible conversion prices is a single known value, as at that point it equals the prevailing stock price (or at least some average stock price calculated over a predefined period approaching that reset date). Assuming a reset downwards only, as one discounts further back along the lattice, the array of possible conversion prices diminishes, capped out by the current prevailing conversion price set at the previous reset date. The process continues until such time as a theoretical value for the stock price at $t0$ is solved for (point C).

Although modeling for stochastic interest rates is feasible in a regular convertible bond model, undertaking the calculation for a resettable bond becomes inordinately complex and extends the calculation time considerably, making it less practical as a trading tool.

7.6 EVOLVING INTO AN EQUITY PROXY

The effect of successive resets downwards is to shift the strike of the long call progressively lower. What starts out as an instrument with a very different pay-off profile to the underlying stock, ends up becoming essentially a stock proxy when reset at or close to its floor.

Take the case of the Sumitomo Bank 0.75%. Its initial pay-off profile (the heavy continuous line in Figure 7.5) demonstrates strong defensive characteristics between the then current conversion price (2255) and the floor, set 50% lower (1128). Intuitively, one would expect that so long as the share price remained above that 50% floor level, parity would get reset back to at least 100% and the bond price would, by implication, trade at or above that level. Weekly empirical data from 5/96 to 5/97 ("x" symbols in Figure 7.5) demonstrate this. The only time the bonds traded below par was as the share price approached the floor level.

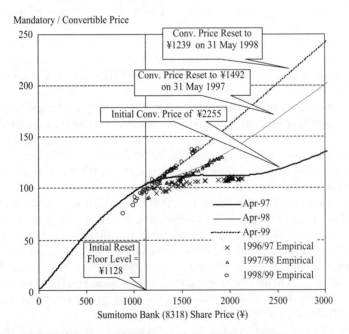

Figure 7.5 Sumitomo Bank 0.75% due 2001

Illustration of the effect of successive conversion price resets downwards on the pay-off profile of the preferred (vertical axis) for given share price movements (horizontal axis). 25% stock volatility assumed in deriving the theoretical pay-off curves for this bond at successively lower conversion prices

Source: Morgan Stanley Dean Witter Research

Upon the conversion price getting reset from 2255 to 1493 in May 1997, the pay-off profile of the bond pivots upwards, with the defensive zone contracting, reflecting a smaller buffer of 32% (1493/1128) above the floor, compared to the initial 100%. Consequently, the equity sensitivity of the bond rises, reflected in the tendency for bonds to trade deeper in-the-money, on the back of some share price strength (Δ symbol in Figure 7.5) during the 5/97 to 5/98 period. Greater equity sensitivity on the upside equates to similar sensitivity on the downside. By May 1998, the Sumitomo Bank 0.75% bonds would be reset downwards again to the current 1239 level, within 10% of their floor. The effect has been to pivot the bond pay-off profile upwards again, making for an almost one-for-one movement between the bond and the underlying stock.

As of writing, midway through the reset recalculation period ahead of the May 1999 reset date, strength in Sumitomo Bank's stock price makes it likely that the conversion price will remain unchanged at its current level. It bears mentioning too the feature in this preferred whereby in May 2001 (the final reset date), the floor steps down to 850 (37% of the original conversion price), reinstating some defensive characteristics to the bond in its final year.

Well over half the original bank reset issues have reset at or close to their floors, with little or no asymmetry between the stock and preferred remaining. Given that coupons are so low for most of these issues, there's often little motivation to be exposed to the stock through the preferred and the tendency has been for many holders to convert, leading to a contracting outstanding issuance pool and deteriorating liquidity.

7.7   TRADING BEHAVIOR OF MANDATORY RESET STRUCTURES

At issuance, most of the bank resets were brought to market on compelling valuations—issued at par, sometimes on premiums as low as 2.5% and theoretical values often in the 115–120% range. On such terms, many holders of the underlying equity found themselves compelled to shift into the preferreds. In hindsight, several years of severe weakness in bank share prices that followed meant holders of these preferreds outperformed strongly relative to their peers retaining exposure via the stock.

While most issues were theoretically cheap at issuance, few, if any, ever traded up to their true values. From the outset, it became clear that a large part of the market didn't have the ability to calculate a theoretical price for these instruments and that was therefore reflected in their market prices. That same market became increasingly dysfunctional when bank share prices weakened significantly in early 1997 and again in the last quarter of 1997. The market's expectation that these resets would trade like convertibles with bond floors was mistaken, with bond prices tumbling as share prices moved towards and below their reset floors.

The degree to which investors exposed to these issues participate on the upside and downside relative to their underlying stock prices can be captured by each bond's delta profile (lower charts in Figure 7.6). Since it has a definable bond floor, the BOT-Mitsubishi Bank issue (on the right) has a more familiar profile to a regular convertible, with the delta curve sloping upwards from left to right in a predictable way with relative steepness in the mid-section dependent on assumed volatility.

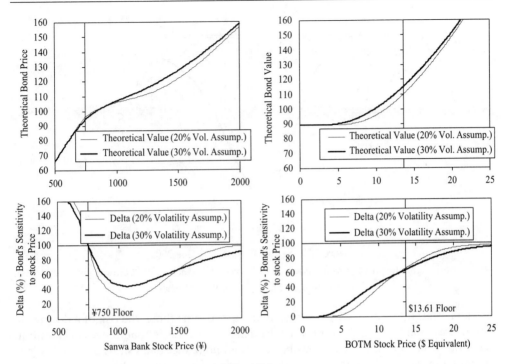

Figure 7.6

Sanwa Bank 1.25% due 2005—Theoretical   BOT-Mitsubishi 3% due 2001—Theoretical
price curves and delta profiles at different   price curves and delta profiles at different
volatility assumption levels   volatility assumption levels

Source: Morgan Stanley Dean Witter Research

The U-shaped delta profile for the Sanwa Bank issue (on the left) is typical of most mandatory resettable structures, with the delta troughing for share prices which are at-the-money (and lie within the defensive zone) before rising dramatically on the downside once reset floors are breached and the reset valuation plays catch-up with parity (reflected in deltas sometimes exceeding 100%).

7.8 "NEGATIVE GAMMA" BECOMING PART OF THE VOCABULARY

This U-shaped delta curve is synonymous with the increased usage of the term "Negative Gamma" in the context of Japanese bank resets. Gamma, the rate of change in delta, is generally positive for convertibles (reflecting the typical upward sloping left to right delta curve), peaking for share price movements in and around the conversion price and predictably rising in value as the embedded option within a convertible approaches maturity.

In the case of mandatory convertible resets, gamma can turn negative for share prices below the floor where the delta curve begins rising (from Figure 7.7). This phenomenon can be particularly dangerous to delta-neutral investors that seek to arbitrage bond and stock asymmetry by going long the bonds and short the stock. As share prices fall, the delta rises, and to remain neutral one is forced to sell more shares, often into an already

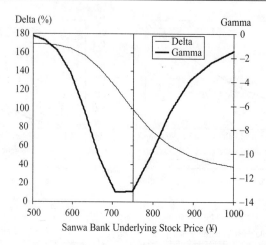

Figure 7.7   Sanwa Bank 1.25% due 2005

Illustration of the 'negative gamma' effect as delta rises for stock prices below a given reset floor
Source: Morgan Stanley Dean Witter Research

weak market. If lots of other investors are doing the same thing, the risk of a downward spiral rises. Similarly on the upside, as the delta reduces (as a bond moves back into its defensive zone), one is forced to buy back shares and reduce one's short position. Again, if many buyers are doing the same thing, reducing that short can become expensive as the stock price moves higher rapidly.

Undoubtedly hedge funds have been active in the Japanese bank reset market, but the perception of their activity levels probably overstates the reality. Latching on to the negative gamma concept, the broader Japanese equity market was quick to condemn hedge funds for precipitating Japanese bank share prices lower. What most failed to appreciate is that to short bank shares, one must first source a borrow in the stock, and this became progressively more difficult as time went on, frustrating any hedge fund's best efforts to set up trades in this reset market.

Negative gamma can also arise in situations where a trader sells options against a long regular convertible position, particularly if there's a large maturity mis-match between the two instruments. Often the gamma on the short option position will be small when the trade is initially set up, but as that option approaches maturity, its gamma can spike if the underlying share price is close to the strike. Maintaining a neutral hedge becomes exceedingly difficult, with one often forced to sell more options away at cheaper levels or buy them back at more expensive levels.

7.9   CONCLUSIONS

In hindsight, the Japanese bank mandatory convertible reset issues proved effective both from an issuer's and an investor's perspective. As a form of financing, they overcame the need to both raise debt or directly tap the equity market in an environment that was conducive to neither. As an investor in these instruments, versus owning the underlying stock, relative outperformance has been strong (see Figure 7.8) with downward resets offsetting often significant share price weakness.

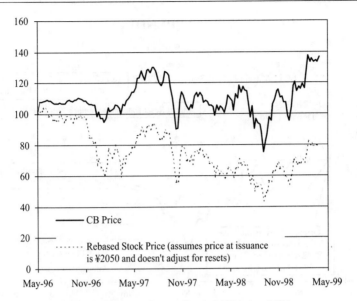

Figure 7.8   Sumitomo Bank 0.75% due 2001

Illustration of the outperformance of the reset structure vis-à-vis the stock in periods of severe share price weakness

Source: Morgan Stanley Dean Witter Research

The bank reset market, capitalized at approximately US$10 billion, came to dominate the Japanese euroyen convertible market, in the absence of much other issuance. The liquidity in this market was remarkable throughout 1997 and 1998, with turnover indicated by Euroclear statistics in the region of US$60 billion and US$40 billion, respectively. The presence of these instruments allowed for an effective market in Japanese bank exposure to operate outside Tokyo market hours and facilitated investors in Europe and the US. Despite certain criticism guided at the overcomplexity of these structures, the reality is that the convertibles market and the flexibility of the product continue to offer novel solutions to issuers with a sophisticated investor base capable of ascertaining value. While opportunities for further mandatory resets in Japan presently look exhausted, their application in the recent government recapitalization preferred share private placement scheme is encouraging.

7.10   APPENDIX

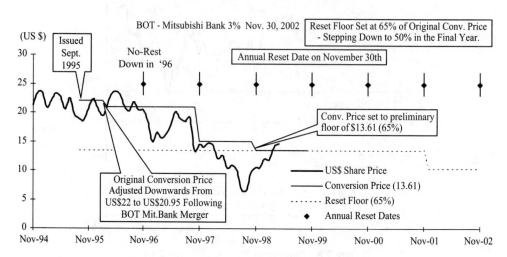

Figure 7.9   BOT-Mitsubishi 3% due 2002—timeline of key reset events
Source: Morgan Stanley Dean Witter Research

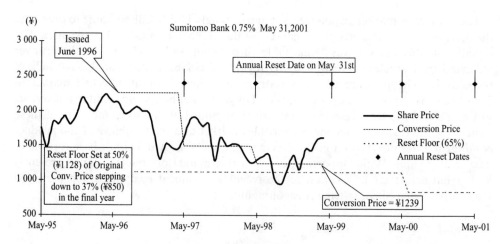

Figure 7.10   Sumitomo Bank 0.75% due 2001—timeline of key reset events
Source: Morgan Stanley Dean Witter Research

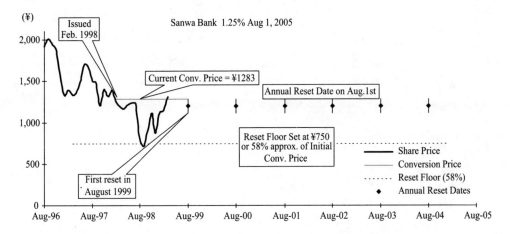

Figure 7.11 Sanwa Bank 1.25% due 2005—timeline of key reset events
Source: Morgan Stanley Dean Witter Research

8

Japanese Reset Convertible Bonds and Other Advanced Issues in Convertible Bonds

"Sometimes it takes a PhD to figure out a structure designed by a high school dropout"

IZZY NELKEN

8.1 INTRODUCTION

Between 1995 and 1998 several Japanese banks issued "jumbo" convertible bonds with large outstanding amounts. In the mid-1990s the Japanese banks were considered quite risky as they had large real estate exposures. As a result of worsening conditions the Japanese banks required more capital. Equity issuance was out of the question since stock markets were depressed. Straight bond issues would have required a high coupon yield. This would have placed a burden on the banks' treasury departments.

Convertible bonds were seen as a reasonable tool to raise capital. Investors in such convertible bonds wanted some sort of "insurance" should the issuing bank's stock decline. The Japanese banks found it much easier to sell convertible bonds if the reset feature was included.

Prior to its merger with the Bank of Tokyo, Mistubishi bank issued a $2 billion US dollar deal in September 1995. The deal had a reset clause since it would have been redeemable for cash if the share price at maturity was less than half of the original conversion price. As operating conditions in Japan worsened, the banks needed to raise more and more capital to operate within the BIS regulatory capital guidelines. More and more reset convertibles were issued.

Currently, reset convertibles are fairly common in the Japanese domestic market and have also been issued in other Asian countries.

The conversion feature is in some cases upward and downward. In most cases, however, it is only downward. A decline in the share price will usually cause a decline in the price of the convertible. By including a reset feature and ensuring that the convertible bond is again convertible to par worth of stock, the convertible's price increases as compared to a non-reset convertible.

Usually the downward reset is limited by a floor. That is, if the issuer's stock declines by a lot, the holder of the convertible will only be compensated for some of the decline. This is to ensure a limit on the potential dilution of the issuer's stock in case of conversion.

Handbook of Hybrid Instruments. Edited by Izzy Nelken. © 2000 Izzy Nelken. Published 2000 by John Wiley & Sons Ltd.

8.2   THE RESET FEATURE

In a reset convertible, the conversion price resets at certain dates as a function of the store price on that date and the stock price evolution during the preceding period. When the conversion price is reset downward, it makes the bond more expensive. This is done to compensate the bond holders for a reduction in the price of the stock. Many convertible bonds exhibit several reset dates. Of course, the conversion price on the second reset date depends on the conversion price which was set on the first reset date. This in turn depends on the initial conversion price. If the bond has three reset dates, the conversion price on the third reset date depends on the conversion price which was set on the second date which depends on the conversion price of the first reset date, etc.

In some convertible bonds, the conversion price may not reset downward below a certain multiplier of the *first* conversion price. Other convertibles, as in our example, allow the conversion price to reset based upon the *previous* conversion price.

Note that in some convertible bonds, the conversion price may also be reset upwards. In our example, this does not happen since the upper limit on the conversion price is set to the previous conversion price multiplied by 1.

8.3   MODELING OF RESET CONVERTIBLES

We analyze convertible bonds using a multi-dimensional tree (or pyramid). Our algorithms have been described before in "Costing the Converts", by Cheung, W. and Nelken, I., *Risk Magazine*, 7, No. 7 (July 1994); "Fervour of the Convert", by Nelken, I., *Asia Risk Magazine* (April 1996); and "Convertible Bonds and Preferred Shares". In Nelken, I. (Ed.) (1997), *Option Embedded Bonds*, Chapter 8. Chicago: Irwin.

When trying to apply tree-based methods to solving Japanese reset convertibles, one realizes that the changing conversion price makes the problem "path dependent". Path-dependent problems are known to be very difficult to price with a tree-based methodology.

The difficulty is that when we arrive at a particular node, there may be very many conversion prices possible at that node. Thus, it is no longer sufficient to know the stock price and interest rate at that node. We also need to know the conversion price. However, there may be very many possible conversion prices as they depend on the past history of the stock.

This is known as "a dropout from high school can easily create a problem that will challenge a PhD."

In any case, we have completed the creation of a model which solves for reset convertible bonds. This is implemented in a kind of "super trees". One of the features of this algorithm is that it does not require much more time than solving for a non-reset convertible. It does not rely on Monte Carlo techniques, neither does it spawn a new tree at each possible reset date. Instead, the tree is "enhanced" so it can keep track of many conversion prices.

It is very tempting to ignore the reset feature. However, as is shown below, the computed bond prices (and Delta hedge ratios) will be quite different between reset and non-reset convertibles.

8.3.1 Example

We examine the relationship between two convertible bonds.

- The non-reset convertible is convertible into seven shares of the underlying stock.
- The reset convertible is initially also convertible into seven shares of the underlying stock (conversion price $142.857 per $1000 face value of bond). In addition, there are three reset dates. On each of those dates, the conversion price may be reset *downward* only.

On 1-Sep-2005 the conversion price resets to be equal to the share price, provided that this will not reset the conversion price to below 50% of its previous value.

This repeats again on 1-Sep-2006 and on 1-Sep-2007.

Assume that on 1-Sep-2005, the share price is equal to $80. The non-reset convertible will have a conversion value of $560 and will be out-of-the-money. It will probably trade close to its bond equivalent basis, probably below par. The reset convertible, on the other hand, will reset its conversion price to $80. The conversion value will be $1000 (by definition) and the convertible will trade above par.

On 1-Sep-2006, the share price has declined some more to $60. The non-reset convertible will have a conversion value of $420 and will be even more out-of-the-money. We can not say for certain what happens to the reset convertible.

If, as in our example, the previous conversion price was $80, the new conversion price will be reset to $60. The new conversion value will be $1000 (by definition) and the convertible will trade above par.

But consider another case where on 1-Sep-2005, the stock price has been $150. In this case, the conversion price was not reset and stayed at $142.857. Now (on 1-Sep-2006) that the share price has declined to $60, we can not reset the conversion price to below 50% of its previous value. The new conversion price will, therefore, be reset to $71.42857. The conversion value of the bond will be $840.

An important feature of these bonds is that the conversion value is path dependent. It is not enough to know the stock price today to compute the conversion value.

If we continue with this analysis to the third reset date, we will have even more possible conversion prices.

8.3.2 Bond Prices

Figure 8.1 is a drawing of the bond prices of the non-reset convertible and the reset convertible. We also plot the "reset premium". This is defined as the difference on prices divided by the price of the non-reset bond.

When the stock price is in the "default region", the reset and non-reset trade close to each other. Even if the reset convertible allows the acquisition of more shares, the shares are close to worthless and do not contribute much to the bond price.

At very high stock prices, the conversion price of the reset is not likely to reset downwards, and again, the reset and non-reset trade close to each other.

At intermediate bond prices, there are substantial differences in price between the reset and non-reset bonds. As Figure 8.1, shows, the differences can be upwards of 10%.

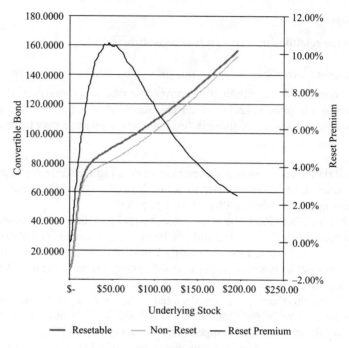

Figure 8.1 Non-reset and reset bonds

8.3.3 Delta Hedge Ratios

It is even more instructive to study the Delta hedge ratios of the reset and non-reset convertible bonds.

Figure 8.2 is a chart of the Deltas of both bonds. Figure 8.3 is a close up in which we have concentrated on the "interesting" region which highlights the differences between the reset and non-reset bonds.

As UBS found out to its dismay, it is the Delta of a reset convertible which causes problems. In a typical (non-reset) convertible, the Delta declines as the stock price declines. Thus as the convertible becomes "out of the money" and moves into the "bond equivalent region" it becomes less sensitive to the stock price.

In the reset convertible, on the other hand, the conversion price declines with the stock price. Thus as the stock price declines below a certain threshold, Delta *increases* (see Figure 8.3). Now, consider a trader with a hedged position. They are long convertible bonds and short stocks. As the share price declines, the Delta increases, the trader is in the difficult position of having to short even more shares. So they need to borrow more shares and sell them short. This, in turn, puts an even greater downward pressure on the share price. Thus the trader is forced to "go against himself". In addition, this strategy is followed by many other convertible hedgers and the stock is caught in a "short squeeze". The short borrow rates move right up and the positive carry that was obtained by a long position in the bond and a short position in the share, turns into a negative carry.

The carry is given by:

$$\text{Carry} = \text{Coupon} - \text{Delta} \times (\text{Dividends} + \text{Stock Borrow Fees})$$

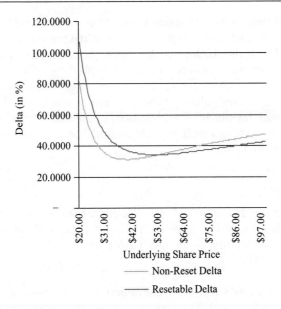

Figure 8.2 Delta for reset and non-reset convertibles

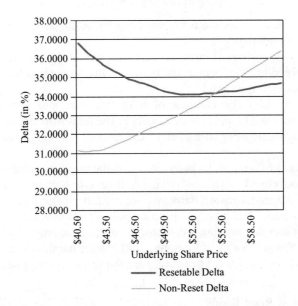

Figure 8.3 Close up of Delta for reset and non-reset convertibles

As the Delta increased and stock borrow fees became very high, the positive carry turned into a negative one.

At extremely low stock prices (the left-hand side of Figure 8.2), we begin to see the effects of the bankruptcy region. Note that extremely low stock prices hurt the reset convertible more than they hurt the non-reset bond. The reason for this is that the reset convertible can only adjust its conversion value so far. In a reset convertible, if the stock price declines to moderately low levels, we can reset the conversion price to the current stock price. However, if the stock price declines to extremely low levels, the conversion price adjusts to the previous conversion price multiplied by a factor (in our case, 50%). Thus at moderately low stock prices, the conversion value is again par. At extremely low stock prices, the conversion value is sub-par. Thus it stands to reason that the price difference in low stock regions for reset bonds will be higher than that of non-reset. Add that to the bankruptcy effect which impacts on both the reset and non-reset bonds and the pattern becomes understandable.

8.3.4 Gamma Ratios

Option traders are usually taught to "avoid negative Gamma like the plague". Gamma is the second derivative of the price of a derivative instrument with respect to the underlying. We review the first terms in a Taylor series:

$$f(x+h) = f(x) + h^*f'(x) + h^2/2^*f''(x) + \dots$$

The trader does not know which way the underlying will move. Suppose the trader is Delta hedged so that $f'(x) = 0$. Then whichever way the underlying moves we have:

$$f(x+h) = f(x) + h^2/2^*f''(x)$$

If $f''(x)$, which is known as Gamma, happens to be negative, the trader will lose whichever way the underlying moves.

On the other hand, positive Gamma adds to the price of the instrument. This leads to the old-timer expression "the 'benter' the better". This means that the more Gamma an option has, the better it is to hold.

In Figure 8.4 we plot the Gamma of both the reset and non-reset convertible. Notice the large negative Gamma which exists in the reset instrument. Also notice that the negative Gamma area begins earlier in the reset convertible than in the non-reset bond.

We call Gamma the "cost of the baby sitter". If the absolute value of Gamma is high then any small movement in the underlying will require a change in the Delta hedge ratio. Therefore, the trader must "baby sit" the hedged position. On the other hand, if Gamma is close to zero, then a hedged position will continue to remain hedged. We note that reset convertibles are instruments whose Gamma is negative and lower than non-reset bonds. The absolute value of Gamma, on the other hand, is higher for reset bonds than for non-reset convertibles. Therefore, they require a lot more hedging.

8.3.5 Conclusion of Reset Bonds

The reset convertible is a very interesting bond. Its price and hedge ratios depend on a variety of factors. These include the reset dates, the stock multiplier on each reset date which is used to determine the conversion price and on the minimal (and maximal) amounts by which the conversion price can be modified.

These relationships are quite complex and an adequate model is essential. Fortunately, such a model has recently become available from Super Computer Consulting Inc. For more information, please give us a call.

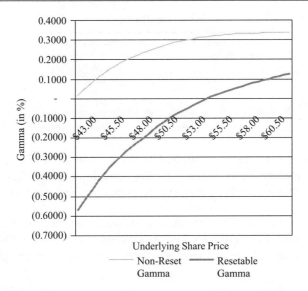

Figure 8.4 Close up of Gamma for reset and non-reset convertibles

8.4 TWO MORE INTERESTING POINTS RELATED TO CONVERTIBLE SECURITIES

8.4.1 Duration

The duration of non-convertible bonds decreases as their coupon increases. This familiar effect is due to the fact that the higher coupon bonds deliver more cash flows near the start of their life as compared to lower coupon bonds which deliver cash flows towards the end of their life. For example, all other things being equal, a 7.5% coupon bond will have a lower duration than a 3.5% coupon bond. A zero coupon bond has the highest duration of all.

Convertible bonds, on the other hand, sometimes exhibit an opposite effect. Raising the coupon causes the duration to *increase*. Let us understand this phenomenon.

Compare a 7.5% coupon bond that is convertible to four shares with a 3.5% coupon bond which is convertible to eight shares. The holders of the 7.5% convertible will have less of a propensity to convert their bonds (as they receive a higher coupon). Thus the expected lifetime of the bond increases which will cause the duration to increase. So with convertibles we have two contradictory effects:

High coupon → Lower duration (as in normal bonds)
High coupon → Lower propensity to convert → Longer lifetime → Higher duration

These two effects are contradictory and it is difficult to ascertain which is the stronger of these. A model is useful in this regard.

8.4.2 Correlation

It is clear that the correlation between stock price and interest rates has an effect on the price of the convertible. A table of correlation numbers and prices follows (Table 8.1).

Table 8.1

Stock/rate correlation	Convertible bond price ($)
1	134.00
0.5	127.57
0	120.79
−0.5	113.82
−1	106.54

In Table 8.1 we see a difference of about 25% between the price of the convertible when the correlation assumption is 1 and −1. This specific example exhibits quite a large sensitivity to correlation. Typical convertible bonds we have observed, may have price differences in the area of 15–20%.

Consider, if you will, another correlation product, the "crack spread option". This option has a payout that is determined by the difference, at expiration, between the prices of raw oil and heating oil. For an example option, we obtain the prices given in Table 8.2.

Table 8.2

Heating oil/crude oil correlation	Spread option price ($)
1	1.24
0.5	2.866
0	3.807
−0.5	4.531
−1	5.117

The spread option's price is, of course, very sensitive to correlation. The higher the correlation between the prices of both underlying instruments, the closer the two underlying instruments are going to be to each other.

Thus the spread option exhibits a price sensitivity to correlation of about 400%, while the sensitivity of the convertible is about 25%. We now explore the sensitivity of the convertible to correlation and why that sensitivity is not as great as the correlation sensitivity of a spread option.

Consider a typical node in a quadranary (quadro) tree which models the convertible bond. At node A, we have a stock price of s and an interest rate of r. One period later, the stock price may rise to s^+ or fall to s^-. Similarly, the interest rate may climb to r^+ or may decline to r^-:

$$B\ (s^+, r^+) \rightarrow \text{Medium}$$
$$C\ (s^+, r^+) \rightarrow \text{Low}$$
$$A\ (s, r) \qquad D\ (s^+, r^-) \rightarrow \text{Medium}$$
$$E\ (s^+, r^+) \rightarrow \text{High}$$

In the quadro tree, node A has four descendent nodes which correspond to the four possibilities:

- Stock Up, Rates Up—Node B
- Stock Down, Rates Up—Node C
- Stock Down, Rates Down—Node D
- Stock Up, Rates Down—Node E

With each node, we also associate a probability of arriving at that node. The four probabilities are P_B, P_C, P_D and P_E.

The precise details associated with the quadro tree have been described in our book *Option Embedded Bonds*, I. Nelken (Ed.) (1997), published by Irwin Professional Publishers, Chicago, IL.

The node B has two effects: the high stock price increases the price of the convertible while the high interest rate reduces it. Therefore, the price of the convertible at node B is medium. At node C, the price is low since the stock price is low (reducing the price) and the interest rate is high, again, reducing the price. At node D the price is medium and at node E the price is high.

Consider a high correlation between stock prices and interest rates. A high correlation will increase P_C and P_E and will decrease P_B and P_D.

So, in effect, we are taking the average of a high number and a low one and the result is in the middle.

On the other hand, suppose the correlation is negative. Now, P_B and P_D are high. So we are taking the average of two medium numbers—the result again is medium.

Of course, the convertible has a lot of embedded options and these will change the price of the bond at each of the nodes so it is hard to generalize from this discussion.

9

A Dictionary of Terms Related to Hybrid Instruments

GARY GASTINEAU AND MARK KRITZMAN

Absolute Call Privilege: The right of an issuer to redeem a bond at any time without any preconditions.

Absolute Priority Rule (APR): A provision of many bankruptcy systems that senior creditors are fully compensated before junior creditors receive anything, and that junior creditors are fully compensated before shareholders receive anything. In practice, lower-ranking creditors and shareholders often receive something as compensation for expediting the settlement process.

Acceleration Covenant: A provision of a debt instrument or swap agreement that requires early payment and termination in the event of default or credit downgrade.

Accretion: (1) Accumulation or accrual of interest, as in a discount bond. (2) Growth by an organic process as in agriculture, or by financial accumulation as in a fund that accumulates and reinvests income.

Accrued Interest: The current value of the earned portion of the next coupon payment due on a bond or note.

Adjustable-Rate Convertible Debt: (1) A convertible bond with no conversion premium and a coupon equivalent to or linked to the dividend on the underlying common stock. This structure was designed to make dividend equivalents deductible by the issuer, but the Internal Revenue Service has held that the coupon on such instruments is paid from after-tax income. (2) A convertible bond or note with a variable (floating-rate) coupon set by reference to a standard index rate (e.g., LIBOR).

Adjustable-Rate Preferred Stock (ARPS): Floating-rate preferred stock with a dividend rate reset based, for example, on the maximum of a series of short- and long-term rates plus or minus a designated spread. Designed to permit US corporate investors to take advantage of the 70% intercorporate dividend exclusion. *Also called Cumulative Auction Market Preferred Stock (CAMPS), Dutch Auction Rate Transferable Securities (DARTS) Preferred Stock.*

Advance Guarantee: A call option.

Aftermarket: The market for a security after an initial public offering. The aftermarket or secondary market may be over-the-counter or on an exchange.

Handbook of Hybrid Instruments. Edited by Izzy Nelken. ©2000 Gary Gastineau. Published 2000 by John Wiley & Sons Ltd. Reproduced with permission. From *The Dictionary of Financial Risk Management* © 1992, 1996, 1999.

Aggregate Exercise Price: The exercise or strike price of an option contract multiplied by the number of units of the underlying security or instrument covered by the option contract. For example, a bond option with a strike price of 101 ($1010 per bond) covering 1000 bonds would have an aggregate exercise price of 1010 times 1000, or $1 010 000.

All-In Premium: *Brit.* The warrant premium expressed as a percentage of the current price of the underlying.

All-Ordinaries Share Price Riskless Index Notes (ASPRINs): Low- or zero-coupon equity index-linked notes with a specified percentage participation in the Australian All-Ordinaries stock index and minimum redemption at par.

Alternative Asset: Any non-traditional investment instrument, style, or category—especially an asset class with returns that are not highly correlated with stock and bond returns. Examples can include precious metals, real estate, and managed accounts using currency, commodity, and long/short stock accounts, or even hedge funds using stock index and debt futures.

American Corporate Accrual Receipts (ACARS): Stripped coupon and principal payments based on corporate bonds. The corporate bond equivalent of STRIPS.

American Option: A put or call that can be exercised at any time prior to expiration. Most listed stock options, including those on European exchanges, are American-style options. Important exceptions are certain low strike price options and/or options on shares with restricted transferability. Most listed options on other instruments are also American-style options, but a number of European-style options have been introduced in recent years, particularly on stock indexes and currencies. The labels, European and American, come from a 1965 warrant article by Nobel Laureate Paul Samuelson.

Analytic: (1) An equation, or set of equations, usually embodied in a computer program, that performs specific calculations too complicated to perform routinely by hand or with a pocket calculator. (2) A problem-solving approach that relies on equations rather than trial and error.

Analytic Model: A model whose solution can be determined by solving an equation or set of equations, as opposed to the use of numeric methods.

Annualization: Translation or conversion of data or a rate calculation for part of a year or more than a year into an annual equivalent amount or rate.

Annualized Return: The rate of return that would occur on average per year given a cumulative multi-year return or a fractional year return and taking into account compounding and discounting. The formula for annualizing a return is: $R_a = (1 + R_u)_{(1/n)} - 1$, where R_a equals the annualized return, R_u equals the unannualized return, and n equals the number of years over which the cumulative return is calculated. When reporting investment performance, it is inappropriate to annualize returns calculated over periods of less then one year.

Anomaly: An unexplained or unexpected price or rate relationship that seems to offer an opportunity for an arbitrage-type profit, although not typically without risk. Examples include the tendency of small stocks to outperform large stocks, of stocks with low price-to-book value ratios to outperform stocks with high price-to-book value ratios, and of discount currency forward contracts to outperform premium currency forward contracts.

Anticipatory Hedge: (1) A long hedging position taken to provide participation in a market before an investor is ready to take a position in the related cash instruments or actuals. *Also called Long Hedge.* (2) A short equivalent position taken to protect against a decline when tax or other considerations force a delay in the sale of the related long position.

Antidilution Clause: A provision of a convertible security that provides for adjustment of the conversion ratio in the event of stock dividends or stock splits, and sometimes in the event of a sale of stock below market value.

Arbitrage: (1) Technically, the action of purchasing a commodity or security in one market for immediate sale in another market (deterministic arbitrage). (2) Popular usage has expanded the meaning to include any attempt to buy a relatively underpriced item and sell a similar, relatively overpriced item, expecting to profit when the prices resume a more appropriate theoretical or historical relationship (statistical arbitrage). (3) In trading options, convertible securities, and futures, arbitrage techniques can be applied whenever a strategy involves buying and selling packages of related instruments. (4) Risk arbitrage applies the principles of risk offset to mergers and other major corporate developments. The risk offsetting position(s) do not insulate the investor from certain event risks (such as termination of a merger agreement or the risk of delay in the completion of a transaction), so the arbitrage is incomplete. (5) Tax arbitrage transactions are undertaken to share the benefit of differential tax rates or circumstances of two or more parties to a transaction. (6) Regulatory arbitrage transactions are designed to provide indirect access to a market where one party is denied direct access by law or regulation. (7) Swap-driven arbitrage transactions are motivated by the comparative advantages that swap counterparties enjoy in different debt and currency markets. For example, one counterparty may borrow relatively cheaper in the intermediate- or long-term US dollar market, while the other may have a comparative advantage in floating-rate sterling. A cross-currency swap can improve both of their positions.

Arbitrage Free: No arbitrage opportunities exist. An arbitrage-free environment requires complete markets.

Arrearage: (1) Unpaid dividends that must be paid to holders of cumulative preferred stock before common stock dividends can be paid. (2) Any other past due obligation.

Ask Price: An abbreviation of "asked price," often necessitated by the limited space available on a display screen. If space is not an issue, asked is preferred (as in bid-asked spread).

Asset Manager: A portfolio manager, corporate treasurer, or other individual responsible for management of the risks and returns associated with a portfolio of securities or other instruments.

At-the-Money: The market price or rate of the underlying and the strike price or rate of an at-the-money option are equal. If the current market price of the stock is $80, an option to buy a stock at a strike price of $80 is at the money. Increasingly, particularly in currency markets, the phrase refers to the forward price associated with the current spot price, as in "at-the-money forward."

Automatic Exercise: A procedure used by many option clearing organizations whereby expiring options that are in the money by a specified amount, or that are cash settled, are exercised without specific instructions from the optionholder.

Automatically Convertible Enhanced Security (ACES): *Also called Debt Exchangeable for Common Stock (DECS), Dividend Enhanced Convertible Stock (DECS).*

Aval: A third-party guarantee, usually by a bank.

Back Bond: A bond obtained through exercise of an option or a warrant.

Back Stub Period: The last interim period in the life of a swap or other periodic reset agreement if that period is different (usually shorter) than preceding periods.

Bank for International Settlements (BIS): An organization dominated by central banks, the BIS is concerned with international payments.

Bank Guarantee: A form of credit enhancement where a bank lends its own credit to assure timely payment of another party's obligation(s).

Basis Point (BP, BIP): 1/100 of a percentage point, also expressed as 0.01%. The difference between a yield of 7.90% and 8% is 10 basis points. When applied to a price rather than a rate, the term is often expressed as annualized basis points.

Beta: (1) A measurement of stock price volatility relative to a broad market index. If a stock moves up and down twice as much as the market, it has a beta of 2. If it moves one-half as much as the market, its beta is 0.5. Because beta assumes a linear relationship, it can be seriously misleading if used in stock option evaluation or comparison. (2) The slope of a regression line. (3) The second tier of stocks listed on the London Stock Exchange. The other tiers are alpha, delta, and gamma.

Bond: Traditionally, a written unconditional promise to pay a specific principal sum at a determined future date, and interest at a fixed or determinable rate on fixed dates. Increasingly, the promise to pay has become conditional, and the principal, interest, and payment dates have become contingent in real world instruments.

Bond Basis: A method of interest calculation using a day count fraction equal to actual days divided by actual days in a year (usually 365). *Also called Day Count Basis.*

Bond Equivalent Yield (BEY): A bond or Treasury bill or other discount instrument's yield over its life, assuming it is purchased at the asked price and the return is annualized using a simple interest approach. Bond equivalent yield is equal to a bill's discount, expressed as a fraction of the purchase price multiplied by 365 divided by the number of days to maturity.

BEY = (discount/purchase price) × (365/days to maturity)

Bond-Over-Bill (BOB) Spread: The yield differential between a specific bond and a given maturity Treasury bill. The inverse of a Bill-Over-Bond (BOB) Spread.

Bond Value: The estimated market value of the fixed-income element of a convertible bond. Bond value excludes the value of the convertible's equity option component, but usually reflects any bond call privilege the issuer retains. *Also called Investment Value.*

Bond With Attached Warrant: A combination of a traditional bond or note and a call warrant on shares of the issuing firm. The warrant can usually be traded separately after the underwriting period. The structure differs from the traditional convertible bond because the life of the warrant continues if the bond is called. Usually, the valuation of the bond with attached warrant is slightly different from that of a convertible bond, because the issuer's bond call provision would be used on the straight bond under different circumstances than it would be used to call a convertible bond. The interest rate on the bond is below straight bond market rates at issuance because of the value of the warrant, making an early bond call unlikely.

Boundary Conditions: In the valuation of financial instruments, boundary conditions are limitations on the value of an option or any other instrument determined by the provisions of the instrument and by the structure and value of any underlying instrument. Relevant boundaries for an option contract include relationships among the underlying price, the intrinsic value or forward intrinsic value of the option, and the stock price. Boundary conditions are usually expressed as equations that describe minimum and maximum values of the instrument under all possible circumstances. If boundary conditions are violated in the market, a risk-free arbitrage opportunity is created.

Building-Block Approach: A generic term for a variety of risk management techniques that separate a financial instrument into simpler components, reaggregate the components into portfolios, and manage specific types of risk in the separate portfolios.

Business Day: In most countries/markets, any day on which banks and/or securities exchanges are open for business. Differences in national holidays have important implications for cross-border transactions and even for the nature and quality of data available from non-domestic markets for use in financial analysis.

Busted Convertible Security: A security trading so far below conversion value that its value as a straight debt or preferred stock obligation is much higher than its conversion value—causing it to trade much like a straight, or non-convertible, security.

Calibrated Model: A valuation model that produces prices consistent with available market information. The model values are forced to fit existing prices by constraining the time-varying parameter specifications, often at the expense of intertemporal insights.

Call-Adjusted Yield: The non-callable bond-equivalent yield on a callable bond. Equal to the basic yield to maturity less the expected opportunity loss (due to exercise of the issuer's call privilege). Similar adjustments are made in the calculation of call-adjusted duration and call-adjusted convexity.

Call Loan: A loan extended with the understanding that it can be called by the lender at will. Most loans collateralized by securities are made on a call basis. At one time, the broker's call loan rate was significant in money markets. Today, most call loans are based on LIBOR-type rates.

Callable Option or Warrant: In the hands of its holder, this is a long call or long put subject to a short call retained by the issuer of the long option. The issuer can limit the holder's profit by exercising its call and terminating the position during the life of the call feature. Ordinarily, the long call or put has a longer life than the option to terminate retained by the issuer.

Callable Securities: Bonds, preferred issues, and occasionally warrants that can be retired by the issuer. The right to call an issue is often subject to conditions such as a time delay and/or the payment of a premium over the face value of the security. If a security is called, the holder may lose some of the market value of the position.

The terms under which the issue can be called are described in the issuance document-ation.

Callable Step-Up Note: A callable debt issue that features one or more increases in a fixed rate or a step-up in a spread over LIBOR during the life of the note. Most issuers of these notes have low credit ratings. Consequently, the purpose of the step-up is usually to encourage the issuer to refinance. If the issuer does not refinance, the higher rate is designed to compensate for the investor's acceptance of credit risk. Occasionally, a highly rated issuer will sell one of these bonds to implement a strongly held view that rates will decline and a replacement bond can be issued at a lower rate.

Called Away: Elimination of an underlying security position through the exercise of a call option (exercised against the position). Examples include a common stock position called away through the exercise of a short call option, and a bond position called by the issuer under call provisions embedded in the bond indenture.

Called Bond: A bond that the debtor declares due and payable on a certain date prior to maturity and in accordance with a call provision in the bond indenture. Investors need to be alert to bond calls because a called bond earns no interest after the payable date.

Common-linked Higher Income Participation Security (CHIPS): A synthetic Preferred Equity Redemption Cumulative Stock (PERCS) issued by a financial intermediary or some other third party.

Compounding: The reinvestment of all periodic return in subsequent periods. For ex-ample, if an investment strategy generates a 10% total return in each of two consecutive periods, and the first return is reinvested in the strategy, then the cumulative com-pounded return over the two periods equals 21%, because the first 10% return generates an additional 1% return in the second period.

Conversion: The exchange of a convertible security for the underlying instrument.

Conversion Premium (on a Convertible Bond): The additional amount or percentage that a convertible bond pays over parity with the underlying. Note the analogy to the concept of premium in the UK warrant market.

Conversion Price: The share price at which the face amount of a convertible bond or convertible preferred is converted into common stock.

Conversion Ratio: The number of common shares an investor receives in exchange for a single convertible bond or convertible preferred share.

Conversion Value: The value of a convertible security if converted immediately—after reflecting any change in the value of the underlying security resulting from the act of conversion. *Also called Parity Value.*

Convertible Adjustable Preferred Stock (CAPS): A floating- rate preferred issue, con-vertible by the holder on dividend payment dates into a variable number of the issuer's common shares. The shares received upon conversion are equal in market value to the par value of the preferred (usually subject to a cap on the number of shares). The convertible feature is designed to give the adjustable-rate preferred investor greater liquidity, and to protect the preferred investor's principal if the credit standing of the issuer declines. If the number of common shares to be issued is not capped, the stock may be subject to a bear raid, forcing the issuance of a large number of shares and even a change in control. *Also called Capital Market Preferred Stock (CMPS).*

Convertible Bond with a Premium Put: A convertible bond issued at nominal or face value with an embedded put that entitles the bondholder to redeem it for more than its face value beginning at some future date. The put is exercised only if the underlying equity fails to appreciate by enough to make the bond worth more alive than dead.

Convertible Capital Note or Security: A fixed-term debt instrument or preferred stock issued by a bank and convertible into perpetual preferred stock. In some issues, conversion to preferred may be encouraged or forced by the issuer, who may have the right to reduce the note coupons or simply to effect conversion. The perpetual preferred stock becomes Tier I bank capital under the Basle Capital Adequacy Directive. These notes are used primarily to assure a bank has access to additional capital in an emergency. *Also called Exchangeable Capital Security (X-Cap), Exchangeable Capital Unit, Preferred Purchase Unit.*

Convertible Exchangeable Preferred Stock: A convertible preferred issue that is exchangeable at the issuer's option for convertible debt with identical yield and identical conversion terms. Designed to permit an issuer to switch to a lower-cost (tax-deductible) obligation when its earnings become taxable.

Convertible Floating-Rate Note: An FRN with an embedded option permitting the issuer to convert the note into long-term fixed-rate bonds.

Convertible Gilts: UK government bonds that give the holder an option to convert them into longer maturity bonds on specified terms.

Convertible Money Market Units (CMMUs): Unlike the more popular return of principal equity-linked notes, convertible money market units provide a high return if an equity-linked instrument appreciates, but provide full participation (except for the accumulated yield) in a downside move if the value of the equity instrument or index declines. While an equity-linked note provides a return pattern often reminiscent of a long call, the pattern of the convertible money market unit is similar to that experienced by a covered call writer. Someday a philosopher or psychiatrist will analyze why institutional investors generally sell covered calls rather than buy puts against their portfolios, but tend to buy equity-linked notes rather than convertible money market units. *Also called Synthetic High-Income Equity-Linked Debenture (SHIELD).*

Convertible Reset Debenture: A convertible bond with a required upward interest rate adjustment, typically effective several years after issuance. The issuer may be required to reset the coupon high enough to give the debentures a market value at least equal to their face or par value. The purpose of the reset is to compensate the bondholder for any credit deterioration. The reset frequently encourages the issuer to refinance, or perhaps forces conversion.

Convertible Security: A bond, preferred stock, or warrant that is convertible under prescribed circumstances into the common stock of a corporation or some other security with or without a supplementary payment of cash or "useable" securities.

Convertible Stock Note: A "debt" instrument that pays coupons and principal in the common stock of the issuer. A variety of mandatory convertible bond.

Convertible Unsecured Loan Stock (CULS): *Brit.* A convertible bond.

Convexity: (1) In a fixed-income instrument, convexity is a measure of the way duration and price change when interest rates change. A bond or note is said to have positive convexity if the instrument's value increases at least as much as duration predicts when rates drop, and decreases less than duration predicts when rates rise. Positive convexity is desirable to investors because it makes a position more valuable after a price change than its duration value suggests. (2) In an option position, convexity is a measure of the way the value of the position changes in response to a change in the volatility or price of the underlying instrument. A position with positive convexity (gamma) maintains or increases its value better than delta predicts when volatility increases or when prices change by a large percentage in either direction. A position with negative convexity loses value relative to delta's prediction when prices change in either direction.

Correlation Risk: (1) The risk that the realized correlation between assets will be different than the assumed correlation, thereby rendering a portfolio riskier than anticipated.

Cost of Carry: (1) The net out-of-pocket cost of holding a cash market position. (2) A model for the pricing of futures contracts, particularly financial futures, describing the fair value of the futures contract in terms of the net cost incurred to hold a long cash position and a short futures position through the settlement date of the futures contract.

Coupon: (1) The nominal annual rate of interest on a bond or note usually expressed as a percentage of the face value. (2) A piece of paper detached from a bearer bond and exchanged for a quarterly, semi-annual, or annual interest payment.

Covariance: A measure of the correspondence between the movement of two random variables such as securities prices or returns. The correlation coefficient is a normalized covariance measure because it is independent of the units of measurement. Covariance is calculated as the product of the variables' standard deviations and their correlation coefficient.

Covenant: A provision of a loan or risk management agreement that requires or prohibits certain actions by a borrower or a financial agreement counterparty. Covenants may limit dividends, require maintenance of working capital, set a ceiling on compensation, etc. If a covenant is violated, the instrument is considered in default.

Covered Warrant: A stock, basket, or index warrant issued by a party other than the issuer of the underlying stock(s) and secured by the warrant issuer's holding in the underlying securities or the warrant issuer's general credit standing. Covered warrants are most common in Europe and parts of Asia. They are often issued by investment banks when transfer of the underlying security is temporarily or permanently restricted, when traditional warrants are not available, or when buyers want security and currency warrant combinations not otherwise available in the market.

Covered Writer: A call option writer who owns the underlying that is subject to option. An investor setting up an option hedge or writing multiple options may be covered with respect to part of the option position and uncovered with respect to the rest.

Cram-Down Rules: Procedures in bankruptcy litigation that allow the bankruptcy court to implement a reorganization plan over the objections of a class of creditors. Specifically, bankruptcy rules provide that secured claimants must retain their liens on the debtor's property, and their liens must be satisfied if the property is sold. The claims of unsecured claimants must receive full value, or no junior claimants will receive anything. Actual practice may deviate from these rules, and cram-down rules give something to junior creditors to secure cooperation.

Credit Crunch: A reduction in the supply of credit that disrupts the credit extension process. Credit crunches are often associated with tightening monetary policy.

Credit Enhanced Debt Securities: Bonds or notes with special investor protection that gives them a better credit standing than the ordinary debt of the issuer would have. To obtain enhanced credit, an issuer may pay a guarantor or endorser for a letter of credit or a surety bond that lends the guarantor's higher credit to the issuer. The purpose of credit enhancement is to achieve a lower net borrowing cost.

Credit Enhancements: Supplementary provisions of a financial contract designed to moderate losses from an adverse credit event or counterparty default. The most common enhancements are third-party guarantees and collateral deposits.

Credit Risk: (1) Exposure to loss as a result of default on a swap, debt, or other counterparty instrument. (2) Exposure to loss as a result of a decline in market value stemming from a credit downgrade of an issuer or counterparty. Credit risk may be reduced by credit screening before a transaction is effected or by instrument provisions that attempt to offset the effect of a default or require increased payments in the event of a credit downgrade. (3) A component of return variability resulting from the possibility of an event of default. (4) A change in the market's perception of the probability of an event of default, which affects the spread between two rates or reference indexes.

Cross-Currency Convertible Bond: A convertible bond denominated and with coupons paid in one currency that is convertible into shares of a common stock denominated and traded in a second currency. Conversion terms are stated as the number of shares exchanged for each bond. Depending on the relationship of the currencies at the bond's maturity, the bond may be converted even if the share price is unchanged or lower than the price at issuance. Alternatively, the bond may be redeemed for cash in the denominated currency, if the share price rises while the shares' nominal currency declines.

Cross-Currency Warrants: Currency warrants in which neither of the two currencies determining the payout is the US dollar, or, alternatively, the investor's base currency.

Cross Hedging: A technique used in a variety of markets to counter the risk of one instrument by taking a risk-offsetting position in another instrument whose risk characteristics do not perfectly offset the position to be hedged. Examples include hedging the risk of a 100-stock portfolio with futures contracts on the S&P 500, or doing a currency hedge on a portfolio of German stocks with Swiss franc forwards or options. Among the risks in a cross hedge are that different maturities of the offsetting positions will lead to a mismatch, that the market for one of the instruments will be highly illiquid, with correspondingly larger price fluctuations, and that differences in credit quality will affect the cross-hedge basis.

Cumulative Preferred Stock: A preferred stock issue that requires payment of all passed dividends on that issue before payment of any common stock dividends.

Cumulative Trust Preferred Securities: Similar to Quarterly Interest Debt Shares (QUIDS), a quarterly dividend version of Monthly Income Preferred Shares (MIPS).

Currency Business Day: Any day on which banks are open for foreign exchange business in the principal financial center for a specific currency.

Currency-Hedged Foreign Bond: A bond with all coupons and principal payments in an investor's domestic currency, but with coupons sensitive to foreign interest rates. Foreign interest rate sensitivity can be achieved by making the coupon equal to a fixed rate plus a domestic floating rate (such as LIBOR) minus a foreign floating rate.

Currency-Linked Notes: Debt structures with returns partly determined by changes in currency rates and, correspondingly, by interest rate differentials across currencies. Currency-linked instruments are available in isolation or combined with a variety of interest rate, equity, or index structures.

Current Coupon: An interest coupon on a bond giving a yield close to current rates on comparable instruments.

Debenture: (1) In the US, an unsecured bond or note. Neither principal nor interest payments are secured by a lien against specific property. (2) In the UK, a secured or collateral-based debt instrument.

Debt Exchangeable for Common Stock (DECS): A debt issue with an embedded short put and long call combined with an interest coupon. The issuer is the issuer (or a block holder) of the underlying common stock; the DECS issue is ultimately convertible into the common. *Compare with Dividend Enhanced Convertible Stock (DECS), which is a preferred stock with a similar return pattern and the same acronym. Also called Automatically Convertible Enhanced Security (ACES), Preferred Redeemable Increased Dividend Equity Security (PRIDES), Protected Equity Participation (PEP), Fixed-Income Equity-Linked Debt (FIELD).*

Debt Instrument or Debt Security: Generically, an obligation to repay a fixed amount, usually with periodic interest. A lump sum interest payment at maturity may be substituted for periodic payments in the case of a zero-coupon debt instrument. A more generalized term than Bond or Note.

Default: Failure to meet an obligation, such as timely payment of interest or principal, maintenance of minimum working capital levels, etc. Upon an event of default, creditors are usually permitted to take steps to protect their interests.

Default Exposure: The loss that would be incurred by a market participant if its counterparty defaulted. Default exposure is often measured using Monte Carlo techniques. Typically, the case associated with the 95% probability limit is defined, somewhat arbitrarily, as the "maximum default exposure." To complicate any loss calculation or estimate further, a default usually reduces the market value of an instrument, but rarely reduces it to zero within a short period.

Default Risk: (1) The probability that a particular interest, principal, or swap payment or set of payments due from an issuer or a counterparty will not be forthcoming on schedule. (2) The cost of a payment default. Different financial transactions have different default probabilities, and because of the different magnitudes of associated net cash flows and principal exposures, different costs associated with the same probability of default. (3) The product of (1) and (2).

Deferred Coupon Note or Bond: A debt instrument that pays no interest for a fixed period and then pays interest at a relatively high rate for the remainder of its life.

Deferred Interest Bond: A bond that pays interest only at a future date or dates. A zero-coupon bond is the ultimate deferred interest bond, because it pays all interest and principal at maturity.

Deferred Pay Securities: Instruments whose value accrues for some time before the issuer has to part with cash. Examples include zero-coupon bonds and payment in kind (PIK) securities.

Delayed Convertible: A convertible security that cannot be converted immediately.

Delta: (1) The change in option price for a given change in the underlying price or rate. The neutral hedge ratio. (2) The smallest-capitalization issues on the London Stock Exchange. Delta stock quotes are not continually displayed on dealing screens. The other size classifications are alpha, beta, and gamma .

Delta/Gamma Hedge: A risk-offsetting position—consisting in part of short-term option contracts—that neutralizes the market risk of an underlying position in an instrument with some embedded option features. The hedge offsets the current delta within a narrow range and attempts to match the change in delta (gamma) of the underlying position over a wider range of possible prices. In contrast to dynamic hedging or delta hedging, which relies on a series of transactions in the underlying, forwards, or futures to match changing deltas, a delta/gamma hedge has an option payoff pattern built in.

Delta-Gamma-Kappa-Rho Hedge: A complex hedge involving at least two options with different expiration dates. This hedge is designed to eliminate exposure to the risks described by all four of these option price sensitivity measures.

Delta Hedge: A risk-offsetting position that matches the market response of the base or underlying position over a narrow range of price or rate changes. Because one side of the net position has option characteristics, the position must be modified to maintain delta neutrality if the price or rate moves beyond a narrow range.

Delta Neutral: A series of related instruments or a portfolio consisting of positions with offsetting positive and negative deltas that eliminate or neutralize the aggregate response to market movements over at least a limited range of prices or rates.

Depth of Market: The number of shares of a security that can be bought or sold at or near the bid and asked prices without causing a dramatic change in price.

Derivative Instrument or Product: (1) A contract or convertible security that changes in value in concert with and/or obtains much of its value from price movements in a related or underlying security, future, or other instrument or index. (2) A security or contract, such as an option, forward, future, swap, warrant, or debt instrument with one or more options, forwards, swaps, or warrants embedded in it or attached to it. The value of the instrument is determined in whole or in part by the price of one or more underlying instruments or markets. *Also called Contingent Claim.* (3) An instrument created by decomposing the return of a related underlying instrument or index. Examples include Americus Trust and Collateralized Mortgage Obligation (CMO) component instruments. (4) Occasionally limited to zero net supply contracts. This restrictive definition excludes warrants, convertibles, and CMO components. (5) In the financial press, any product that loses money.

Detachable Warrants: Warrants originally issued with a bond or other security, that may be separated, traded, and/or exercised independently of the other security.

Dilution: The process that reduces the participation of equity owners in the earnings and market value increase of a company through the issuance or prospective issuance of new common stock or participating instruments. Warrants or other convertible securities issued by a corporation have a potential diluting effect on voting power and earnings per share, because they can lead to new share issuance. Exchange-traded options or third-party options or warrants do not dilute earnings because they are exercised into existing shares. In practice, unless a warrant or convertible issued by the company is quite large (relative to the common stock equivalent capitalization), the dilution effect is not a major consideration in the valuation of the underlying or derivatives on the underlying. Except for rare cases where a warrant or other convertible is sold or exchanged at less than a fair market price, dilution gets more analytical attention than it deserves.

Dirty Price: The price of a bond including accrued interest. Outside domestic US bond markets and the Eurodollar markets, most bonds trade "dirty."

Discount Bond: A debt instrument, such as a Treasury bill or a coupon or principal payment stripped from sovereign or other debt, that pays no periodic interest but trades at a discount from its ultimate settlement value at maturity.

Discount Instrument: (1) A debt instrument, such as a Treasury bill or a coupon or principal payment stripped from sovereign or other debt, that pays no periodic interest but trades at a discount from its ultimate settlement value at maturity. (2) Any fixed-rate bond with a below market coupon, so named because this low-yielding instrument trades at a discount to its par or notional value. (3) A reference to a security selling at less than its theoretically fair or expected value.

Distressed Security: A financial instrument (usually debt) that is in default, or in substantial risk of default, and has lost, or stands to lose, much of its value.

Diversification: An approach to investment management analyzed and popularized by Harry Markowitz and encouraged by widespread acceptance of the usefulness of the capital asset pricing model (CAPM). With diversification, risk can be reduced relative to the average return of a portfolio by distributing assets among a variety of asset classes, such as stocks, bonds, money market instruments, and physical commodities, as well as by diversifying within these categories and across international boundaries. Diversification usually reduces portfolio risk (measured by return variability) because the returns (both positive and negative) on various asset classes are not perfectly correlated.

Dividend Arbitrage: Techniques used to obtain part or all of an investor's return in the form of dividend payments. These techniques are often referred to as dividend capture when practiced in the US Dividend capture may be practiced if dividends are treated more favorably than other forms of investment return for tax, regulatory, or accounting purposes. Certain American, German, and Japanese investors, among others, have found dividends particularly attractive at times.

Dividend Crossover Method: A technique used to approximate the relative attractiveness of a convertible bond and its underlying equity. The dividend crossover method estimates the date on which the rising common stock dividend will equal the convertible coupon. This approach is meaningful only when the convertible is deep in the money and a reliable dividend growth forecast is available.

Dividend Enhanced Convertible Stock (DECS): A preferred stock issue with an embedded short put and long call and a higher-than-market dividend rate. The issuer is the issuer (or a block holder) of an underlying common stock, and the DECS issue is ultimately convertible into the underlying common. *Compare with Debt Exchangeable for Common Stock (DECS)*, a variation of convertible debt with a similar return pattern and the same acronym. *Also called Yield Enhanced Stock (YES), Preferred Redeemable Increased Dividend Equity Security (PRIDES), Equity-Linked Security (ELKS), Automatically Convertible Enhanced Security (ACES).*

Dual Currency Bond: Generically, a fixed-income instrument that pays a coupon in a base currency (usually the currency of the investor) and the principal in a non-base currency (typically the currency of the issuer). This generic structure is subject to many variations. *Also called Adjustable Long-term Puttable Securities (ALPS).*

Duration Bogey: The level of asset or liability duration sought in the management of a portfolio.

Duration Gap: The difference between the duration of an asset portfolio and the duration of its associated liabilities.

Duration Risk Management: The use of modified duration measurements for a group of assets and/or liabilities to quantify and control exposure to interest rate risk.

Early Redemption (Put) Option: An embedded feature of some bonds with both fixed and floating rates that permits the holder to sell the bonds back to the issuer or to a third party at par or close to par if interest rates rise and/or if the quality of the issuer's credit declines. *Bonds with these options are usually called Put Bonds, Puttable Notes, or Puttable Bonds.*

Early Termination Date: The date on which the final obligations of the parties to a risk management agreement are calculated in the event of a default.

Effective Duration: The ratio of the proportional change in bond value to the infinitesimal parallel shift of the spot yield curve. Equal to modified duration if the yield curve is flat.

Efficient Market: A trading market where the current price reflects all available information from past prices and volumes. In this market, past price and volume patterns cannot provide meaningful predictions of future price movement. These minimum features describe a weak form efficient market. More stringent requirements describe semi-strong and strong forms. Efficiency is categorized by the strength of the efficiency that can be proven.

- **Weak Form:** There are no dependencies in past price changes that a technician can use to predict future changes. Prices are a random walk.

- **Semi-Strong Form:** The current price reflects all publicly available information that could affect the price.

- **Strong Form:** The current price reflects all relevant information, whether publicly available or not. *Also called Market Efficiency.*

Embedded Option: An option that is an inseparable part of another instrument. Most embedded options are conversion features granted to the buyer or early termination options reserved by the issuer of a security. A common example is the call provision in most corporate bonds that permits the issuer to repay the borrower earlier than the nominal maturity of the bond. The homeowner's option to repay mortgage principal early—resulting in early liquidation of a mortgage-backed security—is another common embedded option. *Also called Embeddo, Imbedded Option.*

Emerging Market: (1) Any market that has introduced public trading of securities since roughly 1970. (2) Any market that is not one of the ten largest securities markets in the world. There is no uniform standard for inclusion or exclusion from the emerging market category, and small markets are called "emerging" even when trading activity has been declining and economic prospects are grim. There is an element of political correctness to this term. The "emerging nations" where these markets are located have been known variously as developing nations, less-developed nations, underdeveloped nations, the third world, and have-not nations.

Emerging Market Warrants: Covered or guaranteed options or warrants on common stocks, stock baskets, indexes, or bonds traded in an immature market often characterized by some combination of restrictions on foreign ownership, discontinuous trading, inadequate investor protection, and/or limitations on currency convertibility. The creator or writer of these warrants insulates the buyer from some of these undesirable market characteristics in return for a warrant premium that is bigger than volatility alone can justify.

End User: Usually a reference to the entity for which a financial instrument is created or to whom it is sold by a broker or dealer.

Endorsement: In OTC transactions, a creditworthy guarantor sometimes endorses a derivatives contract to guarantee performance. Clearing corporations perform an analogous function for listed options and futures.

Equity Enhanced Dedication: A form of portfolio insurance using a dedicated bond portfolio as the reserve asset and common stocks or stock index futures as the risky asset. This technique is designed to maintain a minimum pension surplus (or a ceiling on underfunding), while providing equity exposure and a chance to increase the ratio of assets to liabilities.

Equity-Linked Note (ELN): A security that combines the characteristics of a zero- or low-coupon bond or note with a return component based on the performance of a single equity security, a basket of equity securities, or an equity index. In the latter case, the security is typically called an equity index-linked note. Equity-linked notes come in a variety of styles. The minimum return may be zero with all of what would normally be an interest payment going to pay for upside equity participation. Alternatively, a low interest rate may be combined with a lower rate of equity participation. The participation rate in the underlying equity instrument may be more or less than dollar for dollar over any specific range of prices. The participation may be open ended (the holder of the note participates proportionately in the upside of the underlying security or index, no matter how high it goes), or the equity return component may be capped. Other things equal, a capped return is associated with a higher rate of participation up to the cap price. *Various versions of this instrument are known as Capital Guarantee Note, Equity-Linked Debt Placement, Equity-Linked Certificate of Deposit (ELCD or ECD), Equity Participation Notes (EPNs), Indexed Notes, Index-Linked Bonds or Notes, Equity Index Participation Note, Equity Index-Linked Note, Equity Participation-Indexed Certificates (EPICs), Index Principal Return Note, All-Ordinaries Share Price Riskless Index Notes (ASPRINs), Geared Equity Capital Units (GECUs), Performance Index Paper (PIP), Customized Upside Basket Security (CUBS), Structured Upside Participating Equity Receipt (SUPER), Portfolio Income Note (PIN), Market Index Deposits (MIDs), Market-Indexed NotE (MINE), Market Index Target-Term Security (MITTS), Stock Index Growth Notes (SIGNs), Stock Index Insured Account, Stock Index Return Security (SIRS), Stock Performance Exchange-Linked Bonds (SPEL-Bonds) Guaranteed Return*

Index Participation (GRIP), Guaranteed Return on Investment (GROI) Certificate, Index Growth-Linked Units (IGLUs), Index Participation Certificate, Protected Equity Note (PEN), Protected Equity Participation (PEP), Protected Index Participation (PIP), Safe Return Certificate, or as a variety of "money back" certificates. While the names may provide a clue to the structures, each issuer seems to have at least one proprietary name for some version of these instruments. Investors must look at the structure and pricing of the units offered and compare them with more familiar names and structures. *Compare with Commodity Index Note.*

Equity-LinKed Security (ELKS): An enhanced dividend, capped return instrument modeled on Preference Equity Redemption Cumulative Stock (PERCS). Unlike PERCS, which are issued by the corporation that issued the underlying, ELKs are issued by a third party, frequently a financial intermediary. *Also called Common-linked Higher Income Participation Security (CHIPS), Yield Enhanced Equity-Linked Debt Security (YEELDS), Performance Equity-Linked Redemption Quarterly Paid Security (PERQS), Convertible Money Market Units (CMMUs) (diagram), Market Index Deposits (MIDs), Synthetic PERCS.*

Equity Option: A put or call, often exchange listed, with a single common stock issue as the underlying. *Also called Stock Option.*

Equity Yield Enhancement Security (EYES): An equity-linked instrument with a single stock as the underlying, a coupon that exceeds the dividend on the underlying stock, and a capped return. The higher coupon is purchased with the proceeds from the cap. A synthetic (dealer issued) preference equity redemption cumulative stock (PERCS). *Also called Yield Enhanced Stock (YES), Performance Equity-linked Redemption Quarterly paid Security (PERQS), Preference Equity Redemption Cumulative Stock (PERCS).*

European Option: A put or call that can be exercised only on its expiration date. The term has nothing to do with where the option is traded or what underlies it. Stock options listed on European option exchanges are usually American-style options in the sense that they can be exercised prior to the expiration date.

Ex-Dividend: Without the dividend. Stocks sell ex-dividend on the first business day when a normal transaction would not lead to settlement in time to give the buyer the right to receive the dividend. A stock normally trades ex-dividend well before the payment date of a dividend.

Ex-Dividend Date: The date on which the buyer of a stock is no longer able to purchase the stock the regular way and still receive a specific dividend payment. A holder of the stock who sells on the ex-dividend date is entitled to retain the dividend when it is paid.

Exchangeable Bond or Note: A bond or note issue that is "convertible" into the shares of a company other than the issuer of the debt instrument. This structure has been used primarily by corporations to sell a large position in the shares of another company. Recent issues have included notes exchangeable for a basket of stocks.

Exchangeable Zero-Coupon Swap: A specialized swap in which the end user who is originally scheduled to receive a fixed sum at maturity (the zero-coupon payment) sells the dealer an embedded option to convert the single payment to a series of fixed payments. The end user benefits from this structure if volatility declines and rates are relatively stable to declining.

Exercise Limit: A limit on the number of exchange-traded option contracts that can be exercised by one holder within a specified time period. Usually equal to position limits.

Exercise Notice: A notification—ultimately reaching an option seller—that the buyer of an option wishes to exercise and obtain the appropriate cash settlement or physical delivery of the underlying.

Exercise of an Option: Purchase or sale of the underlying at the strike price by the holder of a call or put. In cash settled option markets, exchange of the option position for cash.

Exercise Price: In some markets, the term "exercise price" designates the total amount or aggregate exercise price paid in exercise of the option. The exercise price for an underlying unit is more commonly called strike or strike price.

Exercise Procedure: The process detailed in an option contract, or in the rules of an exchange or clearing corporation, for the exercise of an option.

Expiration Date: (1) The date after which an option is void. An option buyer must decide whether to exercise on or before this date. (2) The final settlement date of a futures or forward contract.

Expiry: The British term for (1) the option or futures expiration process, and (2) the expiration date.

Extended Bond: A replacement bond with identical security but a more distant maturity offered to an issuer's bondholders in lieu of repayment of principal on the original bond schedule.

Extendible Note: (1) An open-ended debt obligation that resets every few years to a new interest rate based on negotiations between the issuer and the investor. At each renegotiation date, the investor has the option to put the notes back to the issuer, if the new rate the issuer proposes is unacceptable. (2) A combination of a traditional bond or note and an embedded option that gives the issuer or the holder the right to terminate or to extend the maturity of the note at a prespecified interest rate on one or more exercise dates.

Face Value: (1) Value of a bond or other debt instrument at maturity. *Also called Par.* (2) Notional principal amount of a forward, future, option, or swap.

Fair Value: The amount at which an asset (liability) can be bought (incurred) or sold (settled) in a current transaction between willing parties, that is, other than in a forced or liquidation sale. Quoted market prices in active markets are the best evidence of fair value and should be used as the basis for the measurement, if available. If a quoted market price is available, the fair value is the product of the number of trading units times that market price. If a quoted market price is not available, the estimate of fair value should be based on the best information available in the circumstances. The estimate of fair value should consider prices for similar assets or similar liabilities and the results of valuation techniques to the extent available in the circumstances. Examples of valuation techniques include the present value of estimated expected future cash flows using discount rates commensurate with the risks involved, option pricing models, matrix pricing, option-adjusted spread models, and fundamental analysis. Valuation techniques for measuring assets and liabilities should be consistent with the objective of measuring fair value. Those techniques should incorporate assumptions that market participants would use in their estimates of values, future revenues, and future expenses, including assumptions about interest rates, default, prepayment, and volatility. In measuring forward contracts, such as foreign currency forward contracts, at fair value by discounting estimated future cash flows, an entity should base the estimate of future cash flows on the changes in the forward rate (rather than the spot rate). In measuring financial liabilities and non-financial derivatives that are liabilities at fair value by discounting estimated future cash flows (or equivalent outflows of other assets), an objective is to use discount rates at which those liabilities can be settled in an arm's-length transaction (FASB SFAS No.133, Accounting for Derivative Instruments and Hedging Activities).

Fair Value Basis: The value or range of values of the difference between the forward or futures price and the spot price that offers no opportunity for profitable arbitrage at current carrying costs. For example, if the maximum risk-free lending rate is 6.0%, and the minimum borrowing rate is 6.2%, the fair value basis of a zero-coupon bond future one year out would be a range between 6.0% and 6.2% over spot. The range will be greater after transaction costs. In actual markets, participants' opportunity sets are different, and the fair value basis may range between a single point and a relatively wide interval. In some markets, such as DAX futures in Germany, there are structural arbitrage profits available and these may disappear only slowly over time.

Fair Value of an Option: The option value computed by a probability-type option valuation model. The fair value of an option is the price or premium at which both the buyer and the writer of the option should expect to break even, neglecting the effect of commissions and other trading costs and after an adjustment for risk. Fair value is an estimate of where an option should sell in an efficient market, not where it will sell. The fair value of an option is also defined as parity plus basis plus insurance value. *Also called Fair Value Premium.*

Fallen Angel: A corporate bond whose investment rating has been reduced, usually from investment grade to a speculative rating, as a result of deterioration in the credit quality of the issuing corporation.

Financial Engineering: The development and creative application of financial technology to solve financial problems and exploit financial opportunities. (International Association of Financial Engineers.) The art (with contributions from science) of creating desirable cash flow and/or market value patterns from existing instruments or new instruments to meet an investment or risk management need. The creations of financial engineers are typically based on traditional instruments such as bonds and notes with forward and futures contracts, options, and swap components added.

Financial Instrument: Cash, evidence of an ownership interest in an entity, or a contract that both (a) imposes on one entity a contractual obligation (1) to deliver cash or another financial instrument to a second entity, or (2) to exchange other financial instruments on potentially unfavorable terms with the second entity, and (b) conveys to that second entity a contractual right (1) to receive cash or another financial instrument from the first entity, or (2) to exchange other financial instruments on potentially favorable terms with the first entity (FASB SFAS No. 133, Accounting for Derivative Instruments and Hedging Activities).

Fine Print: Contract provisions, often in a small type font, that may create problems if both contracting parties are not fully alert to their contents.

Firm Price: A price at which a trader is willing to trade for a limited period of time. *Compare to Indicative Price (2).*

Flight to Quality: A reference to attempts by investors to shift from high-risk to low-risk investments in response to a development that stimulates perceptions of increased risk.

Forbearance: A creditor's postponement of legal action when a borrower is delinquent, usually in expectation of favorable action by the debtor.

Force Majeure Clause: A contract provision that excuses one or both parties from part or all of their obligations in the event of war, natural disaster, or some other event outside the parties' control.

Forced Conversion: Involuntary conversion of a warrant or convertible instrument undertaken to preserve the value of the holder's position. Forced conversion occurs when the issuer exercises a bond call provision in a convertible bond or is acquired by another firm for cash.

Forward Yield Curve: An interest rate curve derived point by point from the traditional yield curve, the forward curve is used to price many interest rate derivative instruments. The forward curve shows the implied forward interest rate for each period covered by the yield curve. The diagrams under the listing for yield curve illustrate forward rate curves for both normal and inverted yield curve environments. *Also called Forward Rate, Forward Rate Curve.*

Frequency: The periodic schedule of rate or price readings used to calculate the payoff of an average rate or price option.

Fungibility: The standardization and interchangeability of listed option and futures contracts and certain other financial instruments with identical terms. Fungibility permits either party to an opening transaction to close out a position through a closing transaction in an identical contract. All financial contracts with identical terms are not necessarily fungible, a fact that can increase risk in some markets.

Futures Contract: An agreement, originally between two parties, a buyer and a seller, to exchange a particular good for a particular price at a date in the future. All terms are specified in a contract common to all participants in a market on an organized futures exchange. The contract must be for a specific amount of a good for delivery at a specific time as required by the exchange with the price determined in a public marketplace by "open outcry" or on an electronic limit order book system. Futures contracts can be traded freely with various counterparties without material counterparty credit risk. After a trade is cleared, the exchange clearing corporation is the ultimate counterparty for all contracts, so the only credit risk is the creditworthiness of the exchange's clearing corporation. No credit intermediary is necessary, but margin deposits must be posted as performance bonds with the clearing broker, and, in turn, with the exchange clearing corporation. Typically, variation margin payments mark futures positions to market at least once a day.

Futures Contract on Individual Stock: A simple, single stock futures contract priced, valued, and margined much like a stock index futures contract. These instruments have been introduced in Sweden, Australia, Britain, and Hong Kong. The attraction of single stock futures contracts is based on their generally low margin requirements and the ability to avoid transfer and dividend withholding taxes. Not permitted in the US at this time.

Gamma: (1) The change in delta divided by the dollar change in the underlying instrument's price. The second derivative of the option price with respect to the price of the underlying. A measurement of the rate of change in the option price with respect to the underlying price. If the gamma of a position is positive, an instantaneous move either up or down in the underlying will give the position a higher value than the static delta would predict. A positive gamma indicates a position with positive convexity. *Also called Curvature.* (2) The smallest electronically quoted stocks on the London Stock Exchange.

Geometric Brownian Motion (GBM): A stochastic process in which price changes follow a stationary random walk in continuous time. This specification of price movement implies that, conditioned on the current price, the distribution of continuously compounded returns at the end of any finite time interval will be normal.

Globalization: The trend toward looking at economic and financial issues, instruments, and portfolios from a worldwide rather than a single-country viewpoint.

Greeks: Option derivatives or sensitivities usually (but not always) designated by a Greek letter. Examples include sigma, delta, gamma, kappa, tau, "vega," rho, theta, and omega.

Guarantee: A contractual or statutory commitment to accept responsibility for repayment of another entity's loan or similar obligation.

Guaranteed Bond: (1) A bond on which the payment of principal, interest, or both has been guaranteed by a party other than the issuer. (2) Outside the US, a structured note or bond—usually an equity-linked note—that promises a return of all or most of the original investment at maturity, plus participation in favorable movements in an underlying index or instrument. *Also called Endorsed Bond.*

Guaranteed Exchange Rate Warrant: Covered warrants on non-US stock indexes issued in the US by a sovereign or financial intermediary with the currency exchange rate at maturity fixed at the spot rate in effect at issuance.

Guaranteed Return Index Participation (GRIP): Equity index- linked note, typically with less than 100% participation in the index.

Guaranteed Return on Investment (GROI) Certificate: A combination of a note and collar or equity risk reversal position guaranteeing investors a minimum return with a cap on the maximum return.

Guaranteed Return Structure (GRS): Any structured product that guarantees a minimum value at maturity (e.g., most equity-linked notes) or guarantees a minimum return based on levels reached by the underlying during the life of the instrument (e.g., ladder options).

Guaranteed Warrant: A stock index warrant issued by a sovereign or a corporation in the US market.

Haircut: (1) The margin or, more frequently, the capital tied up when a financial intermediary takes a position. (2) A commission or fee for execution of a transaction (uncommon). (3) The collateral held by the lender in a REPO transaction.

Handle: The first few digits of a financial instrument price or an interest rate or currency exchange rate. These digits change relatively infrequently as prices fluctuate, so a quote will often omit this handle, or "big figure," particularly in a busy trading environment. *Also called Big Figure.*

Hard Call Protection: A period when a bond is not callable for early redemption by the issuer under any circumstances. Hard call protection is often more important with convertible bonds than with straight bonds.

Harmless Warrant: A warrant permanently attached to a callable bond. It usually conveys the right to purchase more of the same bond.

Hazard: A risk or source of risk. Used primarily in insurance.

Hazard Rate: The probability or rate at which an event is expected to occur during a specified interval, assuming it has not yet occurred. The hazard rate is often used to measure default risk in bonds.

Hedge: (1) Among professional traders and position managers, a position or combination of positions taken to profit from an expected change in a spread or relative value; basis arbitrage. (2) In popular use, a position or combination of positions that reduces some type of risk, usually at the expense of expected reward. Risk hedging is typically accomplished by making approximately offsetting transactions that largely eliminate one or more type of risk. (3) In the narrower sense, the term often indicates partially offsetting a long position in one security with a short or short equivalent position in a related security.

Hedge Account: (1) An account in which a risk reduction position is carried. (2) Designation of a trader's futures position as a hedge account can be important in obtaining favorable margin requirements and an exemption from speculative position limits on futures contracts.

Hedge Fund: A private pool of assets managed intensely and often aggressively. A wide variety of financial instruments may be used and the managers of the fund are typically paid a percentage of any profits. In spite of the name, many such funds do little or no hedging, and risk exposures vary greatly. Funds offered in the US have a limited number of holders (usually limited partners), and partners must meet certain requirements in terms of net worth, minimum investment, etc.

Hell or High Water Clause: A guarantee, usually by a parent corporation or an unaffiliated guarantor, to meet bond or lease obligations if the primary obligor does not perform. The guarantee is not contingent on the performance of any other obligation by any party.

Historical Volatility: The variance or standard deviation of the change in the underlying's price, rate, or return during a designated period in the past. Historical volatility may or may not be a useful indicator of future volatility, but it is often used as such.

Hockey Stick Payoff Pattern: The traditional kinked return pattern of an option strategy valued at expiration. Also the return pattern of an immunized portfolio.

Hung Convertible: A convertible bond or preferred stock issue whose conversion cannot be forced by the issuer, usually because it is selling below parity or because the issue is protected from calls until a certain date or price level is reached.

Hurdle Rate: (1) The minimum or required rate of return that a proposal must exceed to justify a capital investment. (2) The minimum return an investment manager must achieve before she starts to earn an incentive or performance fee.

Hybrid Debt: Any combination of a debt instrument and an equity, currency, or commodity forward, option, or swap. A variant of hybrid security.

Hybrid Instrument Rules: Regulations adopted by the Commodity Futures Trading Commission (CFTC) exempting certain instruments that have some characteristics of a security and some characteristics of a future from regulation by the Commission under the Commodities Exchange Act. The most important common thread in these rules is that the commodity- or futures-linked value must be less than 50% of the value of the hybrid instrument.

Hybrid Security: Generically, a complex security consisting of virtually any combination of two or more financial instrument building blocks—bond or note, swap, forward or future, or option. Often, the return is a function of two or more underlying instrument returns, such as equities and interest rates or equities and exchange rates.

Illiquid: Not readily convertible into cash. Illiquid assets can only be sold with difficulty or at a lower value than their nominally quoted price.

Immunization of a Portfolio: A risk management technique designed to ensure that a portfolio of debt instruments will cover a liability coming due at a future date or over a period in the future. The typical approach to immunization is to invest in a portfolio with a Macaulay duration equal to the duration of the liabilities and a present value equal to the present value of the liabilities. This technique implicitly assumes that any shifts in the yield curve will be parallel shifts.

Implied Correlation: A factor in the pricing of multimarket financial instruments, implied correlation reflects a dealer's expectation of the relationship between two or more primary valuation parameters. For example, evaluating a swaption in terms of caps or floors requires analysis of the correlations among volatilities of a number of forward rates. Implied correlations among currency exchange rate pair volatilities are reflected in the pricing of their cross-rate options.

Implied Default Probability: Default probability expressed as a function of credit spreads in the market.

Implied Volatility (IV): The value of the price or rate volatility variable that would equate current option price and fair value. Alternatively, the value of the volatility variable that buyers and sellers appear to accept when the market price of an option is determined. Implied volatility is calculated by using the market price of an option as the fair value in an option model and calculating (by iteration) the volatility level consistent with that option price. Volatility is nearly always stated as annualized standard deviation in percentage of face amount or rate. *Also called Implied Standard Deviation (ISD).*

Imputed Value: Information about the value of a non-traded asset inferred from information about the values of traded assets.

In-the-Money: A term referring to an option that has intrinsic value because the current market price of the underlying exceeds the strike price of a call or is below the strike price of a put. For example, a call exerciseable at $100 is said to be 3 points in the money when the underlying bond is selling at $103.

In-the-Money Forward: A reference to an option that is "in-the-money" when the spot price or rate of the underlying is compared to the forward price or rate used in valuing the option at expiration.

Index Growth-Linked Units (IGLUs): A combination of a note and a collar or equity risk reversal position. As the name implies, the underlying is usually an index, but it may also be a small basket of stocks.

Index-Linked Bonds or Notes: Debt instruments with principal and/or interest payments linked to the performance of an inflation or stock market index. *Also called Equity Index-Linked Note, Real Yield Security (REALS).*

Index Participation Certificate: An equity index-linked note—usually one that provides more or less than 100% participation in the movement of the index and more or less than a full return of principal at maturity.

Index Warrants: Put and call options on an index or index futures contract with an original life of more than one year. Index warrants are issued by corporate or sovereign entities or cleared and guaranteed by option clearing houses. Pricing of these instruments in the marketplace often depends on investors' ability or inability to sell the warrants short or on the ability of new issuers to license an index to supply new warrants. *Also called Equity Index Warrants.*

Initial Margin: The collateral deposit or performance bond deposited with a broker at the time a derivatives position or an underlying security position is taken. Initial margin may be set by government regulators by the exchange where the instrument is traded. If the broker carrying the position and handling the trade feels the minimum margin does not give her firm and its customers adequate protection, she may set a higher minimum margin.

Insurance: (1) A risk/return pattern characteristic of options that limits (or insures against) price or rate movements through a predetermined (strike) price or rate in exchange for the explicit or implicit payment of an option (insurance) premium. (2) The component of an option or of a more complex instrument that provides this risk limitation feature. In contrast to a straight hedging transaction that eliminates risk symmetrically over all price ranges, an insurance position creates an asymmetric risk/ return pattern. (3) An arrangement under which one party to a contract (the insurer) in return for a consideration (the premium) indemnifies another party (the insured) against a specific loss, damage, or liability arising from specified uncertain events.

Interest: Money paid for the use of borrowed funds.

Interest Rate Parity: The principle by which forward currency exchange rates reflect relative interest rates on default risk-free instruments denominated in alternative currencies. Currency forward rates and interest rate structures reflect these parity relationships. Currencies of countries with high interest rates are expected by the market to depreciate over time, and currencies of countries with low interest rates are expected to appreciate over time, reflecting (among other things) implied differences in inflation. These tendencies are reflected in forward exchange rates as well as in interest rate structures. Any opportunity to earn a certain profit from interest rate discrepancies will be arbitraged away by hedging the currency risk. If interest rate parity holds, an investor cannot profit by borrowing in a low interest rate country and lending in a high interest rate country. For most major currencies, interest rate parity has not held during the modern floating-rate regime.

Interest Rate Reset Notes: Interest on these notes is reset several years after issuance to the greater of the initial rate or a rate sufficient to give the notes a market value greater than the face amount. The reset provision is designed to offer the buyer of a long-term debt instrument some protection from loss of principal due to rising interest rates or a decline in the issuer's debt rating.

Interest Rate Risk: (1) An adverse variation in cost or return caused by a change in the absolute level of interest rates, in the spread between two rates, in the shape of the yield curve, or in any other interest rate relationship. (2) Exposure to accounting or opportunity loss as a result of a relative or absolute change in interest rates. Varieties of interest rate risk include prepayment risk, reinvestment risk, volatility risk, call risk, and long-term rate risk. A variety of instruments are available to reduce or eliminate most kinds of interest rate risk.

Internal Rate of Return (IRR): (1) The discount rate that equates the present value of future cash flows with the market value of a financial instrument, or the present valued cost of an investment. More than one internal rate of return may be consistent with a given set of cash flows. (2) A compound interest rate at which the net present value of cash inflows from a project is equal to the net present value of cash outlays. Net present value analysis and real option analysis are increasingly replacing IRR calculations as the basis for capital expenditures.

Intrinsic Value of an Option: The amount, if any, by which an option is in the money.

Issuer: The legal entity that issues and usually assumes any obligations of a security or other financial instrument.

Issuer's Option Bond: A debt instrument that, in return for a higher yield than the issuer would otherwise have to pay, gives the issuer an unusual option. The option may range from a put requiring the investor to accept the issuer's common stock for the bond's principal at maturity, to the right to retire the issue at maturity, partly with cash and partly with a new issue of bonds. In the latter case, the issuer's option may be an option to extend maturity.

Junk Bond: A bond carrying a rating below Baa (Moody's) or BBB (S&P). Some speculative bonds are originally issued with below investment-grade ratings, and others, known as "fallen angels," decline from their initial investment-grade ratings.

Kappa k: Change in option price in response to a percentage point change in volatility. Kappa measures the sensitivity of option value to a change in implied volatility. Tau, vega, and zeta are also used to designate this relationship.

Know Your Customer (KYC) Rule: A requirement in many regulatory regimes that a broker or dealer be familiar with the investment or funding objectives and policies of a customer, and actively discourage or even reject transactions that may be inappropriate or hazardous for the client—or for the broker/dealer.

Lambda l: The percentage change in an option price, divided by the percentage change in an underlying price. A measurement of the option's leverage—equivalent to the leverage factor.

Legal Risk: The most important legal risks in financial risk management are legal capacity, or *ultra vires* risk (the risk that a counterparty is not legally capable of making a binding agreement), and regulatory risk (the risk that a statute or a policy of a regulatory body conflicts with the intended transaction).

Letter Stock: (1) Common or preferred stock sold subject to an investment letter from the purchaser who agrees not to sell it in the open market until a future date, when the company promises to register it for public sale or when the restriction on sale expires through the passage of time. These shares may be bought and sold by sophisticated investors before they are registered, but they usually trade at a discount to fully registered shares.

Leverage: An investment or operating position subject to a multiplied effect on profit or position value from a small change in sales quantity or price. Leverage can come from high fixed costs relative to revenues in an operating situation, or from debt or an option structure in a financial context.

Leverage Factor: The expected or actual percentage price change in value of an option or other derivatives position in response to a 1% change in the cash value of the underlying. Equal to gearing if the option delta equals 1. For all values of delta, leverage equals delta times underlying price, divided by warrant or option price per underlying unit. Sometimes expressed as a ratio rather than as a percentage.

Liability: An obligation to make a payment to another.

Lifetime: The term or tenor of a financial instrument or agreement.

Liquid Yield Option Note (LYON): A zero-coupon convertible, callable (by the issuer), puttable (by the investor) bond issued by a corporation. The combination of LYON features usually assures a positive return—at least until the expiration of the last opportunity to put the security back to the issuer at a premium over the issue price. The total return, if the company prospers and the common stock performs well, will be less than the return earned by common shareholders. The payout pattern of a LYON is roughly similar to some types of equity-linked notes.

Liquidate: Close a position.

Liquidation Value: The amount (typically in cash or the equivalent) that can be realized by selling an asset or project quickly.

Liquidity: A market condition where enough units of a security or other instrument are traded to allow large informationless transactions to be absorbed by the marketplace without significant impact on price stability.

Liquidity Ratio: A measure of the trading volume of a security associated with a 1% change in its price. The higher the ratio, the more shares that apparently can be traded with little change in price. Not a very consistent or useful measure.

Liquidity Risk: (1) An adverse cost or return variation stemming from the lack of marketability of a financial instrument at prices in line with recent sales. Liquidity risk may arise because a given position is very large relative to typical trading volumes, or because market conditions are unsettled. Liquidity risk is usually reflected in a wide bid-ask spread and large price movements in response to any attempt to buy or sell. (2) In a depository institution, the cost or penalty associated with unanticipated withdrawals or the failure to attract expected deposits. Liquidity risk is usually managed by limiting holdings of illiquid positions, by matching asset and liability maturities, and by limiting any maturity gap. *Also called Marketability Risk.*

Lock-In Clause: A provision in a subordinated loan agreement preventing payment of interest or repayment of principal (even at maturity) if the payment brings the issuer's capital below a designated level imposed by law or regulation.

Long: (1) Ownership of an investment position, security, or instrument. (2) A position that benefits from a rising market. (3) An investor whose position is such that she benefits from a rising market.

Long Dated Forward: A forward contract with a settlement date more than one year in the future.

Long Dated Option: Traditionally, any option with an initial life of more than a year. Today, the term usually refers to instruments with an initial life in excess of two or three years.

Long Hedge: A risk-offsetting position that protects an investor or liability manager from an opportunity loss in the event of price appreciation in an underlying before a desired position can be established. An example might be a long call or a long futures or forward position taken in anticipation of a cash inflow that will finance a cash market investment.

Long Position: (1) The holdings of the buyer of a security or other instrument. (2) A holding that appreciates in value when market prices increase, such as long stocks, bonds, futures, or call options, or short put options. Note that the holder of a put is long the contract or instrument, but profits when the market price declines.

Long-term Equity AnticiPation Securities (LEAPS): Exchange- traded options with an original life of two years or more. Both puts and calls are available, and LEAPs become fungible with ordinary exchange-traded options as their remaining life falls into the maturity range of traditional exchange-listed options.

Long the Basis: A hedged position consisting of a long position in the cash instrument or actual and a short position in a future or forward. The opposite position would be short the basis.

Macaulay Duration: The present value-weighted time to maturity of the cash flows of a fixed payment instrument or of the implicit cash flows of a derivative based on such an instrument. Originally developed as a market risk measurement for bonds (the greater the duration or "average" maturity, the greater the risk), duration has proven useful in analyzing equity securities and fixed-income options and futures. The diagram shows Macaulay duration as a balancing of present values of cash flows.

Maintenance Margin: In addition to the initial margin, or performance bond, posted in futures, options, and securities markets, each market requires participants to post additional margin if the initial margin is not adequate to ensure that participants will meet their obligations. There is usually no maintenance margin requirement on long option positions, because they must be fully paid for in most markets. Maintenance margin is usually called variation margin in futures markets.

Making a Market: Posting continuous two-sided (bid and asked) prices and being prepared to trade at those prices during normal market hours.

Mandatory Convertible: An equity-like instrument that provides a higher yield or whose principal is denominated in a stronger currency than the underlying common stock at the time of issuance. On or before a contractual conversion date, the holder must convert this instrument into the underlying common stock. Mandatory convertibles are used when a traditional equity issuance would not be possible without placing severe market pressure on the underlying stock, or because the common stock yield or the stock's native currency is unattractive to potential purchasers. *Also called Preferred Purchase Unit, Debt with a Mandatory Common Stock Purchase Contract, Equity Contract Notes, Issuer's Option Bond.*

Margin: The required equity or other performance bond that an investor must deposit to collateralize an investment position.

Margin Call: A demand from the broker or dealer carrying a customer's position for additional cash or collateral to guarantee performance on a position that has moved against the customer.

Mark to Market: To value a position or portfolio at current market prices. Marking to market is the only way to monitor risk and profit and loss effectively, and most enterprises are moving to daily marks to market of financial instruments. Marking positions to market is required with increasing frequency by accounting standards-setting bodies and regulators around the world.

Mark to Model: To price a position or portfolio at prices determined by using a financial model to interpolate between or among the market prices readily available. A mark to model is less reliable than a mark to market, because it depends on the realism of the assumptions in the model and may attribute a degree of liquidity to the instruments being priced that may not be present. With many complex financial instruments, where no ready market is available, a mark to model is the only practical valuation technique.

Market: (1) Prices at which a market maker is willing to buy and sell a particular instrument. If a market maker is willing to buy XYZ at 10 1/2, and sell XYZ at 11, his market is "10 1/2 at 11" for XYZ. A market maker's quote usually indicates size as well as price. (2) Location (physical or electronic) where transactions take place.

Market Index Deposits (MIDs): Bank certificates of deposit or deposit notes with a return linked to the performance of an index, usually a stock market index.

Market Index Target-Term Security (MITTS): An equity-linked note, usually without periodic coupon payments and with a single payoff at maturity.

Market-Linked CD: An equity-linked certificate of deposit.

Market Maker: (1) Any dealer who regularly quotes both bids and offers and is ready to make a two-sided market. (2) A trader on the floor of an exchange who enjoys certain trading privileges in exchange for accepting an obligation to help maintain a fair and orderly market.

Market Neutral Investment Strategy: An approach to portfolio management that relies on the investment manager's ability to make money through relative valuation analysis, rather than through market direction forecasting. Although approaches vary, market neutral investment techniques usually generate gains in all or nearly all market scenarios. Market neutrality can be implemented with offsetting futures positions or with offsetting short and long positions. The offset is not necessarily measured in units of dollar exposure, but rather in relative variability units. Market neutrality does not insure non-volatile returns or positive returns.

Markov Process: A stochastic process with the property that its present value alone provides just as much information about its future value as does its entire history up to and including the present value. A Markov process implies that only the present value is needed to forecast future values.

Markovian: The absence of memory in a time series. Also called time independence.

Martingale Process: (1) A stochastic process with a finite first moment and the property that, conditioned on the entire history up to and including the present, the expected value of all future increments is zero. This is equivalent to the assumption that the expected value at any future moment equals the value of the process at the present moment. Stock prices are considered to follow a martingale process, because if currently available information implies that the expected value of a future increment is positive, then investor demand will drive up the current price, thereby eliminating the expected gain. *Also called Diffusion Process.* (2) Interestingly, this term has its earliest applications in probability and random processes as the name of a betting system in which the gambler doubles his wager at each loss until a win gains him a net amount equal to his original bet—or he goes bankrupt. This usage was common in the nineteenth and early twentieth centuries.

Matched Hedge: A hedge that uses a financial instrument based on the same asset as the asset to be hedged in the underlying portfolio. This type of hedge contrasts to a cross hedge, which uses a different but correlated financial instrument to hedge an underlying asset, or a basket hedge, which uses a group of financial instruments collectively correlated with the asset to be hedged.

Matrix Price: An estimated price or value for a fixed-income security. Matrix prices are based on quoted prices for securities with similar coupons, ratings, and maturities, rather than on specific bids and offers for the designated security. The name "matrix price" comes from the practice of interpolating among values for similar instruments arranged in a matrix format. These model prices must be used with care and with understanding that a specific position may be highly illiquid.

Maturity: The date on which the life of a financial instrument ends through cash or physical settlement or expiration with no value.

Model Verification: An important risk management function that requires testing and verifying the accuracy and appropriateness of the valuation models used to price derivative transactions. A bad model can lead to a large, potentially unprofitable position because it may give the impression that the position is very attractive, encouraging a large commitment.

Modeling Risk: An adverse variation in cost or return stemming, usually indirectly, from errors in the assumptions built into a model or from a failure to model the behavior of an instrument, index, price, or rate correctly.

Modified Duration: A measurement of the change in the value of an instrument in response to a change in interest rates. The primary basis for comparing the effect of interest rate changes on prices of fixed-income instruments. The formula shows the small difference between modified and Macaulay duration. Many applications are not sensitive to the difference, and modified and Macaulay duration numbers are often used interchangeably. *Also called Adjusted Duration.*

$$D_{mod} = [1/(1 + [y/f])]D_{mac}$$

where D_{mod} = modified duration; y = yield to maturity; f = frequency of coupon payment, and D_{mac} = Macaulay duration.

If Macaulay duration is 6, yield is 7% (0.07), and the bond pays interest twice a year:

$$D_{mod} = [1/(1 + [0.07/2])]6 = 5.8$$

Modigliani–Miller Hypothesis: The proposition (largely responsible for winning Nobel prizes for its proposers) that, in an efficient capital market with no tax distortions, the relative proportion of debt and equity in a corporate capitalization does not affect the total market value of the firm. Corporate financial officers and financial engineers continue to search for market inefficiencies and tax-related opportunities that can lower a corporation's cost of capital in the real world.

Money Back Certificates: Hybrid instruments that promise the investor the return of her original investment at a minimum. Cash that might ordinarily be paid as yield goes to pay for exposure to any of a variety of equity, interest rate, commodity, and/or currency exposures. These hybrids are usually best analyzed by dividing the original investment into a zero-coupon bond that will appreciate to the value of the original investment over the life of the instrument to provide the money back component and the balance used to buy an option, invest in a commodity pool, etc.

Money Back Options or Warrants: Similar to money back certificates, but the warrant structure may permit only a partial refund of the warrant investment in the event of an adverse move in the underlying.

Moneyness: (1) The characteristic of being sufficiently like cash to be used as a medium of exchange in the settlement of transactions. (2) The degree to which an option is in the money and behaving more like a forward contract than an option.

Monthly Income Preferred Shares (MIPS): A complex instrument based on an intra-company loan between a limited liability issuer and its parent company. The instrument is designed to give the parent equity treatment for regulatory, rating, and capital purposes, and tax deductibility for the coupon on the instrument. Some versions of this instrument may achieve the desired tax objective, but all tax issues have not been resolved. *Also called Exchangeable Preferred Income Cumulative Shares (EPICS), QUarterly Income Capital Securities (QUICS), QUarterly Income Preferred Securities (QUIPS), Trust Preferred Stock Units (TruPS), Trust Originated PReferred Securities (TOPRS).*

Moral Obligation Bond: A municipal security backed by the issuer's or a related entity's stated intention to repay, but not by its full faith and credit.

Mule: An apparently innocent domestic currency bond from a highly rated issuer with embedded swaps, options, or forward contracts linking it to a foreign stock, bond, or currency position that an investor could not legally take directly. The name is a reference to the front-line carriers of illegal drugs.

Multi-Step-Up Callable Bond or Note: A callable step-up note with more than one coupon increase set over the life of the note to "step-up" the pressure on the issuer to refinance and call the note.

Multifactor Model: One of three types of models that try to explain risk/reward relationships based on two or more factors. Macroeconomic factor models use observable economic time series as measures of the factors correlated with security returns. Fundamental factor models use many of the measurements generated by securities analysts, such as price/earnings ratios, industry membership, company size, book-to-price, financial leverage, dividend yield, etc. Statistical factor models generate statistical constructs that have no necessary fundamental or macroeconomic analogs, but that explain, in the statistical sense, many of the relationships of security returns from the security return data alone. Factor models are used to predict portfolio behavior, and in conjunction with other tools, to construct customized portfolios with certain desired characteristics, such as the ability to track the performance of indexes or other portfolios.

Municipal Convertible: A combination of selected features of a zero-coupon bond and a coupon bond, these instruments typically pay no interest in the early years, and become a traditional coupon-paying municipal bond later in life. These bonds trade under a variety of names and acronyms, with stepped tax-exempt appreciation on income realization security (STAIRS) as common as any.

Municipal Embedded Derivative Security (M-Beddo): A municipal note with an embedded swap, cap, or other structure. The final instrument may be relatively complex.

Near Month: The next futures or options contract due to expire.

Negative Carry: The net cost of carrying a position when the cost of funds is greater than the yield on the securities.

Negative Pledge Clause: A provision of a bond indenture designed to protect the bondholder's position from deterioration as a result of the issuer's actions. For example, unsecured notes may provide that those notes will be secured equally with any secured debt issued in the future.

Neutral Hedge Ratio: The fraction of a point by which the price of an option contract is expected to change in response to a one-point change in the price of the underlying instrument. Mathematically, the first partial derivative of the option price with respect to the underlying price. If its neutral hedge ratio is 0.5, an option contract should change in price by about $0.50 per underlying unit for each $1 change in the price of the underlying. This relationship is the primary basis of risk management with instruments with option payoff patterns. Of course, higher derivatives, such as gamma and other relationships, must also be monitored and evaluated in an effective risk management program. *Also called Delta (1) Hedge Ratio.*

Ninety-Ten (90-10) Strategy: A multiperiod option purchase plan that avoids large losses in any single investment period by committing 10% of portfolio assets to the purchase of options and investing the balance of the portfolio at interest. Variations from the ninety-ten ratio are common in practice.

No Arbitrage Condition: A boundary condition on option and underlying price relationships that eliminates the possibility of risk-free arbitrage between and among puts, calls, and underlying instruments.

No Arbitrage Hypothesis: The notion that there is never a situation when the simultaneous purchase and/or sale of assets can result in a riskless profit.

Non-Call Life (NCL) Bonds: Bonds not callable for redemption under any circumstances not specifically noted in the indenture.

Non-Cumulative Preferred Stock: A preferred issue that is not entitled to payment of passed dividends before common dividends can be resumed.

Non-Detachable Warrants: Warrants that cannot be separated from their carrier bond and cannot be traded separately.

Normal Distribution: A probability distribution that describes the behavior of many natural and man-made phenomena. The normal distribution is particularly useful because it can be described with a relatively simple equation, and analyzed to reveal detailed characteristics of segments of the distribution. For example, about 68% of total observations fall within one standard deviation on either side of the mean of a normal distribution. About 95% fall within two standard deviations, and more than 99% fall within three standard deviations of the mean. If a population distribution is not normal, a sample standard deviation will not have these distribution characteristics, which are often used to estimate the confidence an investigator can have that an observation falls inside or outside the population described by the distribution.

Normal Price of an Option: The option price predicted by an econometric model or any similar technique used to estimate typical underlying price–option price relationships. The normal price is an estimate based on the assumption that relationships that existed in a prior period are still meaningful. Normal price is a prediction of what an option price will be, not necessarily what it should be if fairly valued relative to likely payoffs at expiration. In contrast to a market neutral-hedged position taken at fair value, a position taken at normal price does not necessarily offer an investor the expectation of earning the risk-free rate if the neutral hedged position is maintained (without frictional costs) through expiration. *Also called Average Price of an Option.*

Notice Day: On many futures exchanges, one or more days on which a notice of intent to deliver may be filed.

Notional Principal Amount: The nominal value used to calculate swap payments and on which many other risk management contract payments are based. In an interest rate swap agreement, each period's rates are multiplied by the notional principal amount to determine the value of each counterparty's payment.

Off-Balance Sheet (OBS) Instrument: A notional principal contract that changes an economic unit's risk structure without appearing as an asset or liability on a traditional balance sheet. Swaps, forward rate agreements, and various currency contracts are common OBS instruments. The fact that the balance sheet is not affected does not mean that the instrument is not reported. The size and impact of these instruments in the aggregate is usually summarized in a footnote to financial statements. Financial accounting standards-setting boards in most developed countries and regulators setting capital requirements for financial intermediaries have largely eliminated any disclosure advantage these instruments once had.

Offer Price: The price at which a trader or market maker is willing to sell a security or future.

Omega: (1) The third derivative of the option price with respect to the price of the underlying. The derivative of gamma with respect to underlying price. *Also called Speed.* (2) Currency risk of an option on an instrument denominated in a different currency. (3) One of the less frequently used option sensitivities; specifically, the sensitivity of the percentage change in option value to the percentage change in the underlying price.

Omega Risk: (1) Currency risk associated with an option contract on an underlying instrument priced in a different currency. (2) Currency risk associated with translating the value of a currency option position in a different currency to a base currency. (3) Currency correlation risk.

One-Time Put Bond: A bond with a single opportunity to put it back to the issuer.

One-Way Floater: A floating-rate note with a coupon that can only increase in response to changes in an index rate. The coupon cannot decrease.

Opening: The start of a trading session.

Opportunistic Investment Manager: A portfolio manager who will invest in any market or any asset class that he believes will provide a superior return.

Opportunity Loss or Cost: The value of a lost chance or a potential profit that was not realized because a course of action was taken that did not permit the investor to obtain that profit. The actual or expected cost of following one course of action measured relative to the most attractive alternative. Opportunity loss is not reflected in an accounting statement. An example of an opportunity loss would be the $20 per share profit forgone by a covered call writer who sells a call with a $45 strike price for a $5 premium, only to see the underlying stock jump to $70 in response to a takeover bid.

Option: (1) A stipulated privilege of buying or selling a stated property, security, or commodity at a given price (strike price) within a specified time (for an American-style option, at any time prior to or on the expiration date). A securities option is a negotiable contract in which the seller (writer), for a certain sum of money called the option premium, gives the buyer the right to demand within a specified time the purchase (call) or sale (put) by the option seller of a specified number of bonds, currency units, index units, or shares of stock at a fixed price or rate called the strike price. Many options are settled for cash equal to the difference between the aggregate spot price and the aggregate strike price rather than by delivery of the underlying. In the US and many other countries, stock options are usually written for units of 100 shares. Other units of underlying coverage are standard in other option markets. Options are ordinarily issued for periods of less than one year, but longer-term options are increasingly common. (2) Any financial contract that changes in value like an option (asymmetrically), even if the terms of the contract do not state the price relationship in terms of a right or privilege or in other language usually associated with options.

Option-Adjusted Duration: A modified duration calculation that incorporates the expected duration shortening effect of an issuer's embedded call provision.

Option-Adjusted Internal Rate of Return: An estimate of the internal rate of return adjusted to reflect the expected impact of an embedded option on the investment's cash flows.

Option-Adjusted Spread (OAS): An alternate way to calculate the call-adjusted yield of callable bonds by comparing the option-adjusted yield to the non-callable bond equivalent yield and its spread versus the Treasury yield curve.

Option-Adjusted Yield: The expected yield to maturity of a bond or note after adjusting for the probability-weighted impact of an embedded option, usually an issuer's call provision.

Option Contract: In over-the-counter options, a contract document sets forth the provisions of the option. The terms of a listed option are stated in clearing corporation documents. The buyer's evidence of ownership of an exchange-traded option is his confirmation slip from the executing broker.

Option Hedge: A partially or fully price-hedged position where the investor sells more than one risk-offsetting option against each corresponding underlying unit. The net effect of this position is to maximize the option seller's profit when the underlying sells at the strike price at expiration. The rate of return at expiration declines if the shares sell either above or below the strike price. The writer loses money only if the stock rises or falls beyond a break-even point at expiration. *Also called Ratio Write, Variable Hedge, Hedge.*

Option Premium: (1) In the US, and sometimes other markets, the amount of money an option buyer pays for a conventional put or call or the quoted price of a listed option. (2) The amount by which the price of an option exceeds its intrinsic value. For example, if an option to buy XYZ Corporation at $100 is selling at $9, and the stock is selling at $103, the premium is said to be $6. To avoid confusion between (1) and (2), the term "option price" or "premium" is used to designate the market price of an option, and the term "premium over intrinsic value" is used to designate the amount by which the stock price must rise before the expiration date for the option buyer to break even, neglecting commissions. Premium over intrinsic value is also called time value, volatility value, or opportunity value, with differing degrees of accuracy and usefulness.

Option Replication: (1) A technique to create an option- like payoff pattern through a series of transactions in the underlying or in related futures contracts as in dynamic hedging and traditional portfolio insurance. (2) Creating a long-term option out of a sequence of baskets of short-term options. As the price of the underlying moves, there may be a need to trade the replicating options dynamically, but long-term option replication with short-term options generally requires fewer portfolio adjustments than option repli-cation with the underlying or with related futures contracts. *Also called Synthetic Option.*

Out-of-the-Money: Refers to an option with no intrinsic value because the current underlying price is below the strike price of a call or above the strike price of a put. For example, a put at $100 when stock is selling at $105 is said to be 5 points out of the money.

Over-the-Counter (OTC): A security or other instrument that is not traded on an organized exchange or a market that is not part of an organized exchange. OTC instruments can be created with any provisions allowed by law and acceptable to counterparties. OTC markets and instruments are less closely regulated in some ways than exchange markets and instruments.

Par: The face value or nominal value of a security. Used more frequently for bonds and other fixed-income securities than for stocks.

Parallel Shift: A movement of each point on a yield curve up or down by the same distance. Many duration-matching and control strategies assume that any yield curve shifts will be parallel.

Pari Passu: Two securities or obligations that have equal rights to payment are said to rank pari passu.

Parity: (1) The condition in which a bond sells at its nominal or face value. (2) The condition in which an option sells at its intrinsic value. The maximum of zero or spot minus strike for a call and the maximum of zero or strike minus spot for a put.

Partial Duration: A technique for applying some of the principles of duration analysis to rate changes that affect only part of the yield curve, typically the shorter end of the curve. Partial durations sum to a value that is usually close to the overall effective duration. *Similar concepts are Reshaping Durations, Key Rate Duration.*

Partially Protected Equity-Linked Note: A variation on the participating equity-linked note (ELN) in which the investor has full participation on the upside but only partial protection (or partial participation) on the downside.

Participation Bond: A bond with a minimum required coupon and an additional payment based on the issuer's profitability. In contrast to a convertible bond, which participates in the price action of the underlying common stock, a participation bond has a variable interest rate, some of which is linked to corporate earnings.

Participation Certificate: (1) A security issued by a corporation with a payoff pattern similar to an equity-linked note. (2) A security issued by a corporation to create an additional class of equity shares with a different dividend rate or reduced restrictions on share transfer. *Also called Bearer (Participation) Certificate.*

Path Dependency: A situation where the terminal value of an option or a dynamic hedging strategy depends on the particular path of the underlying risky asset's price changes. By contrast, a path-independent strategy's terminal value depends only on the terminal value of the underlying risky asset.

Path-Dependent Option: While the value of a traditional option depends only on the price of the underlying on the day of exercise or expiration, the value of a path-dependent option depends partly or exclusively on the price pattern the underlying follows in reaching exercise or expiration. Asian (average price or rate) options, lookback options, and barrier options are all examples of path-dependent options. If early exercise could be appropriate for an American option under certain circumstances, that option is also path-dependent in a sense.

Performance Equity-linked Redemption Quarterly pay Security (PERQS): Synthetic (dealer-issued) preferred equity redemption cumulative stock (PERCS). *Also called Synthetic High-Income Equity-Linked Debenture (SHIELD), Short-Term Appreciation and Investment Return Trust (STAIR). Compare to Equity-LinKed Security (ELKS).*

PERformance Linked to Equity Securities (PERLES): A synthetic equity based on the performance of an index or an individual stock. PERLES may also be interpreted as securitized swaps because of their symmetric payout structure. The underlying equity is usually a cross-border investment to the PERLES holder, and withholding tax avoidance is usually one reason behind selection of this structure.

Performance Plus Shares: Synthetic common stock or stock index instruments issued by a financial intermediary that promises the buyer the total return from the underlying security or index plus an additional return based on a dividend withholding tax credit, a stock loan premium, or some other element of return that the intermediary can obtain more easily than the buyer of these special shares.

Perpetual Preferred Stock (Perp): A fixed-rate equity instrument with no participation in the issuer's profit and no promise of principal repayment. Issued directly or in conversion of other instruments by banks subject to the Basle Capital Adequacy Directive. Perps are counted as Tier I capital.

Perpetual Warrant: A warrant granting the right to buy shares of common stock at a fixed price with no expiration date. A perpetual warrant is only exercised if the stock's dividend rate is high enough and safe enough to entice the warrant holder to exercise and claim the forward dividend stream.

Pick-Up: A gain in yield from the sale of one security and the purchase of another. Used primarily in the bond market.

Pips: Basis points. The term is used primarily in currency markets. *Also called Points (1), Tick.*

Points: (1) Digits added to or subtracted from the fourth decimal place (basis points) to convert a spot exchange rate to a forward rate or to reflect the trading basis in a currency market. (2) Multiples of the minimum price fluctuation or tick in any market. (3) Payments by a mortgagee to prepay servicing costs and obtain a lower net interest rate.

Positive Carry: The net gain from carrying a position when the cost of funds is less than the yield on the securities held.

Preference Equity Redemption Cumulative Stock (PERCS): A limited-term, limited participation convertible preferred stock with an enhanced dividend. PERCS shares are convertible at maturity into one share of the underlying common stock if the common stock is selling below the PERCS strike price, and into a fractional share equal in value to the PERCS strike value if the common is selling above the strike. After three years, the PERCS shares are converted to common automatically on these terms, and the dividend drops back to the regular common stock dividend. PERCS were the most successful financial product of 1991, because they provided a relatively high current yield in a declining yield environment. As the illustration indicates, the PERCS is essentially a covered call structure. Synthetic PERCS have been issued by third-party issuers, largely investment banks. *Also called Mandatory Conversion Premium Dividend Preferred Stocks (MCPDPS), Participating Equity Preferred Stock (PEPS), Preferred Income Participation Security (PIPS), Equity Redeemable Bond, Common-linked Higher-Income Participation Security (CHIPS), Equity Yield Enhancement Security (EYES), Short-Term Equity Participation Units (STEP Units).*

Preferred Stock: An equity or ownership instrument with certain preferences or priorities over common stock as to dividends and/or distribution of assets upon liquidation.

Premium: (1) In the US, and most continental European markets, the amount of money an option buyer pays or an option writer receives for an OTC put or call or the price of an exchange-listed option. (2) In warrant markets based on the traditions of the UK, premium is the amount by which the value of an investor's position would decrease if the option or warrant were exercised immediately. (3) The amount by which the price of an option exceeds its intrinsic value. For example, if an option to buy XYZ Corporation at $100 is selling at $9, and the stock is selling at $103, the premium is often said to be $6. To avoid confusion between (1) and (3), the term "option price" or "premium" is used to designate the market price of an option, and the term "premium over intrinsic value" is used to designate the amount by which the underlying price must move beyond the strike price (for out-of-the-money options) or the current price (for at- or in-the-money options) before expiration for the option buyer to break even, neglecting commissions.

(4) The amount by which a coupon-bearing debt instrument sells over par because its coupon provides an above market yield. (5) The quality or credit yield differential that an issuer must pay above the rate on a government bond with a comparable maturity. (6) The amount by which the price on a futures contract exceeds the price of another contract or the underlying cash instrument. (7) The consideration paid for an insurance contract.

Premium Bond: A bond selling above par because its coupon is higher than current market levels.

Premium Put Convertible Bond: In addition to the traditional features of a convertible bond, this instrument has an embedded put that permits the investor to redeem it at a premium over parity at some point(s) over the life of the bond. A feature of the liquid yield option note (LYON).

Pricing by Arbitrage: The value of any replicable claim is uniquely determined by no-arbitrage constraints.

Principal: (1) Par or face value of a debt instrument or preferred stock. (2) The value of funds invested, the base for a return on investment calculation.

Principal Exchange Rate-Linked Securities (PERLS): A variation on a dual currency bond that pays both coupon and principal in the base currency, but sets the variable principal payment according to a redemption formula that links it to movements in currency exchange rates between the issue date and maturity. PERLS' principal payments increase as the foreign currency appreciates relative to the base currency, and decrease as the foreign currency declines. Reverse principal exchange rate-linked securities' (Reverse PERLS') principal payments increase as the base currency appreciates relative to the foreign currency, and decrease as the base currency depreciates.

Principal Protected Note: Any note that promises—at a minimum—to return the investor's initial or principal investment. The most common type of equity-linked note.

Principal Risk: The risk of losing some of the nominal or face amount or some of the purchase cost of an investment.

Protected Equity Participation (PEP): (1) Principal guaranteed equity-linked note with upside participation in an individual stock or a basket of stocks and with no cap on return. Identical in structure to a protected index participation (PIP). *(2) Another name for Debt Exchangeable for Common Stock (DECS).*

Protected Exchangeable EQuity-linked Securities (PEEQS): An exchange-traded, equity- or index-linked note that can be cashed out substantially earlier than its stated maturity at a value reflecting the interim performance of the underlying. The purpose of the early cash-out privilege is to assure that the non-interest-bearing note does not trade materially below the contemporaneous cash value of the underlying.

Protected Growth Securities (Pro-GroS): A callable equity-linked note with principal protection and upside participation, but with no interest coupon or other payment until the note matures or is called.

Protected Index Participation (PIP): Principal guaranteed equity index-linked notes with upside index participation but with no cap on return. The instrument's rate of participation in the upside movement of the index varies with the dividend rate on the stocks in the index, interest rates, market volatility, yield on the note (if any), and life of the PIP.

Put Guarantee Letter: A collateralization mechanism to assure performance by the seller of a put option. A bank issues a guarantee that it holds and is prepared to deliver segregated cash equivalent to the aggregate strike price of the put.

Put Option: The right but not the obligation to sell an underlying at a particular price (strike price) on or before the expiration date of the contract. Alternatively, a short forward position with an upside insurance policy.

Put Warrant: A security that, in contrast to a conventional warrant, gives the holder the right to sell the underlying or to receive a cash payment that increases as the value of the underlying declines. Put warrants, like their call warrant counterparts, generally have an initial term of more than one year.

Puttable Extendible Notes: At the end of each interest period, the issuer may redeem these notes at par or attempt to extend the maturity on terms that he believes the noteholder will accept. The noteholder can put the notes back to the issuer if the new rate is unacceptable. Holders also may have one or more additional put options during the initial interest period.

Puttable Notes: A traditional bond or note with an embedded put that permits the bondholder to sell the notes back to the issuer, usually at par. This put gives the holder some protection from loss of principal due to higher interest rates or credit deterioration of the issuer. *Also called Puttable Bonds, Adjustable Tender Securities.*

Quantitative Investment Management: A portfolio management style that applies mathematical and statistical techniques to a single market sector (i.e., equity or debt) or to asset allocation. Quantitative tools vary greatly in sophistication and the underlying variables evaluated may be fundamental or technical.

Quanto Note: An equity-linked note in which the percentage change of a foreign equity or equity index is translated into the currency in which the note is denominated (the investor's base currency) for accounting and reporting convenience, and, sometimes, for regulatory necessity. *Also called Fixed Exchange Rate Equity Note.*

R (Correlation Coefficient): A measure (ranging in value from -1 to 1) of the association between a dependent variable and one or more independent variables. If one variable's values are higher than its average value when another variable's values are higher than its average value, their correlation is positive. By contrast, if one variable's values are lower than its average value when another variable's values are higher than its average value, their correlation is negative. A correlation coefficient is not necessarily a measure of causality, but it does indicate the strength of a relationship. A correlation coefficient of 1 implies that the variables move perfectly in lockstep; a correlation coefficient of -1 implies that the variables move inversely in lockstep; a correlation coefficient of 0 implies that the variables, as calibrated, are uncorrelated.

R_2 (Coefficient of Determination): In regression analysis, the fraction of variation in the dependent variable that is explained by variation in the independent variable or variables. R_2 is calculated as the ratio of the sum of the squared differences between the predicted values for the dependent variable, and the average of the observed values for the dependent variable to the sum of the squared differences between the observed values for the dependent variable and the average of those values. R_2 ranges in value from 0 to 1. A high value indicates a strong relationship between the dependent and independent variables, while a low value indicates a weak relationship.

$$R_2 = [S(\text{Predicted } y - \text{Mean } y)_2]/[S(\text{Observed } y - \text{Mean } y)_2]$$

Random Walk Hypothesis: The random walk hypothesis is a variant of the efficient market hypothesis. It holds that stock prices follow a random walk pattern, and, consequently, historic prices are of no value in forecasting future prices.

Realized Yield: The return actually earned on an investment in a security over a period of time, including the return on reinvested interest or dividend payments.

Rebalancing: Periodic revisions to a portfolio necessitated by the effect of the passage of time on asset and liability duration, changes in the constitution of an index, portfolio cash flows, or market-driven departures from a target allocation.

Red Herring: A preliminary prospectus for a securities offering in the US. The red herring usually has full details of the offering except price and, perhaps, size. It has comprehensive financial data on the issuer. The name comes from a required note usually printed in red ink stating that the issue cannot yet be sold because the registration statement is not effective.

Reinvestment Rate: The interest rate or yield at which any cash flow from coupon or principal payments can be reinvested.

Reinvestment Risk: Exposure to an unfavorable variation in return as a result of an investor's inability to invest an interest coupon or principal repayment at a rate as favorable as the original return on the instrument generating the cash flow.

Remarketed Preferred Stock: Perpetual preferred stock with a dividend rate that resets at the end of each dividend period to a level determined by a remarketing agent, subject to certain maximums relative to commercial paper rates. Dividend periods and payments may be variable even within a single issue to meet issuer and investor needs. Similar to other adjustable-rate preferred structures except for the rate reset and redistribution mechanism.

Replicable Position: A condition that can be reproduced by constructing a portfolio with a value at maturity identical in all circumstances to the value of the contingent claim, with all changes in the composition of the portfolio self-financed.

Replicating Portfolios: Combinations of stock, cash, and borrowing that reproduce the return pattern of an option or option-based instrument and form the basis for portfolio insurance and other dynamic hedging strategies or synthetic structures.

Reset Option or Warrant: Typically, a stock or equity index call option or warrant whose strike price may be reset to a lower strike, or a put whose strike price may be reset to a higher strike, at some point during the life of the instrument if the option is out of the money on the reset date. There may be a limit to the magnitude of the strike price adjustment and the reset may be triggered by a specific price on the underlying rather than set on a specific reset date. *Also called Strike Reset Option or Warrant.*

Reset Performance Equity-linked Redemption Quarterly pay Securities (Reset PERQS): These differ from standard PERQS in that the exchange ratio at maturity is reduced by the ratio of a stated first-year cap price to the actual first-year closing price if the first-year closing price exceeds the cap price.

Return On Capital (ROC): The rate of return on a financial institution's regulatory capital.

Return On Equity (ROE): Net income divided by net worth.

Return On Risk-Adjusted Capital (RORAC): Similar to risk-adjusted return on capital (RAROC), except that the rate of return is measured without a risk adjustment, while the capital charge varies depending on the risk associated with the instrument or project. One of a number of risk-adjusted performance measures (RAPM).

Reverse Dual Currency Bond: A bond that pays coupons in a non-base currency (typically the currency of the issuer) and pays principal in the base currency (the currency of the investor).

Rho: (1) The dollar change in an option price in response to a percentage point change in the risk-free interest rate. (2) Greek letter often used to denote the correlation coefficient.

Rising Star: A bond whose rating has been increased by a rating agency as a result of improvement in the credit quality of the issuer.

Risk: Exposure to uncertain change. In popular usage, adverse change is appropriately emphasized. Annualized standard deviation of return is the generic measurement of risk in most markets, but both asset and liability managers increasingly add other statistical measures, such as skewness and kurtosis, to a risk profile, or, even better, look at the entire probability distribution of returns and the maximum cost of adverse developments.

Risk-Adjusted Performance Measures (RAPM): A reference to one or more of Return On Capital (ROC), Return On Risk-Adjusted Capital (RORAC), Risk-Adjusted Return On Capital (RAROC), or Risk-Adjusted Return On Risk-Adjusted Capital (RARORAC).

Risk-Adjusted Return On Capital (RAROC): A technique for risk analysis and project evaluation that requires a higher net return for a riskier project than for a less risky project. The risk adjustment is performed by reducing the risky return at the project or instrument return level, rather than by adjusting the capital charge. One of a number of risk-adjusted performance measures.

Risk-Adjusted Return On Risk-Adjusted Capital (RARORAC): A combination of risk-adjusted return on capital (RAROC) and return on risk-adjusted capital (RORAC), in which specific risk adjustments are made to the return stream and the capital charge is varied to reflect different expectations of risk in different businesses. While this may seem like double-counting, the adjustments on each side of the process usually cover different risks. One of a number of risk-adjusted performance measures.

Risk-Free Rate: Modern portfolio theory postulates the existence of at least one risky asset and one risk-free asset, usually taken to be Treasury bills or comparable short-term sovereign debt. The risk-free rate is the rate of return on the risk-free asset. This risk-free rate is lower than the expected return on the risky asset, because issuers have to offer a risk-averse investor the expectation of a higher return to induce him to abandon the risk-free asset for an investment with uncertain returns or, say, credit risk.

Risk Neutral: An attitude toward risk that leads an investor to be indifferent between an investment with a certain outcome and a risky investment with the same expected value but an uncertain outcome. A risk neutral investor's indifference curve is flat in dimensions of expected return and risk.

Risk Neutral Pricing: Valuing a derivative by taking discounted expectations under the assumption of risk neutral probability.

Risk Neutral Probability: A probability distribution of future price structures used in derivatives pricing (valuation) that meets two conditions: (a) Prices occurring with positive probability under risk neutral probability should be identical to prices that occur with positive probability in the original model; and (b) the expected return on all assets in the model should be the same. *Also called Equivalent Martingale Measure.*

Risk Neutral Valuation: A valuation process based on the ability to establish a perfect hedge either dynamically or through a buy and hold strategy. Although this valuation assumes that the expected growth rate is equal to the risk-free rate, because risk neutral investors do not demand a risk premium, the solution applies to all investors regardless of risk preference.

Risk Premium: (1) An additional required rate of return due to extra risk incurred from investing in an asset. (2) The difference between the expected total return from a risky investment and the risk-free rate.

Rocket Scientist: The popular press' designation for the creators of risk management products and services and for the managers of risk management programs. Frequently used as a pejorative.

Rolling Hedge: Using the relatively high liquidity in exchange-traded futures and option contracts to maintain a continuous (relatively short-term) risk-offsetting position by closing contracts as they approach maturity and opening more distant positions.

Rolling Over: (1) The process by which an investor closes an option or futures contract with a near-term expiration and opens a contract on the same side of the market (long or short) with a more distant expiration. (2) More generally, substituting a position with a different expiration date and/or a different strike price for a previously established position. The process is called rolling up when substituting an option with a higher strike price, rolling down when substituting an option with a lower strike price, and rolling forward when substituting an option or futures contract with a more distant expiration.

Round Trip: A purchase followed by a sale or a sale followed by a purchase of a cash instrument or a derivative security.

Samurai Bond: A yen-denominated bond issued by a non-Japanese company in Japan. Analogous to Yankee bonds in the US and Bulldog bonds in the UK.

Samurai Warrants: European-style capped calls convertible into non-voting equity. The non-voting feature is usually linked to restrictions on foreign ownership or control.

Second Generation Duration: A measure of duration in which the relevant cash flows are discounted not by the yield to maturity of the instrument in question, but rather by the yields associated with zero-coupon bonds that mature simultaneously with each cash flow.

Secondary Market: In contrast to the primary market, where new security issues are sold to investors, the secondary market is the traditional exchange or over-the-counter market where previously issued securities are bought and sold by individual and institutional holders with brokers and dealers as intermediaries. *Also called After-Market.*

Securitized Options: Packaged stock or stock index options combined with another security such as a note.

Security: A negotiable financial instrument other than cash or a futures contract.

Seller's Option: (1) A put option. (2) A securities transaction settlement arrangement by which delivery and payment can be arranged at a time of the seller's choosing (within limits).

Sensitivity: A measurement, description, or graph of the relationship between or among two or more of the variables determining option value or option value derivatives.

Settlement Currency: The currency in which a settlement is paid.

Settlement Date: The date on which the exchange of cash, securities, and paperwork involved in a transaction is completed.

Settlement Price: (1) A price, typically the exact or approximate opening or closing price, on which any maintenance or variation margin payment or cash exercise settlement is based. (2) The final delivery price used to evaluate contracts held to maturity. *Also called Delivery Price, Exchange Delivery Settlement Price (EDSP).*

Short: (1) A position whereby an investor incurs rights and obligations that mirror the risk/return characteristics of another investor's asset position, and, consequently, change in value in opposite directions to that asset position. (2) An investment position that benefits from a decline in price. (3) An investor whose position benefits from a decline in the market.

Short Hedge: A risk-offsetting position that protects an investment or a liability against the adverse effects of a price decline.

Short Position: (1) A position that appreciates in value when the underlying market price decreases. Examples include selling a stock short, selling a future, buying a put, or selling a call. (2) The position of the stock or futures short seller or of the writer or seller of an option contract. Note the anomalous position of the short put that benefits from an increase in the price of the underlying.

Short Proceeds: The cash received from the short sale of a security. The interest return from investment of the short proceeds is usually divided between the short seller, who gets partial "use of proceeds," and the securities lender.

Short Sale: The sale of a security or other financial instrument not previously owned by the seller in the expectation that it will be possible to repurchase that instrument at a lower price some time in the future. The term "short sale" is ordinarily applied only to the sale of securities, but an equivalent synthetic short position can be attained through the sale of an uncovered call option and the purchase of a put or by selling a forward or a future.

Short Squeeze: An upward movement in the price of an instrument stimulated by shorts rushing to cover their positions in response to a fundamental or technical development or in response to a request from a lender for the return of borrowed stock.

Short-Term Appreciation and Investment Return Trust (STAIR): A synthetic PERCS-type structure consisting of long positions in Treasury securities and short in-the-money puts on a portfolio. STAIRs have a payout pattern equivalent to PERCS and short-term equity participation units (STEP units). *Also called Performance Equity-Linked Redemption Quarterly Paid Security (PERQS).*

Short-Term Equity Participation Units (STEP Units): A synthetic PERCS structure using a portfolio or index rather than a single stock. The basic structure features a higher yield than the underlying instrument(s) and full participation in the value of the underlying up to the capped price. The proceeds from the sale of a cap (call) are invested in an annuity to pay the higher dividend yield. A minor tax feature defers tax on the incremental yield until maturity, typically three years. At expiration of the trust, large unit holders can elect to receive stock; otherwise, shares will be sold and proceeds distributed. Unlike PERCS, these synthetics raise no new capital for issuers. *Also called Packaged Equity Trust Securities (PETS).*

Short-Term Instruments Linked to Treasuries (STILTs): A principal protected note with a variable coupon linked to the absolute or relative performance of one or more Treasury instruments or index rates.

Sigma: The standard deviation or volatility of the price or rate of an instrument, frequently the instrument underlying an option.

Single Point Adjustable-Rate Stock (SPARS): A floating-rate preferred stock with a dividend reset every forty-nine days at a specified relationship to high-grade commercial paper.

Sinking Fund: A provision of a bond indenture that commits an issuer to call bonds prior to maturity or to purchase them in the open market. Option theory has been applied to evaluate a sinking fund provision to determine how best to meet the sinking fund obligation when the issuer has some flexibility.

Skew: A reference to a graph or table of the at- and out-of-the-money strike implied volatilities structure of put and call options with a common underlying and common maturity. Less frequently, a reference to the term structure of volatility.

Skew Measure: The change in volatility (standard deviation) for a 1% change in option strike or exercise price ($\Delta s/DE$). *Sometimes called Iota (I).*

Skewness: A measure of the non-symmetry of a distribution. Symmetrical distributions have a skewness value of zero. A distribution with negative skewness has more observations in the left tail (left of the peak or mode), and a distribution with positive skewness has more observations in the right tail.

Soft Call Protection: A limited premium to parity that an issuer must pay to call a bond after any period of hard call protection has passed. Non-convertible bonds can usually be called at a premium that declines gradually as the bond approaches maturity. Atypical soft call provision might require a 50-basis point per year premium for an early call.

Speculation: (1) A term of opprobrium applied to any financial instrument or transaction of which the speaker or writer disapproves. (2) A financial transaction characterized by the acceptance of greater exposure to price change than might be usual or appropriate for the individual or entity taking the position. (3) A technical term characterizing certain transactions on a futures or commodity exchange in which the entity taking the position is increasing rather than reducing exposure to a specific category of price risk. (4) A position taken because it offers the prospect of capital gain. (5) Purposeful ownership of a less than fully diversified portfolio in pursuit of a superior risk-adjusted return. See "Exactly What Do You Mean by Speculation?" by Martin S. Fridson, *The*

Journal of Portfolio Management, Fall 1993, pp. 29–39, for illustrations of the difficulties of defining speculation adequately.

Speed: An option derivative or sensitivity calculation that measures the change in gamma in response to the change in the price of the underlying, *ceteris paribus*: $\Delta g/Dx$. The third derivative of option price with respect to the underlying price. *Also called Omega.*

Spot Market: The market for a cash or current (as opposed to forward) commodity or financial instrument taking the form of (1) an organized, self-regulated central market; (2) a decentralized over-the-counter market; or (3) a local organization that provides a market for a small region.

Spot Price: The current market price. For example, the current price of a stock, bond, or currency for normal delivery or of a cash commodity for prompt delivery.

Spread: (1) The difference between the bid and the asked price in any market. (2) The difference between the yields or prices of two financial instruments. (3) The price or rate difference between two delivery months in a futures market. (4) A transaction designed to profit from a narrowing or widening of a price or yield spread. *Also called Spread Position, Spread Warrant.* (5) For listed options: The purchase of one option and the sale of another of the same type on the same security or index. The investor setting up the spread hopes to profit from a favorable change in the difference between the prices of the two options. If the number of options purchased is not equal to the number sold, the position may be called a ratio spread or a variable spread. (6) The difference between the price investors pay an underwriter for a new securities offering and the proceeds of the financing paid to the issuer. (7) In the old conventional stock option market (largely pre-1973): A straddle-like position in which the put side and the call side were struck at different prices. Typically, the put strike was below and the call strike was above the market price of the stock at the time the spread was established. In the listed option market, this position is called a *Spraddle* or a *Strangle*. (8) The difference between a bank's lending rate and its borrowing rate.

Squeeze: Pressure (usually upward) on a price resulting from a temporary shortage of supply. An extreme shortage might lead to a corner.

Standard & Poor's 500 Depositary Receipts (SPDRs, pronounced "spiders"): A warehouse receipt structure, similar to the Toronto Exchange's TIPs, that provides the investor with an interest in the holdings of a trust designed to track the return of the S&P 500 index. SPDRs were introduced by the American Stock Exchange as a replacement for their ill-fated index participations. They have become one of the fastest growing fund products in history.

Standard & Poor's Index Notes (SPINs): (1) Originally, a fixed coupon note with a below market yield and the principal payment linked to the value of the S&P 500 stock index. *Also called Stock Performance Exchange-Linked Bonds (SPELBonds).* (2) A zero-coupon equity-linked note with an American-style early exercise and settlement feature available when the index is above the embedded strike.

Standard & Poor's-LInked Trust Shares (SPLITS): An S&P 500-based participating equity-linked note.

Standard & Poor's (S&P) "r" Symbol: A lower case "r" added to S&P's ratings of certain derivatives and hybrid instruments to alert investors to the possibility of high volatility or dramatic fluctuations in expected returns.

Standard Deviation (SD, s): The square root of the mean of the squared deviations of members of a population from their mean. The most widely used measurement of variation about a mean, and, for many purposes, a proxy for risk. The standard deviation of normally distributed random variables has many useful characteristics that, unfortunately, do not usually apply to distributions truncated or skewed by option payoff patterns.

Standardization: (1) A characteristic of exchange-traded derivatives instruments and publicly traded corporate offerings that makes it possible for buyers and sellers to learn the pertinent characteristics of an instrument based on a few words of description or a security identification number or symbol. (2) A constant (usually the mean) is subtracted from each number in a distribution to array all numbers around a new mean. Each number is then divided by a constant (usually the standard deviation) to simplify further comparisons. *Also called Normalization.*

Start Date: The date—spot or forward—when some feature of a financial contract becomes effective or when interest payments or returns begin to be calculated. *Also called Effective Date.*

Step-Down Coupon Note: A debt instrument with a high coupon in earlier payment periods and a lower coupon in later payment periods. This structure is usually motivated by a low short-term rate environment, regulatory, or tax considerations.

Step-Down Option or Warrant: A stock or equity index call warrant with a downward strike price reset during a limited period, at a specific future date, and/or as a consequence of a drop in the underlying to a predetermined level. Specific terms vary with the issue.

Step-Down Preferred Stock: A very high-coupon instrument designed to pay a partially tax-sheltered dividend that, in effect, liquidates the principal before the payment drops to a nominal level and the issuer is recapitalized, often through a merger of affiliated companies. The Internal Revenue Service has challenged this structure.

Stock Market Annual Reset Term (SMART) Note: A variable-rate note with the periodic coupon dependent on the performance of a stock market index rather than on an interest rate or rate spread. *Generically, a Coupon-Indexed Note.*

Structured Enhanced Returns Trust (STEER): A mechanism designed to permit an institutional investor to enter into a swap indirectly or to obtain indirect participation in an instrument that it might not be able to acquire directly. An intermediary organization (the "Trust") purchases an instrument to serve as the basis for a swap, and the return on that instrument is swapped with a third party to provide the exposure the investor seeks. The STEER structure is more cumbersome and generally more costly than the simple purchase of a structured note with appropriate embedded return characteristics.

Structured Financial Transaction: (1) A security backed by financial assets such as loans or lower-quality bonds or notes. The security may trade on a limited basis or be the subject of a public offering. (2) A combination of a conventional security and an embedded derivative. (3) A packaged guaranteed series of payments issued by an insurance company in settlement of litigation, an insurance closing, or a long-term lottery payout. The nominal value of the settlement is usually much greater than the present value of the scheduled payments.

Structured Note: A debt obligation, usually in the form of a medium-term note or bank certificate of deposit, with one or more embedded risk/return modification components (swaps, forwards, options, caps, floors, etc.) that change its return pattern. A corporation or government agency that issues a structured note usually buys the risk/return modification components from a financial intermediary, but the issuer remains ultimately responsible for all payments to the holder of the note. *Also called Hybrid Debt.*

Structured Product: An over-the-counter (OTC) financial instrument created specifically to meet the needs of one or a small number of investors. The instrument may consist of a warrant, an option, or a forward embedded in a note or any of a wide variety of debt, equity, and/or currency combinations. *Also called Structure.*

STRuctured Yield Product Exchangeable for Stock (STRYPES): A specialized form of debt exchangeable for common stock (DECS) used to facilitate the public sale of a low-dividend stock by increasing the yield for a few years at a sacrifice in upside price participation.

Structurer: An unpretentious rocket scientist or financial engineer.

Stub: (1) The highly leveraged common stock remaining after a leveraged buyout or other recapitalization. The stub's value is affected by the issuance of debt to replace much of the original common stock. The stub is difficult to evaluate except as an option on the firm. (2) An interim period at the beginning or end of a swap or other periodic reset agreement that is of non-standard length. For example, a two-month stub at the end of a quarterly reset swap. *Also called Back Stub Period, Front Stub Period.* (3) The ex-warrant bond originally issued with a detachable warrant. (4) A package of three consecutive one-month LIBOR contracts used to create a synthetic three-month Eurodollar position on the Chicago Mercantile Exchange.

Synthetic Asset: A package of risks and returns created by combining other instruments to approximate very closely the package of risks and returns available in a traditional security. A position that behaves like a put, call, or some other standard instrument but has been created using different positions or dynamic trading techniques. For example, portfolio insurers create synthetic puts, equity portfolio managers often create synthetic stock or synthetic calls, index arbitrageurs may create synthetic Treasury bills, and bond futures traders may create synthetic bonds.

Synthetic Bond: A combination of financial instruments or components designed to behave like long-term bonds. Examples might include money market instruments plus bond futures, a long bond call combined with a short bond put and a money market position, or any of a variety of other risk equivalent combinations.

Synthetic Call Option: Typically, a combination of a long put and a long position in the underlying. The put strike is the strike of the synthetic call.

Synthetic Convertible Debt: (1) A debt and warrant package structured to resemble a traditional convertible debt issue. The components of the package may be separable, unlike traditional convertibles, or they may be in the form of an equity-linked note. (2) An equity-linked note issued by an entity other than the issuer of the underlying equity instrument.

Synthetic Equity: A derivative instrument with the essential risk/reward characteristics of a direct investment in a stock, a specific basket of stocks, or an appropriately weighted basket of stocks equivalent to a stock index.

Synthetic Foreign Bond: A domestic currency-denominated bond with all payments marked to the market in terms of a foreign currency. All coupons are computed against the principal denominated in the foreign currency value at the issue date, and converted into the domestic currency at the spot exchange rate on the coupon payment date. Repayment of principal is converted into the domestic currency at the spot rate at maturity. In short, the only difference between this instrument and a true foreign bond is that the issuer is responsible for conversion of all payments into the investor's domestic currency.

Synthetic Forward: A combination of a long European call and a short European put with the same expiration date and strike price. This combination provides the functional equivalent of a forward contract on the underlying. *Also called Synthetic Futures Contract.*

Synthetic Guaranteed Investment Contract (Synthetic GIC): A guaranteed account secured by a pool of assets owned by the investor (the assets are segregated to protect them from claims by the financial institution's general creditors) with a separate guarantee issued by the institution.

Synthetic High-Income Equity-Linked Debenture (SHIELD): Comparable in structure to preference equity redemption cumulative stock (PERCS), but issued by an entity other than the issuer of the underlying stock. *Also called Convertible Money Market Units (CMMUs), Performance Equity-Linked Redemption Quarterly Paid Security (PERQS).*

Synthetic PERCS: Similar to Equity-Linked Security (ELKS). *Also called Yield Enhanced Equity-Linked Debt Security (YEELDS), Common-linked Higher Income Participation Security (CHIPS), Synthetic High-Income Equity-Linked Debenture (SHIELD).*

Synthetic Zero-Coupon Convertible Bond: A combination of a zero-coupon note and a detachable warrant with an equal term to expiration. The notes are usable to exercise the warrants and the issuer may enjoy an advantage in interest deductibility over other issuers of zero-coupon convertibles. *Also called Super-LYONS.*

Tau τ: The sensitivity of the value of an option to changes in the volatility variable. Usually expressed as the dollar change in the value or price of an option for a percentage point change in the standard deviation of the underlying. Also commonly known as vega. Although vega is not a Greek letter, it starts with a "v" and sounds acceptable to most market participants.

Term Sheet: A written summary of the characteristics of a financial instrument, usually prepared by an underwriter in the case of a public offering, or by the issuing dealer in the case of an OTC derivatives instrument. While term sheets are not usually technically binding on offerings for which a prospectus or other offering circular is prepared, they are frequently incorporated into the contractual terms of an OTC instrument.

Term Structure of Interest Rates: The pattern, usually represented graphically as a yield curve, of interest rates on sovereign or other consistent quality debt of various maturities. Where sovereign debt is not actively traded at appropriate maturities, the swap curve may be the best indicator of the term structure of interest rates in a specific currency. The term structure also sets relationships for arbitrage-free debt instrument option models.

Term Structure of Volatility: A curve, broadly analogous in purpose to an interest rate yield curve, that illustrates the relationship of yield or price volatility to maturity or duration. Much like the term structure of interest rates, the curve illustrates the pattern of implied volatilities of representative (usually at-the-money) options as option maturities extend forward. A term structure can be calculated or estimated for any strike, spot, or forward.

Term to Maturity: The life of a financial instrument. The period until an instrument is to be exercised or converted into cash or an underlying position.

Theta θ: The sensitivity of an option's price to the passage of time with the price of the underlying and implied volatility unchanged. A measurement of the "wasting asset" characteristic of an option, i.e., its rate of time decay (Dp/Dt).

Time Decay: The loss in value of an option or an instrument with an embedded option as the expiration date approaches.

Tombstone Advertisement: A starkly simple advertisement run by an underwriting syndicate or investment banker to claim credit for a role in the completion of a financial transaction.

Total Return: (1) For most assets, income plus any principal gain or minus any principal loss during a measurement period divided by principal (investment) and expressed as a percent. (2) For bonds held to maturity, the discount rate at which the initial investment in the bond will grow to the total value available at maturity with interim cash flows invested at an assumed reinvestment rate.

TRust Automatic Common Exchange Securities (TRACES): The functional equivalent of Automatically Convertible Enhanced Security (ACES) or Debt Exchangeable for Common Stock (DECS) (diagrams). The structural difference is a trust entity between the issuer of the underlying common stock and the investor.

Trust for Income Participation from Stocks (TIPS): A synthetic PERCS structure renamed package equity trust securities (PETS) before issuance because of a name conflict with the Toronto Stock Exchange's index deposit receipt product.

Trust Preferred Stock Units (TruPS): Trust units combining a preferred share and a purchase contract that requires the holder to buy a comparable preferred share upon the scheduled maturity of the initial preferred issue. The trust holds debt of the ultimate issuer. The structure combines features of other offerings that qualify as regulatory capital (e.g., mandatory convertibles) and structures that attempt to make preferred stock dividends deductible [e.g., Monthly Income Preferred Shares (MIPS)].

Two-Factor Option Pricing Model: While the traditional Black–Scholes model allows for one stochastic variable (volatility), a two-factor model used to evaluate a traditional equity option or, perhaps, an option embedded in a bond, provides for a second stochastic variable—usually an interest rate. The final value of the security is a function of both variables as well as the other inputs in the option valuation mechanism.

Underlying: The security, cash commodity, forward, futures, swap, or other contract or instrument that is the subject of a derivatives contract or instrument.

Underwriter: (1) An investment banker who purchases securities for his own account with the express intention of reselling them in the open market. (2) An insurer who undertakes to furnish an insurance contract in exchange for a premium.

Underwriting of Securities: The process by which an underwriting syndicate of securities firms, or less frequently, a single security firm, guarantees the sale of an issue of securities by purchasing it at a stated price from the issuing enterprise for resale to public customers at a slightly higher price.

Unit: Often a derivative security is combined with a conventional security at the time of initial issue to create a unit. This unit structure can be broken up and the derivative and conventional components traded separately.

Value Date: The date on which parties to a financial instrument calculate and exchange payments to settle their respective obligations.

Value of a Basis Point (PV 01 or PVBP): A measure of a bond's price/yield relationship that specifies the dollar value of a basis point change in yield. Also called value of an "01," and abbreviated PV 01 or DV 01. *Also called Dollar Value of a Basis Point (DV 01), Price Value of a Basis Point (PV 01 or PVBP).*

Variable Cumulative Preferred Stock: A floating-rate preferred with an issuer option to select between a Dutch auction reset and a remarketing reset arrangement at the end of each dividend period.

Variable Redemption Bonds: Bonds with both fixed and variable components of principal redemption. The variable portion is linked to an index or rate. Examples include "heaven and hell" and other currency-linked bonds.

Variance: The mean of the squared deviations of each observation from the mean. The square of the standard deviation.

Volatility Point (Vol Point): 1% of annualized standard deviation. Over-the-counter options often trade on the basis of bid/asked spreads expressed in vol points.

Volatility Risk: The risk that the holder or seller of a standard or embedded option incurs if actual volatility or the market's expectations for future volatility change. Other things equal, an optionholder benefits from an increase in actual or expected volatility and suffers from increased price or rate stability. An option seller is hurt by an increase in volatility and helped by a decrease. Some compound, barrier, and average rate options can provide protection from various types of volatility risk.

Volatility Skewness: (1) A measure of the relationship between the implied volatility of options and the strike prices of those options. According to the Black–Scholes option pricing model and its underlying assumption of costless trading, implied volatility should not vary with the strike prices of options. Empirically, however, implied volatilities of options on stocks and stock indexes tend to increase on out-of-the-money options. (2) The tendency of the volatility of an underlying stock or stock index to be inversely correlated with stock price or the tendency of interest rate volatilities to be inversely correlated with the level of interest rates.

Volume: The number of shares, bonds, notes, or contracts traded in a market. Along with units outstanding and open interest, volume is one of the few measures of the liquidity in a market available to an outside observer.

Warrant: An option to purchase or sell the underlying at a given price and time or at a series of prices and times outlined in the warrant agreement. A warrant differs from a put or call option in that it is ordinarily issued for a period in excess of one year. Warrants are issued alone or in connection with the sale of other securities, as part of a merger or recapitalization agreement, and, occasionally, to facilitate divestiture of the securities of another corporation. Ordinarily, exercise of a common stock warrant sold by the issuer of the underlying increases the number of shares of stock outstanding, while a call or a covered warrant is an option on shares already outstanding. Index warrants and many put warrants are cash settled. *Also called Stock Purchase Warrant, Term Stock Right (TSR)*.

Warrant Dilution: Covered warrants and exchange-traded or OTC options do not result in dilution of the interest of common shareholders because the shares underlying these instruments are outstanding shares: no new shares need be issued upon their exercise or settlement. Warrants issued by a corporation as part of its capitalization can dilute the interest of prior shareholders. The best way to estimate this dilution is to divide the market value of the warrants by the market value of the corporation's common shareholders' equity plus the market value of other convertible securities— in the simplest case, the market value of the warrants. The resulting fraction expressed as a percent will give a good measure of the dilution attributable to the warrants. If a warrant dilutes the interest of the shareholders, the value of the warrant itself is reduced.

Weekend Effect: (1) A tendency for implied volatilities (calculated on the basis of calendar days to option expiration) to rise from Friday to Monday. (2) A mild tendency for the US stock market to rise slightly on Friday and to decline on Monday.

Widgets: (1) A generic name for hypothetical products used in an example, often for teaching purposes. (2) Synthetic basket instruments issued by an investment bank and usually listed on an exchange to permit one or more investors to avoid dividend with-holding taxes or foreign ownership restrictions.

Wild Card: Provisions in several futures contracts whereby the investor who is short the contract can deliver any of a number of securities or commodities in settlement of the delivery obligation, can choose the instruments to be delivered at the last moment, and/or can deliver anytime within a prescribed period. The option to change the item delivered or the time of delivery enhances the flexibility of the short's position, and occasionally exacerbates price volatility in the underlying near expiration.

Yield: A percentage rate of return.

Yield Curve: A graph illustrating the level of interest rates as a function of time— obtained by plotting the yields of all default-free coupon bonds in a given currency against maturity, or, occasionally, duration. Yields on debt instruments of lower quality are expressed in terms of a spread relative to the default-free yield curve. In the diagrams, a normal yield curve on the top features short-term yields lower than long-term yields. The inverted yield curve on the bottom illustrates short-term rates in excess of long-term rates and characterizes periods when the central bank is attempting to restrict growth in the money supply and, hence, the level of economic activity. Forward curves derived from each yield curve are also illustrated.

Yield Curve Twist: An interest rate shift characterized by a change in the spread between two interest rates at different maturity points along the yield curve. Yield curve twists can cause problems if an investor or risk manager uses tools that rely on all interest rate changes being characterized by parallel yield curve shifts.

Yield Decrease Warrant: An interest rate warrant that increases in value as long bond yields decline, and, conversely, declines in value when yields rise. Similar to a call on a bond, but the strike and the payment are based on yield changes.

Yield Enhanced Stock (YES): A synthetic PERCS issue.

Yield Enhancement: Any of a variety of strategies used to increase the actual or apparent yield of a debt instrument. Frequently these strategies are based on continuous option selling programs that may increase apparent yields during most periods, but can substantially reduce returns from time to time and in the long run. Occasionally, yield enhancement strategies are based on arbitrage-type transactions, where the probability of return enhancement is quite high during any period the position is in place.

Yield to Maturity: The compound rate of return obtained by holding a bond to maturity under certain assumptions. The yield to maturity calculation assumes that any coupon payments received before maturity can be reinvested at this yield.

Yield to Worst: The yield to maturity under the least desirable bond repayment pattern assuming that market yields are unchanged. If market yields are higher than the coupon, the yield to worst would assume no prepayment. If market yields are below the coupon, yield to worst would assume prepayment at the earliest call date.

Yield Value of a Price Change: The difference in a yield measure that is consistent with a specific price change in a bond or note. The yield value of a price change is the difference in the yields calculated at the two price levels.

Zero-Coupon Convertible Debt: Convertible bonds that are typically puttable to the issuer during the early years of their lives and convertible into the issuer's common stock on terms calculated to provide a return somewhat less than the return on common stock with significantly reduced risk. In the US, the issuer has been able to deduct an implied interest payment even if the instrument is converted and no interest is actually paid.

Zero-Coupon Yield Curve: A graph of the term structure of default-free zero-coupon rates.

Appendix

ConvB CD ROM Installation Guide

ConvB – INSTALLATION GUIDE

- The attached CD ROM is self-installing.
- Insert the *ConvB++ CD* ROM into the disk drive.
- Follow the prompts on the install program, choose the type of system you have, the version of Excel you are using, etc.

Note: This is a sample disk. You can only compute prices of bonds with ten years to maturity, stock volatility of 30% and interest rate volatility of 15% (or 0%).

To Run

To run ConvB, simply start Excel. From Excel perform File... Open... convb\convb.xls. It may be a good idea to setup a special Windows icon for ConvB which would automatically open the file in Excel.

Note:
Excel may ask you to link to other files. At the prompt, please answer with a NO.

Call us with any comments, questions or suggestions.

Super Computer Consulting Corporation

presents

ConvB

User's Manual for the Excel Interface

Introduction

ConvB is a program designed to price and hedge single bonds or portfolios of convertible bonds and/or preferred shares. The program is designed around the Quadranary tree approach developed by Super Computer Consulting Corporation, see "Costing the Converts", *Risk Magazine*, July 1994 and "A Convertible Primer", *AsiaRisk*, April 1996 and "Assessing the Reset", *AsiaRisk*, October 1998.

Handbook of Hybrid Instruments. Edited by Izzy Nelken. © 2000 Super Computer Consulting, Inc. Published 2000 by John Wiley & Sons Ltd.

The program has very many features and can handle bonds with a variety of features. These include:

- Convertible bonds and preferred shares
- Japanese Reset Convertibles
- Credit Guaranteed Instruments
- Return on Capital calculations
- Call options (hard calls and soft calls) and put options
- Any type of mandatory convertible, including: PEPs, DECs, ELKs, PERCs and Collars
- "Double DECs"
- Warrants (European and American style exercise)
- Call and Put options
- A quick one factor model or a full blown multifactor model
- Conversion into stocks, shares or a combination of both
- Dual currency convertibles
- The dilution effect
- Accounting for stock borrowing costs (for hedgers)
- Use of a blended discounting rate: a combination of the risky and risk free rate
- Step up, step down or changing coupon
- If shares fall to really low levels, corporate spreads usually rise. The program handles this phenomenon
- Accrued interest is computed according to a variety of different conventions
- In addition to computing the price of an instrument, the program also computes the risk parameters: Delta, Gamma, both Vegas, duration and convexity as well as functional (key-rate) duration and convexity
- Simple easy hooks and connections to real time date feeds and to databases (e.g. Reuter's Real Time feed, Value Line's convertible database, IDC on-line database)
- Pricing of Convertible bonds with a credit guarantee (e.g. CrEDITS)

Single Bond Screen

You can double click a bond at any time and bring up the "Single Bond Screen". Alternatively, place the cursor on the bond of interest and activate the single bond screen. This screen allows the user to concentrate on a specific bond. All the relevant information for that specific bond can be found and modified on this single screen.

Convertible Wizard

This can be opened by choosing ConvB . . . Convertible Wizard from the pull down menu. The wizard allows the users to:

- Add bonds and delete bonds—under the portfolio function
- The user can also add a new bond which looks like an existing bond
- All the data required for a bond can be entered through the spreadsheets (as described below) or through the convertible wizard.

Many users find the convertible wizard extremely easy to use. Try it!

There are special wizards to facilitate manipulation of the various yield curves.

Example

The Excel spreadsheet opens with the file CONVB.XLS. In this file, there are several sample bonds. We will focus on the two called Example1 and Example2. In the next few pages, we will show how the data for these bonds was entered. The spreadsheet also contains some other bonds, denominated in several currencies. Note that the prices computed on the sheet may be different from the prices which you will get, as the settlement dates are different.

Computation

In the Excel spreadsheet top menu you will find a pull down item called "ConvB".

- *Compute Price*, computes the value of the current bond (the one which is indicated by the cursor). The item *Compute All Prices* will compute the value of selected bonds.
- *Implied Volatility* will find the volatility of the share implied by the price of the convertible.
- *Compute Matrix* will create a five by five matrix of convertible bond prices given a range of values for the underlying stock and a range of values for the volatility of the equity.

The manual will go into these options in more detail.

Settlement Date

This is given in the third row. This is where the settlement date, or the date at which the portfolio should be evaluated appears. Note that the formula computes $T + 3$, adjusted for holidays.

> Settlement Date: 15-Feb-1998

Bond Identifier

This could be a ticker symbol or the CUSIP of the security. Alternatively, it could be the full name of the issuer.

> Bond
> Identifier
Example1
Example2

Code Name

This field is used in conjunction with the Value Line database. When the user inputs the code into the cell, the machine will retrieve all information regarding that bond.

> Code
> Name

CUSIP Number and Code

These fields, used with the Value Line database, are used to enter the CUSIP number and code relating to the security.

CUSIP   CUSIP
Number   Code

Face Value

In this cell, enter the Face Value of the instrument. For most convertible bonds, this should be $1000. However, for preferred shares or other structures, the face value may be different.

Face Value	
$	1000.00
$	1000.00

Redemption Value

In this cell, enter the Redemption Value of the instrument. For most convertible bonds, this should be equal to the face value. However, there are some "premium redemption structures" which redeem at above face value.

Redemption Value	
$	1000.00
$	1000.00

Instrument Type

In this cell, enter a 1 for convertible bonds, 2 for preferred shares, 3 for mandatory convertibles and 4 for warrants.

Instrument Type
1
1

Perpetual

In this cell, enter a "Y" if this is a perpetual bond which never returns its principal. Otherwise, enter an "N". Most convertible bonds are not perpetual instruments while some preferred shares are perpetual.

Reset Convertible

In this cell, enter a 1,2,3 or 4 if this is a convertible bond whose conversion features may reset (e.g. a Japanese reset convertible). A 0 indicates that this is not a reset bond.

Maturity Date

In this field, enter the final maturity of the bond.

Maturity Date
15-Feb-2008
15-Feb-2008

Coupon Payment Frequency

This is a code for how often the coupon is paid out.
A – annual (for some European convertibles)
S – Semi-annual (for most US convertibles)
Q – Quarterly
M – Monthly
W – Weekly

Frequency (A/S/Q/M/W)
S
S

Coupon payment dates are determined by the maturity date and the payment frequency. We assume that a coupon is paid out on the maturity date and on consecutive periods before that. The principal is paid out on the maturity date. On some preferred shares, the principal is not paid out on the same date as the last coupon. Payment of the principal is delayed until a short time after the last coupon is paid. There is a special field: "Delay for principal" to account for that fact.

Stock Price

The share price of the underlying stock. Note that this field (as well as other fields) could be tied in to a real-time feed.

Stock Price
$ 100.00
$ 21.25

Stock Borrow Rate

The user enters the stock borrow rate of the underlying shares in this field. It is entered as a percentage. For example, a rate of 3% would simply be entered as 3.00. If you are unsure, simply enter a zero. The stock borrow rate is the rate charged to hedgers wishing to hedge their exposure to the convertible by shorting the shares. Higher stock borrow rates would reduce the value of the convertible since it is harder to hedge it.

This rate is entered as a semi-annual rate.

Stock Borrow Rate (hedgers)
0.00
0.00

Bond Borrow Rate

The user enters the bond borrow rate of the convertible bond in this field. It is entered as a percentage. For example, a rate of 5% would simply be entered as 5.00. If you are unsure, simply enter a zero. The bond borrow rate is the rate charged to hedgers wishing to short the convertible bond. Higher bond borrow rates would increase the value of the convertible since it is harder to short it.

This rate is entered as a semi-annual rate.

Bond Borrow
Rate(hedgers)
       0.00
       0.00

Volatility of Stocks

The user enters the volatility of the underlying shares in this field. It is entered as a percentage. For example, a volatility of 30% would simply be entered as 30.00.

     Stocks
    Volatility
      30.00
      30.00

In this example, both convertibles have underlying stocks whose volatility is 30%.

Rate Volatility

In this cell, the user types in the volatility of interest rates. This is the volatility of the corporate rates which the issuer pays. A volatility of 20% is input as 20.00. A rate volatility of zero causes the machine to operate with a one factor model. This reduces the run time required by the algorithm.

     Rates
    Volatility
      15.00
        0

In the first example, the volatility level is set to 15%. In the second example, the interest rate volatility is zero. This indicates to the algorithm that we are working in a one factor mode. The one factor computation is much faster but slightly less accurate.

S/R Correlation

In this cell, the user types in the correlation coefficient between interest rates and the stock price. For most stocks, this correlation is somewhat negative as companies tend to do well in low interest rate environments. Of course, this parameter is only used in the two factor model.

S/R Correlation

       –
     (0.20)

The correlation is a number between −1 and 1.
A negative correlation indicates that when rates go up, the stock tends to decline and vice versa.
A positive correlation means that rates and the stock price move up and down in tandem.
A correlation of zero means that movements in the stock are not tied to interest rates.

Dual Currency

A dual currency bond is a bond which is denominated in one currency (the domestic currency) whose underlying stock is denominated in a different currency (the foreign currency). For example, the Bangkok Land 4.50% of 12/97 are denominated in Swiss Francs but the underlying shares are denominated in Bangkok Baht.

In this cell is a switch that should be switched to "Y" or "N" for "Yes" or "No".

If the bond is dual currency, the user should enter a "Y", otherwise an "N".

For dual currency bonds, we assume that the bond, its coupons, call and put features are all denominated in the domestic currency. The share and its dividends are denominated in the foreign currency.

Dual Currency?
(Y/N)
Y
N

Domestic Yield Curve

This is the name of the domestic yield curve which is to be found under the "Yields" sheet.

Domestic
Yield Curve
DOM1
DOM2

Our first example uses a curve called "DOM1" and the second example uses a curve called "DOM2". For all practical purposes, we can name these curves after the credit ratings which they refer to (e.g. "FINAA" could refer to AA rated financials).

Foreign Yield Curve

This field is only used in the case of dual currency bonds. In other cases it could have a dummy argument. It refers to the foreign currency yield curve shown under the sheet "Foreign".

Foreign
Yield Curve
FOR1
FOR1

In this cases, both foreign curves refer to FOR1, however, only the first bond is of dual currency. The foreign curve is ignored in the case of the second bond.

In cases of a bond which is not dual currency, enter FOR1 in this cell. The foreign interest rate curve will be ignored.

Compute Investment Premium?

If you want the program to compute investment premium, enter a "Y". Otherwise, enter an "N".

Compute Inv.
Premium (Y/N)
N
N

Accrued Interest on Calls

When bonds are called, do they pay the accrued interest on top of the call price?

If the answer is "Yes", type a "Y". Otherwise, type an "N".

Calls Acc.
Interest (Y/N)
N
N

Accrued Interest on Puts

When a bond is put back to the issuer, do they also have to pay the accrued interest?

Puts Acc.
Interest (Y/N)
N
N

Most bonds do not pay accrued interest when the holder puts them back to the issuer.

Accrued Interest Type

In this field, the user indicates the type of accrued interest.

1 – actual / actual
2 – actual / 360
3 – actual / 365
4 – 30/360
5 – 30/365

Acc. Interest
Type
1
1

Credit Guarantee

In the emerging markets, many bonds are issued with a "credit guarantee". For example, the "Credit Enhanced Debt Indexed to Stock" (CrEDITS) structures which were issued by the Indian Petrochemical Corporation (IPCL) and the Taiwanese technology company (GVC) among others.

If a guarantee exists, the user should enter the name of the guarantor in this cell. Otherwise, enter "none" or simply leave the cell blank.

Credit
Guarantee
none
BANK1

Time Step

This parameter determines the distance (in time measured in years) between successive levels of the tree. Therefore, it controls the speed and accuracy of the algorithm. When the time step is small, the pricing algorithm is more precise but it requires more resources (memory and CPU time). With large, coarse time steps the algorithm slightly loses in accuracy but gains much in speed. We recommend that the choice of time step be governed by the final maturity of the bond.

Final Maturity	Time Step
More than 30 years	0.5 years
15–30 years	0.25 years
5–15 years	0.125 years
Less than 5 years	0.0625 years

The idea is to have a tree which is rich enough in nodes to catch the various possible states of the world with reasonably accurate probabilities.

Note that for a one factor model (when interest rate volatility is set to zero), we can use much smaller time steps.

Time Step
0.125
1

In our example, we used 0.125 years for the first bond (as we are using a one factor model) and 1 year for the second bond (as we are using a two factor model).

Equity Participation

This input controls the output of the equity participation table shown on the sheet "Eq Partic".

Equity Participation
5
0

If the parameter is non-zero, the program will compute a result in the "Eq Partic" sheet that looks like this:

	Example1	
Stock price	Bond price	Participation %-age
$32.50	$121.4559	25.4
$35.00	$122.4907	27.0
$37.50	$123.7695	28.6
$40.00	$125.3888	29.7
$42.50	$127.0783	31.1
$45.00	$129.107	31.4
$47.50	$131.1834	31.7
$50.00	$133.2981	0.0
$52.50	$135.6642	35.5
$55.00	$138.1505	36.4
$57.50	$140.4907	36.0
$60.00	$142.9591	36.2
$62.50	$145.6587	37.1
$65.00	$148.2344	37.4
$67.50	$150.9643	37.9

The machine moves the stock price by increments of 5%. For each stock price, the machine prints the corresponding bond price (the "dirty price"). The output also includes the percentage participation in the move. For example, when the stock price is $50, the bond price is $133.2981 and when the stock price is $55, the bond price is $138.1505. This is a difference of 3.64%.

Thus when the stock price changed by 10%, the bond price moved by 3.64%. We say that the bond participated in 36.4% of the stock price move.

Percentage Change for Delta

The program automatically calculates not only the price of the bond but also its sensitivity to price movements in the underlying stock. It does this by moving the price of the stock by a certain increment, re-running the algorithm and re-computing the result. The increment by which the stock price moves is computed as a percentage of the current share price.

For example, if the stock price is $20 and the percentage is 10, the increment is determined as 10%*$20=$2.

The program would compute the bond price when the share is priced at $20 and this will be the price which will be displayed. The program also computes the bond price when the share is priced at 18$ and also at $22. These two numbers are used to compute Delta and Gamma, see below.

Delta % Change
5
5

In most cases, a 5% figure is reasonable. However, this could be increased for highly volatile stocks and decreased for low volatility shares.

A zero in this field indicates to the program to compute an "Approximate Delta" by referring directly to nodes within the tree.

There are two methods to compute Delta and Gamma.

a) A numerical method in which we move the initial stock price and re-compute the price of the convertible.
b) By referring directly to adjacent nodes within the tree. We examine the computed price at two adjacent nodes and convert that difference to Delta.

The second method requires less time (since the nodes are already computed). The first method is more flexible as it gives the user control over the size of the movement of the underlying share.

Vega Change

This is used to compute the "vega"—the sensitivity to the volatility. Vega1 is the sensitivity to the volatility of the share price and vega2 is the sensitivity to the volatility of the interest rates.

If these are set to zero, the corresponding vega is not computed.

Vega1 Change	Vega2 Change
1	0
1	0

Additional Inputs

The remaining columns in the "main" sheet are used to display the output of the algorithm. Before describing them, we continue to describe the additional inputs which are placed in the succeeding sheets.

Coupon Schedule

The user needs to input the coupon rates. This should be entered in the sheet marked "Coupons". For normal bonds, this would be a single number. However, some bonds have step-up, step-down or a varying coupon. For these, a coupon schedule is required. In our example, the first bond is a step-up bond. The coupon level starts out at 7% but after two years it increases to 8%. The second bond has a coupon of 5% until maturity.

	Example1		Example2	
term	rate (%)	term	rate (%)	
1-Jan-1995	7.0	1-Jan-1995	5.0	
1-Jan-1997	8.0			

Bond "Example1" has a coupon of 7% beginning on 1-Jan-95. This lasts for two years. Beginning on 1-Jan-97, the coupon changes to 8%. Bond "Example2" has a coupon of 5% beginning on 1-Jan-95. The coupon is unchanged until expiry.

The date entered for "term" is the date at which the coupon is set at that level. The actual coupon payment dates are determined by the maturity date. We assume that a coupon is paid at maturity and at predefined time intervals before maturity. For example, if the coupon payment frequency is "S" for semi-annual and the bond matures on 31-Dec-2010, coupons will be paid out on 31-Jun-**** and 31-Dec-**** until the maturity date.

Therefore, on normal bonds the "term" of the first coupon should be set well in the past (a long time before the settlement date). If the bond has an irregular first coupon (e.g. short first coupon) then enter a first coupon date of zero and then enter the date at which interest starts to accrue as the second coupon.

For example:

Settlement is 28-Jan-1998

Coupon rate 5%

The bond was announced on 25-Nov-97

Coupons are paid out on 15-Feb-**** and 15-Aug-****

Bond matures on 15-Feb-2015

The coupon field would appear as:

1-Jan-96   0
25-Nov-97   5

This tells the machine to start accruing the 5% coupon only as of 25-Nov-97.

Coupon payment dates are determined by the maturity date and the payment frequency. We assume that a coupon is paid out on the maturity date and on consecutive periods before that. The principal is paid out on the maturity date. On some preferred shares, the principal is not paid out on the same date as the last coupon. Payment of the principal is delayed until a short time after the last coupon is paid. There is a special field: "Delay for principal" to account for that fact. Enter the number of days by which principal payment is delayed until after the last coupon date.

Call Schedule

The next item is the call schedule for the bond. There are two types of calls: "protected calls" and "unprotected calls". A protected call allows the issuer to call the bond only if the underlying stock has risen to above a pre-determined level. An unprotected call allows for an unrestricted call option. If the issuer utilizes their call option, the investor may convert the bond into common shares. This is known as "forced conversion". Of course, the program takes this into account.

	Example1				Example2	
% over:	10			% over:		
	days out of				20	Days out of 30
Term	Price	Min.stock	Term		Price	Min.stock
1-Jan-2000	$100.00	$130.00	1-Oct-2003		$100.00	$32.00
1-Jan-2001	$100.00	$125.00				

Bond "Example1" is callable at par beginning in 1-Jan-2000 but only if the stock price is above $130. This call option lasts until 1-Jan-2001. Beginning on 1-Jan-2001, the bond is callable at par but only if the stock price has climbed above $125.

For protected calls, there is an option of requiring the stock to be above the call trigger "X days out of Y" before the call is announced. Typically, the company may call if the stock price is above the trigger 20 days out of 30.

The bond labeled "Example2" is callable at par beginning in 1-Jan-2000 but only if the share price is greater than $32. If we were to change this to an unprotected call, our input section would be:

	Example2	
Term	Price	Min.stock
1-Jan-2000	$100.00	

That is, the bond is callable at par without regard to the share price.

Another parameter is the "% over".

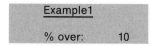

Example1	
% over:	10

There are two cases where a company may call its bonds.

1) To redeem them for cash (e.g. if interest rates are low).
2) To force conversion.

The company will force conversion whenever the conversion value of the bonds is just over the call price. However, the company issues the call notice and then the bond holders respond. If the stock price falls in that interval of time, the bond holders will prefer cash. So the company does not call (in order to force conversion) unless the share price is such that the conversion value is around 10% over the call price. For highly volatile companies, this percentage may rise to 20%.

However, if interest rates are lower and the company can refinance at a lower price, they will call without regard to the "% over".

Put Schedule

The bond's put schedule is entered in this sheet. If a bond is puttable, enter the put date and the put price.

Example1		Example2	
Term	Price	Term	Price
1-Jan-1998	$120.00		
1-Jan-2000	$100.00		

Bond "Example1" is puttable on 1-Jan-1998 for $120.00 and on 1-Jan-2000 for $100.00. The bond "Example2" is not puttable at all.

Conversion Schedule

Note: there are special conversion structures for Mandatory convertibles, Warrants and also for reset convertibles. See below.

Bonds may be converted into:

1. Shares
2. Cash
3. A combination of shares and cash.

The user should enter the date at which the conversion option begins and then the number of shares and cash amount to which the bond may be converted. If the bond is convertible to shares only, the cash amount should be entered as zero.

The conversion number is always entered per the face value amount.

Example1			Example2		
Term	Shares	Cash	Term	Shares	Cash
1-Jan-1995	8	$0.00	1-Jan-1995	40	$0.00
23-Oct-1999	10	$50.00			

The bond Example1 is convertible to eight shares any time until 23-Oct-1999. After that, it is convertible to a combination of ten shares and $50.00 in cash beginning on 23-Oct-99. The bond Example2, is convertible to 40 shares (and no cash). The holder has the right to convert throughout the life of the bond. Note that these are conversion numbers per the face value amount. That is, in Example2, $1000 of bonds are convertible to 40 shares.

Dividends

This is the place to enter the dividend stream enjoyed by the share holder. Dividends may be fixed or there might be precise projections for them.

	Example1			Example2	
Term	Cash	Rate (%)	Term	Cash	Rate (%)
23-Dec-1997	$2.00		1-Jan-1995		2.00
23-Dec-1998	$2.00				
23-Dec-1999	$2.00				
23-Dec-2000	$2.00				
23-Dec-2001	$2.00				
23-Dec-2002	$2.00				
23-Dec-2003	$2.00				

The stock which underlies bond "Example1" will pay a $2.00 dividend every year on 23-Dec. The dividend will last until 23-Dec-2003. Thereafter, there will be no dividends. The stock which is the underlying to bond "Example2" will pay a dividend rate of 2% for its entire life. Dividends are assumed to be paid out continuously and they are quoted as a percentage of the underlying share price.

Domestic Yield Curve

Next, the program needs the domestic yield curve. This is entered as the risk free par bond curve and a corporate spread component. One source of par bond yield curves is the Bloomberg system.

So for each benchmark Government bond, enter its maturity date, the equivalent par bond yield and the corporate spread for this maturity. Note that you must give each yield curve a specific name. This could be USAA for United States AA rated bonds. This name is used in the Main sheet when the bond is being described. Note that many bonds can refer to the same yield curve.

		DOM1				DOM2	
		perturb what? (Y/S) =				perturb what? (Y/S) =	
	perturb	0.0			perturb	0.0	bps
	amount =				amount =		
Term	Yield	Spread	Term	Yield	Spread	pert?	
15-Feb-1998	0.0529	50.0	2-Aug-1997	0.05	0.0		
15-May-1998	0.0538	50.0	1-Nov-1997	0.05	0.0		
15-Nov-1998	0.0546	55.0	1-Feb-1998	0.05	0.0		
15-Nov-1999	0.0571	60.0	1-May-1998	0.05	0.0		
15-Nov-2000	0.0573	70.0	1-Aug-1998	0.05	0.0		
15-Nov-2002	0.0579	80.0	1-Jun-1999	0.05	0.0		
15-Nov-2007	0.0584	90.0	1-Jan-2002	0.05	0.0		
15-Nov-2027	0.0607	100.0	1-Jan-2005	0.05	0.0		
			1-Jan-2015	0.0506	0.0		
			1-Jan-2025	0.0506	0.0		

The yield curve DOM1 is composed of eight benchmark bonds. For example, the benchmark bond which matures on 15-Nov-2000 has a yield of 5.730%%. The corporate spreads are also entered. This means that a corresponding corporate bond which matures on 15-Nov-2000 would yield 6.430%, at a seventy basis points spread to the Treasury.

The yield curve DOM2, is composed of a straight line discounting at 5%. There is no corporate spread.

Note that all yields are entered as semi-annual as per US convention.

Foreign Yield Curve

This input is only required when pricing dual currency bonds. We distinguish between two currencies:

- The Domestic currency which pertains to the bond, its coupon and any embedded features such as call, put or conversion options.
- The Foreign currency which pertains to the share price and any dividends received from the stock.

The user needs to enter the spot exchange rate between the two currencies. Our convention is easy to remember:

one unit of domestic currency = X units of foreign currency.

The curve itself is entered in a format similar to that of the domestic yield curve. That is, the user should enter the foreign par bond yield curve. In this case, the program does not need the corporate spreads and only the yield curve should be entered.

1 domestic unit = x foreign units

FOR1

x = 2.00

Term	Yield
1-Mar-1995	4.676%
1-Jun-1995	5.114%
1-Jan-1996	6.192%
1-Jan-1997	6.540%
1-Jan-2000	6.908%
1-Jan-2006	7.261%

Note that the benchmark par bond matures on 1-Jan-2000 and yields 6.908% (semi-annual yields).

Guarantee

There are structures in which a bank guarantees the performance of a convertible bond. The bank essentially issues an irrevocable letter of credit that guarantees the timely payments of the coupons as well as the principal. Most market participants have modeled this as a bond that has been issued by the bank (e.g. an exchangeable bond). However, this is incorrect.

Consider the two cases:

A) Bank B issues a convertible bond which is convertible to shares of Company C.
B) Company C issues a convertible bond that is guaranteed by Bank B.

To see the difference between the two structures, consider the case in which Bank B defaults and Company C does not. In the first case, the holder of the bond will lose their coupons and principal. In the second case, the holder of the bond will continue to receive them.

To properly model the second case, we need to consider the "joint default" scenario. What is the probability of Company C defaulting *and* Bank B defaulting as well?

Even in the case of joint default, the holder of the guaranteed bond is better off than the holder of a non guaranteed bond. The holder of the guaranteed bond has a recovery rate of:

$$R_B + (1 - R_B) * R_G$$

Here R_B is the recovery rate of the bond and R_G is the recovery rate of the guarantor.

For example, if R_B is 60 cents on the dollar and R_G is 70 cents on the dollar. Then in the case of joint default, the holder of the bond will collect 60 cents from the bond issuer. Then, they still have a claim on 40 remaining cents from the guarantor. Since the guarantor has defaulted and its recovery rate is 70, the bond holder will be able to collect 70% of their claim. This amounts to 70%*40 = 28.

In the case of joint default, the holder of the bond can expect to recoup 60 + 28 = 88.

name of guarantor	**BANK1**
recovery rate of bond (0–100)	50
recovery rate of guarantor (0–100)	80
default correlation (L,M or H) L	
credit spd of guarantor (in bps)	40

The following input parameters are needed:

- Recovery rate of bond—In case of default, the recovery rate of the bond.
- Recovery rate of the guarantor. These are entered as numbers between 0 and 100. A recovery rate of 0 means that in case of default, the holder of the bond is not expected to receive anything. Conversely, a recovery rate of 100 means that in case of default, the holders of the bond will receive all payments which are due to them.
- The model also accepts a default correlation. Imputing a numerical value for default correlation is very difficult. However, it is simple to estimate if the default correlation is High (H), Medium (M) or Low (L). For example, if a Japanese bank guarantees a company which belongs to the same consortium their default correlation is high. On the other hand, if a US bank guarantees the same company, then their default correlation is low.
- Finally, the model requires the credit spread of a one year obligation by the guarantor.

Dilution Effect

For some convertibles, when the holders choose to convert, the issuer simply issues more stock and gives it to the bond holders (in exchange for their bonds—of course). This causes an increase in the number of shares outstanding and a corresponding drop in the price per share.

If a bond exhibits the dilution effect, the algorithm expects to know the number of bonds outstanding as well as the number of shares outstanding. In addition, not all retail clients exhibit "rational" behavior. That is, even when it makes economical sense to convert, some holders may choose not to (e.g. for taxation reasons). So the user should also input the percentage of holders that would convert when it makes economical sense to do so.

Bond Identifier	Dilutions? (Y/N)	# Outstanding Shares	Amount (in $) of Outstanding Bonds	Conversion Percentage (%)
Example1	Y	1 000 000	10 000 000	50
Example2	N	1 000 000	10 000 000	50

The bond Example1 exhibits the dilution effect. So the corresponding column is marked "Y". There are 1 000 000 shares outstanding and $10 000 000 dollars (face value) worth of bonds which are outstanding. The conversion ratio is 50%. That is, when it makes sense to do so, 50% of the bond holders will convert. When $5 000 000 face value of bonds are converted, the issuer would issue more shares. This would increase the amount of outstanding stock to 10 000 000 plus these bonds times their conversion ratio.

The new number of shares is given as:
N + M*number*conv %

N—old number of outstanding shares
M—number of bonds = face value of outstanding bonds / face value of one bond
number—conversion number
conv %—conversion percentage

The bond Example2 does not exhibit the dilution effect.

Stock Price Drops—Standard Model

If share prices drop to very low levels, bond investors may fear increased risk of bankruptcy. Therefore, corporate spreads would rise. This, of course, would have an adverse effect on the price of the bond. The program has a standard model which deals with this phenomena. To activate it, the user should place an "S" (for standard model) and the recovery value of the bond (a number between 0 and 100).

Example1	Example2
(S = standard)	(Recovery)
if stock	spread
falls below	rises by
S	50

For example, a seven year bond whose recovery value is 40 would exhibit a spread stock relationship as illustrated in the graph. Currently, the stock price is $30 and the spread is 50 basis points. As the stock price falls, the spread increases.

Stock Price Drops—Manual Mode

Another alternative is for the user to enter the stock spread relationship manually. The information is presented as follows:

If share prices dip below xxx, spreads increase by yyy basis points.

Of course, the more share prices drop, the higher the spread increase.

	Example1		Example2	
if stock	spread			
falls below	rises by			
19	400		5	10
15	800			

For bond Example1, if share prices drop below $19, spreads would rise by 400 basis points. Further, if the share price dips below $15, spreads would increase to a level 800 bps above where they originally were. The original spreads were given in sheet "Yields".

Bond Example2 suffers much less from this effect. If share prices dip below $5, spreads only rise by 10 basis points. Given that the spot price of the share is currently $20, there is only a low probability of a drop to below $5. Even if such a drop were to occur, spreads would rise by only 10 bps.

Mandatory Convertibles

The software handles all the types of mandatory convertible instruments, including:

- DECS – Debt Exchangeable to Common Stock

DECS are also known as:
  - PEPS: Preferred Equity Participation Securities
  - PRIDES: Preferred Redeemable Increased Dividend Equity Securities
  - MARCS: Mandatory Adjustable Redeemable Convertible Securities
  - SAILS: Stock Appreciation Income Linked Securities
  - TAPS: Threshold Appreciation Price Securities
  - TIMES: Trust Issued Mandatory Exchange Securities
  - TRACES: Trust Automatic Common Exchange Securities

- PERCS – Preferred Equity Redemption Cumulative Stock

PERCS are also known as:
  - MCPDPS: Mandatory Conversion Premium Dividend Preferred Stock
  - TARGETS: TARgeted Growth Enhanced Term Securities
  - YES: Yield Enhanced Stock
  - ELKS: Equity Linked Debt Security
  - PERQS: Performance Equity-linked Redemption Quarterly-pay Securities
  - YEELDS: Yield Enhanced Equity Linked Debt Securities
  - And in Europe: Reverse Convertibles

- Collar

- Double DECS and other structures

These instruments are mandatory convertibles. If the holder of the note holds it to maturity, he must convert at the pre-defined ratios. PEPs, DECs and PERCs may be callable by the issuer prior to maturity. If the issuer calls, the holder may convert as defined by the formulas below.

PEPS

The payoff for the PEPS is defined:

a S	if S < L	—the payoff is tied to the level of the share
C	if L <= S <= H	—constant payoff
b S	if S > H	—the payoff is tied to the level of the share

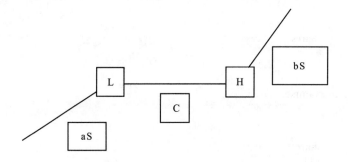

Where the following relationship holds:
C=a L=b H

The following is the conversion data for a PEPS.

PEPS

term	shares	cash
1-Jan-1996	0.80	
1-Jan-1996		$40
1-Jan-1996	0.50	

If the share closes below $50, the PEPS is convertible to 0.8 shares. If it closes above $50 and below $80, the holder will receive $40 in cash (or in shares) and if the share closes above $80, the holder of the PEPS will receive 0.5 shares.

DECS

The payoff for the DECS is defined:

S	if S < L	—the payoff is tied to the level of the share
C	if L <= S <= H	—constant payoff
b S	if S > H	—the payoff is tied to the level of the share

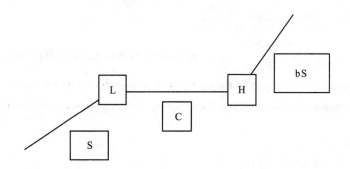

Where the following relationship holds:
C = L = b H

The instrument type for DECS is 3.

The following is the conversion data for a DECS:

DECS

term	shares	cash
1-Jan-1996	a	L
1-Jan-1996	b	H

Let us look at an example:

DECS

term	shares	cash
1-Jan-1996	1.00	
1-Jan-1996		$100
1-Jan-1996	0.8333	

If the share closes below $100, the DECS is convertible to one share. If it closes above $100 and below $120, the holder will receive $100 in cash (or in shares) and if the share closes above $120, the holder of the DECS will receive 0.8333 shares.

Conversion Rights of DECS Holders

There are three types of conversion rights which may be granted to the holder of a DECS.

1) No early conversion

To signal this to the machine, enter a conversion structure which looks like:

DECS
term	shares	cash
1-Mar-2010	1.00	
1-Mar-2010		$100
1-Mar-2010	0.8333	

This instrument can not be converted by the holder prior to maturity.

2) Early conversion at the lowest ratio

To signal this to the machine, enter a conversion structure which looks like:

DECS
term	shares	cash	
1-Mar-2010	1.00		
1-Mar-2010		$100	
1-Jan-1996	0.8333		← note the early date on the final conversion

This instrument can be converted by the holder prior to maturity for 0.8333 shares.

3) Other instruments allow the holder to convert early according to the conversion schedule of the DECS.

DECS
term	shares	cash	
1-Jan-1996	1.00		
1-Jan-1996		$100	
1-Jan-1996	0.8333		← note the early date on all of the conversions

This structure can be converted early by the holder.

Note that the machine does not consider the actual dates on the conversion record. The only important thing is whether a date occurs before the settlement date or after it.

PERCS and ELKS—"Reverse Convertibles"

The payoff for the PERCS is defined:

a S if S < L   —the payoff is tied to the level of the share
C if L <= S   —constant payoff

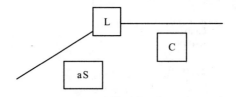

Where the following relationship holds:

C = a L

the PERCS may be called by the issuer prior to maturity but the ELKS may not be called.

The following PERCS is convertible to one share until the share price reaches $100. If the share is over $100, the holder will receive $100.

PERCS
term	shares	cash
1-Jan-1996	1	
1-Jan-1996		$100

Collars

The payoff for the Collar is defined:

C1	if S < L	—constant payoff
a S	if L <= S <= H	—the payoff is tied to the level of the stock
C2	if H < S	—constant payoff

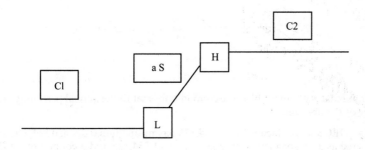

Where the following relationship holds:

C1 = a L
C2 = a H

The collar has the following data structure:

Collar

term	shares	cash
1-Jan-1996		C1
1-Jan-1996	a	
1-Jan-1996		C2

For example, the following collar guarantees the receipt of at least $80 in cash or shares. If the share closes between $80 and $100, the holder will receive one share. If the share closes above $100, the holder of the collar will only receive $100.

Collar

term	shares	cash
1-Jan-1996		$80.00
1-Jan-1996	1.00	
1-Jan-1996		$100.00

Other Mandatory Convertibles (e.g. Double Decs)

With this interface, one can create arbitrarily complex mandatory convertible structures. In this structure, the payoff is as follows:

If S < 100, receive one share
If $100 <= S <$120, receive $100
If $120 <= S <$144, receive 0.8333 shares
If $144 <= S <$150, receive $120
If $150 <= S, receive 0.8 shares

Complex

term	shares	cash
1-Jan-1996	1.00	
1-Jan-1996		$100.00
1-Jan-1996	0.8333	
1-Jan-1996		$120.00
1-Jan-1996	0.80	

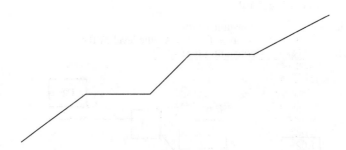

Note that for mandatory convertibles, the coupon rate is set to the annual percentage rate received by the holder of the instrument.

For example, a DECS with a face value of $54.125 paying an annual dividend of 7.875% or $4.262 would be entered as an instrument with a face value of $54.125 and a coupon of 7.875%.

Warrants

Warrants are easily evaluated with Instrument type set to 4. The "conversion" sheet gives the terms of the warrant.

The following warrant allows the holder to receive one share for $100 (so the strike is $100). If the warrant is European, set the "term" to be equal to the expiration date. If the warrant is American, set the term to be the settlement date (or before).

Warrant
term	shares	cash
30-Jan-2000	1.00	−$100.00

Put Options

A put option is also available. You may sell the share for $100.

Warrant
term	shares	cash
30-Jan-2000	−1.00	$100.00

Reset Convertibles

The following example is a reset convertible. The initial conversion price is quoted as 1189 JPY.

On 26-Feb-2000, we examine the stock price. Say it is 1000 JPY.
The new conversion price becomes 1000*1.025 = 1025 JPY.

However, the new conversion price can not fall below the previous conversion price multiplied by 0.80. So the new conversion price can not be below 951.20 JPY. So if the stock price declined to, say, 800, the conversion price would be the maximum of 800*1.025 = 820 and 951.20. The conversion price would hence be set to 951.20.

When the conversion price is reset downward, it makes the bond more expensive. This is done to compensate the bond holders for a reduction in the price of the stock.

The conversion price may also be reset upwards. In our example, this does not happen since the upper limit on the conversion price is set to the previous conversion price multiplied by 1.

	Takase resettable (JPY/ SFR)		
Date	Initial Conversion Price/Stock Price Multiplier	Not Below Previous Conversion Price* Multiplier	Not Above Previous Conversion Price* Multiplier
1-Jan-1996	1189 JPY		
26-Feb-2000	1.025	0.80	1.00
21-Jul-2001	1.025	0.80	1.00

Our bond has a second reset date. Again, the company will examine the share price as of 21-Jul-2001 and reset the conversion price. Note that the new conversion price depends on the conversion price which was set on 26-Feb-2000.

Note: for reset convertibles, we use an "Initial conversion price". For non-reset convertibles we use a conversion ratio.

Assume that 1SFR=78.09 JPY. Then, the conversion ratio is given by
50 000*78.09 / 1189 = 3283.52

An equivalent non-convertible bond is also shown.

Types of Reset Convertibles

There are four types of reset convertibles. On a reset date, the conversion price can reset up or down. It resets based on the current stock price. However, as explained above, the new reset price can not deviate from a floor and a ceiling. The floor is the minimal new reset price. The ceiling is the maximal new reset price. The floor and the ceiling may be determined either by the initial conversion price or by the previous, this is the last current conversion price which is in effect.

Reset Type Code	Minimal New Conversion Price	Maximal New Conversion Price
1	Initial	Initial
2	Previous	Previous
3	Initial	Previous
4	Previous	Initial

For example, most Japanese bank convertibles can reset down based on the Initial conversion price. Thus, no matter what, the conversion price can never decline below 700 JPY (say). On the other hand, once the conversion price has adjusted down, it can not adjust up. So the maximal new conversion price is based on the previous conversion price. For example, if on the first reset date, the conversion price has been reset to 00 JPY, then there can be no more readjustments of the conversion price.

We model this with a reset type of 3. The conversion price resets down based on the initial price but resets up based on the previous conversion price.

Output (Computed Results)

In this section, we review the output of the program.

Full Price

This gives the full (dirty) price of the bond, including accrued interest.

Full Price
$115.2478
$95.8923

Market Price

This cell gives the clean price, not including accrued interest. In case of preferred shares, this is calibrated to the face value of the share. For example, if a preferred share has a face value of $50, the market price will be adjusted to reflect that face value.

Market Price
$115.2036139
$95.86466622

Conversion Value

This is the conversion value of the bond. How much money we could make if we were to convert the bond right now into shares. The conversion value is given by:

(Conversion number * current stock price + conversion cash) / Face value * 100

Conversion Value
$80.0000
$42.5000

Bond Example1, can be converted to eight shares where each share is trading at $100. The conversion value is $800 (per $1000 face value) or $80 per par face value.

Conversion Premium

This is the difference between the market price of the convertible and its conversion value.

Conversion
Premium
$35.2036
$53.3647

Note that conversion premium can be negative as we are taking the difference between the market price and the conversion value. We know that the full price of the convertible can not be less than the conversion value but the market price (that does not include accrued interest) may be smaller than the conversion value.

Conversion Premium %

This is the ratio of the conversion premium to the conversion value.

Conversion Premium %
44.0045
125.5639

In Example1, the conversion premium is $35.20 while the conversion value is $80. Hence, $35.20 is 44% of $80.

Payback

This is defined as the length of time (in years) required to earn back the conversion premium. Payback = Conversion premium / (Coupon of bond – Stock Dividend * Conversion Number).

Note that payback is defined only for stocks which pay a continuous dividend rate. It is not defined for stocks that pay lumpy dividends. Therefore, we do not have an answer for bond Example1.

To illustrate the concept, change the bond Example2 to a single currency bond by changing the "Dual Currency flag" to "N".

Example2 has a conversion premium of $28.20. The coupon of the bond is 5% while the dividend rate of the stock is 2%. The conversion ratio is 40 stocks per $1000.

Payback
- - - - -
8.5480

We take $28.20 (the conversion premium) and divide by the yield advantage of the convertible over the stock.

The convertible pays a 5.00% coupon or $5.00 per year.

The stock pays a 2% dividend. The price of the stock is $21.25 and the conversion ratio is 40 stocks per $1000 of bonds. Purchasing stock would yield:

2% * $21.25 * 4 = $1.70

We now take $28.20 / ($5.00–$1.70) = 8.54 years

Expected Maturity

This is the expected maturity of the bond. When do we expect the bond to mature, be called, be put, or converted either by choice or by forced conversion. The expected maturity gives a measure of how long do we expect the debt to last before it is no longer outstanding.

Expected Maturity
4.4690
7.2130

Cash Payback

This is a special version of the traditional cash payback number. The formula is
(100–stock price*conversion number) / (stock price—dividends rate*stock price*conversion number)
If cash payback is negative, it is not displayed.

Cash Payback
0.2000
$0.7672

In Example1, the stock does not have a dividend rate. So we take, 100–stock price*conversion number. The stock is trading at $100 and the conversion number is 0.8. We obtain 20/100 = 0.2.

In Example2, we have (100–4*21.25) / (21.25–2%*21.25*4) = 15/19.55=0.7672

This is a special formula used by one of our clients.

Delta

Delta is expressed in dollars per share. That is, if the share price changes by one $1, the convertible's value will change by:
Delta
If delta is 62%, then we have the following. For every $1 change in the underlying stock, the price of the convertible will move by $0.62.

However, if the stock only moves by $0.10, we expect the convertible to change by $0.062.

Delta is computed by moving the price of the underlying stock up and down by the dollar amount which is implicated by the input in the column labeled "percent change for delta", computing a new price for the convertible and normalizing.

How to Set Up a Hedge

Usually, a trader will go long a convertible bond and short an appropriate number of shares. Not all convertibles are appropriate for a short hedge strategy. We need the following features:

- The convertible should have a reasonable exposure to the stock price—a busted convertible (for example) would not be a good candidate for this strategy
- The convertible should not be a likely call candidate
- We expect the yield curve to remain stable
- The underlying common stock should be liquid and easy to borrow
- The convertible should have a yield advantage over the common stock. Investors selling a yield paying common stock are required to pay the dividend on the shorted stock. If the common stock's dividend is higher than the income stream produced by the coupon of the convertible, there will be a loss of income.

Convertibles which have a positive leverage, that is they earn more when the share price increases than they lose when it decreases, are even better candidates for this strategy.
In Example1, we observe the following prices:

Stock Price	Convertible Price
$95	$130.01
$100	$132.88
$105	$136.22

Delta is shown as 62.11%. This means that for a ten dollar move in the stock (from $95 to $105), the convertible's price moved by $6.21. A $1 move in the share price would correspond to a $0.62 move in the price of the convertible (per $100 face value).

If one was to buy $100 face value of convertible bonds, you would short 0.62 shares.

If the common moves to $95, you would make 0.62*$5 on the short stock position, or $3.10 and lose $132.88–$130.01=$2.87 on the convertible position. This would result in a profit of $0.23.

If the common moves to $105, you would lose 0.62*$5 on the short stock position, or $3.10 and make $136.22–$132.88=$3.34 on the convertible position. This would result in a profit of $0.24.

Our convertible pays a coupon of 8% or $8.00 per annum for $100 face value of bonds. We need to short 0.62 shares with an annual dividend of $2.00. Thus we also have a positive carry of $6.76 per year.

From this carry cost, we should subtract any borrowing fees for the stock.

Gamma

This measures how much delta will change if the underlying moves by $1.
The actual new delta can be computed by:

New delta = delta + gamma*change

In the case of Example1, gamma is 1.27% or 0.0127

Stock Price	Delta
$99	0.6013
$100	0.6211
$101	0.6263

As the stock price changed by $2, the delta changed by 0.025. We expect that the delta would change by:

$2*0.0127 = 0.0254.

Vega1

This is a measure of the sensitivity of the bond's price to a 1% change in the volatility of the stock. If we increase the share price volatility by 1%, the convertible bond price will increase by Vega1. Note that Vega1 is given in %, so divide by 100.

Example: with stock volatility at 23.8%, the current bond price is $105.94, Vega1 is 2.7166%

When stock volatility increases to 24.8%, we expect the bond price to increase to $105.94 + 2.7166/100 = $105.96717

The actual bond price increased to $105.9652.

Vega2

This is a measure of the sensitivity of the bond's price to a 1% change in the volatility of the interest rates. If we increase the interest rate volatility by 1%, the convertible bond price will increase by Vega2. Note that Vega2 is given in %, so divide by 100.

Example: with rate volatility at 15%, the current bond price is $133.08, Vega2 is 5.92%

When stock volatility increases to 16%, we expect the bond price to increase to $133.08 + 5.92/100 = $133.13

The actual bond price increased to $133.14.

Note: Vega2 can not be computed by the single factor model.

Duration

If the entire yield curve shifts in parallel, what will be the effect on bond prices.

The formula is:
(Lo-Hi) / (Bond Price * 2 * Shift Amount)

Where:
Lo—is the bond price when rates were moved down
Hi—The bond price when rates were moved up
Shift Amount—How much the rates were moved

A shift amount of 1% is calibrated as 1.
So duration is measured as the percentage shift in bond prices for a 1% change in rates.

Take Example2 and turn off the dual currency flag. We compute Duration and Convexity for a 100 bps perturbation. Then we observe the following prices:

Interest Rates	Convertible Price
4% flat	$124.75
5% flat	$119.62
6% flat	$114.78

The duration is taken as ($124.75 – $114.78) / (2*119.62) = 0.0416.

Example2
        duration   convexity
        0.0418   0.0022

Convexity

The machine also computes convexity. How much will duration change when rates move.

Interest Rates	Convertible Duration
4% flat	0.0463
5% flat	0.0418
6% flat	0.0406

The convexity is
$(0.0463–0.0406) / 2 = 0.00225$

Duration and convexity can be measured for changes in yields and for changes in credit spreads.

How to Control Duration and Convexity

In the "Yields" sheet, the user inputs what to perturb: yields ("Y") or spreads ("S")? The user also inputs the number of basis points by which the rates are supposed to be moved.

perturb what? (Y/S) =   Y
perturb amount =   100 bps

To disengage the computation of duration and convexity, blank out the cell which is supposed to have Y or S and also enter zero (0) as the perturb amount.

Key Rate Duration and Convexity

These are computed for each benchmark bond identified by the user. The user enters a Y or S next to the benchmark bond which is supposed to be manipulated. Key rate duration and convexity is shown on a separate sheet "Durations".

Example2
        duration convexity
        0.0418   0.0022

	duration	convexity
1-Nov-1997	0.0003	0.0000
1-Feb-1998	0.0025	0.0000
1-May-1998	0.0000	0.0000
1-Aug-1998	0.0003	0.0000
1-Jun-1999	0.0053	−0.0063
1-Jan-2002	0.0080	−0.0026
1-Jan-2005	0.0225	0.0014
1-Jan-2015	0.0058	0.0002
1-Jan-2025	0.0000	0.0000

This table shows the relative change in bond price as the different benchmark bonds are perturbed by 100 bps. Note that the bond is most exposed to the 1-Jan-2005 benchmark. If we change the yield of that benchmark to 6%, we would expect a decline of 2.25% in the price of the convertible.

Thus we would expect that the convertible would be priced at $119.62 – 2.25%*$119.62 = $116.93. The actual price of the convertible is $117.01.

A better estimate would result if we were to also use the convexity of the bond: $119.62 – 2.25%*$119.62 + 0.0014*$119.62/2 = $117.01.

The formula for the price change is:

New Price = Old Price + Duration * Old Price * Change in Yield + Convexity * Old Price * (Change in Yield)^2/2

Change in yield is calibrated to 1% so a 1% change in yield is considered 1.

Equity Participation

The user can compute the instrument's share in equity participation. Simply put the percentage movement you are interested to look at. This is placed in the main sheet under

The example output looks like this:

Stock price	Example1 Bond price	Participation %-age
$32.50	$121.4559	25.4
$35.00	$122.4907	27.0
$37.50	$123.7695	28.6
$40.00	$125.3888	29.7
$42.50	$127.0783	31.1
$45.00	$129.107	31.4
$47.50	$131.1834	31.7
$50.00	$133.2981	0.0
$52.50	$135.6642	35.5
$55.00	$138.1505	36.4
$57.50	$140.4907	36.0
$60.00	$142.9591	36.2
$62.50	$145.6587	37.1
$65.00	$148.2344	37.4
$67.50	$150.9643	37.9

The machine moves the stock price by increments of 5%. For each stock price, the machine prints the corresponding bond price (the "dirty price"). The output also includes the percentage participation in the move. For example, when the stock price is $50, the bond price is $133.2981 and when the stock price is $55, the bond price is $138.1505. This is a difference of 3.64%.

Thus when the stock price changed by 10%, the bond price moved by 3.64%. We say that the bond participated in 36.4% of the stock price move.

Cash Flow Screen

This will display the hypothetical cash flow screen for a hedger who is long the bond and short shares. There is a final scenario date as well as the margin required ("haircut" ratio). The simplistic assumption is that the various market parameters remain constant throughout the period.

ConvB++	Cash Flow Screen
Settlement Date	30-Dec-1998
Bond Name	Example1
Price is per	$100.00
Maturity Date	29-Dec-08
Scenario Date	21-Aug-01
Stock Price	$50.00
Bond Price (dirty)	$134.0200
Value of bonds	$13 402 000.00
Bond Coupon (%)	7.0000
Interest Rate	5.29%
Stock Borrow Rate (%)	0.50
Input Required Margin (haircut)	15%
Hedge Ratio (delta)	91.1521
Currency Conversion Ratio	1.00
Bond Amount (face value)	$10 000 000.00

In this section of the spreadsheet, are the input parameters. The computation is based on those inputs.

Number of shares to short	91 152.10
Value of bonds	$ 13 402 000.00
Value of short shares	$ (4 557 605.00)
Total value of portfolio	$ 8 844 395.00
Margin to put up	$ (1 326 659.25)
Cost to borrow	$ (196 232.06)

Based on the purchase of $10 000 000 face value of bonds, the hedger would have to short 91 152 shares. This is computed as follows: the hedge ratio (delta) is 91.152%. Hence for every $100 face value of bonds, the hedger should short 0.91152 shares.

$10 000 000/100*0.91152 = 91 152$

The bonds are priced at $134.02 so the value of the bonds is $13 402 000. The value of the short shares is given by 91 152*$50 = $4 557 600, since each share costs $50.

The value of the portfolio (long minus short) is:
$13 402 000–$4 557 600 = $8 844 400

The hedger would need to place on deposit a margin which is given by the haircut ratio. The margin which should be placed on deposit is:
$15\%* \$8 844 400 = \$1 326 660$
This is given as a negative number since the hedger must place this on deposit.

The hedger can borrow this margin amount at a cost given by the short interest rate multiplied by the period for which the amount must be borrowed. The cost to borrow the $1 326 660 at interest rate of 5.29% is:
$(196 232.06)

Now, we consider the carry for the hedger. On the positive side, the hedger collects the coupons from the bond. These are displayed as:

Date	Total Bond Coupons and Principal		$ 1 619 410.19
	Cash Flow	PVCF	
29-Jun-99	$ 350 000.00	$ 341 035.89	
29-Dec-99	$ 350 000.00	$ 332 230.12	
29-Jun-00	$ 350 000.00	$ 323 651.73	
29-Dec-00	$ 350 000.00	$ 315 294.83	
29-Jun-01	$ 350 000.00	$ 307 197.62	

We take the coupons (which are given semi-annually) and discount them at the interest rate of 5.29% to arrive at the present value of the cash flows. The total value of the coupons is $1 619 410.19.

The hedger is short shares. Each share pays a dividend payment of $2.00.

Date		Total Stock Dividend		$ (493 612.41)
	Dividend Amount	Cash Flow	PVCF	
23-Dec-99	$2.000	$ (182 304.20)	$ (173 209.29)	
23-Dec-00	$2.000	$ (182 304.20)	$ (164 380.01)	
23-Dec-01	$2.000	$ (182 304.20)	$ (156 023.11)	

We obtain that the hedger has a liability with a present value of $493 612.41 due to the dividends on the stock.

The hedger also has to borrow stock. As the borrow rate is 0.50% the cost associated is $60 529.85.

Stock Borrow Rate	0.5000
Amount Borrowed	$ (4 557 605.00)
Cost of Borrow	$ (60 529.85)

The final step is to sum all the inflows and outflows:

Cashflow	Dollars	Pts
Coupons	$ 1 619 410.19	12.08
Dividends	$ (493 612.41)	(3.68)
Stock Loan	$ (60 529.85)	(0.45)
Cost of Funds	$ (196 232.06)	(1.46)
Expected Return	$ 869 035.87	6.48
Initial Margin	$ 1 326 659.25	
ROE	24.79%	

The expected return is simply the amount of inflow (the coupons) minus all of the outflows:

- Dividends
- Stock borrow fees

- Cost to borrow the margin

The net result is $869 035.87. This represents a return of 24.79% per annum on the initial margin.

Notes:
- The computation assumes that all market variables stay the same. In particular there is no change in the bond price, stock price or hedge ratios.
- For example, if interest rates rise, the bond price can fall without any change in the stock price.
- The computation uses one risk free rate to discount all the cash flows. In some situations, one may wish to discount each cash flow by the appropriate zero coupon rate.

Yield to Call, Yield to Put, Yield to Maturity (YTC, YTP and YTM)

This is the yield to the first call, to first put or to maturity. The user has to input what type of yield computation is desired:

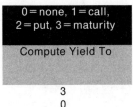

```
        3
        0
```

0 – none
1 – YTC (yield to call)
2 – YTP (yield to put)
3 – YTM (yield to maturity)

The yield is displayed in percentage.

Premium (theoretical)

This is computed as
Bond price / (share price * conversion number)

It is a measure of how much extra are we paying for the bond as opposed to buying straight stock.

Premium (at par)

This is computed as
100 / (share price * conversion number)

It is a measure of how much extra are we paying for the bond as opposed to buying straight stock. All this assuming that we would buy the bond for 100.

Investment Premium

This is the difference in price between the convertible bond and a similar bond which is not convertible. It will only be computed if the cell "Compute Investment Premium" is turned on. Investment premium is only computed for convertible bonds and preferred shares. It is not computed for mandatory structures or for options.

Accrued Interest

This gives the accrued interest on the bond. The accrued interest can be computed according to several conventions as input by the user.

Implied Volatility

The program can calculate implied volatility. That is the volatility which would result in a given market price. Place the cursor over the relevant bond and choose Implied Volatility. Enter the market price you are interested in and press enter. The machine will compute the share price volatility which would result in the given market price. This computation may be quite lengthy.

When implied volatility is found, the user is given a choice whether to accept or reject it. If accepted, that volatility will be displayed in the sheet. The new market price will be very close to the one which the user input.

If implied volatility can not be found, none of the parameters will change.

Matrix

The matrix function computes a five by five matrix of bond prices given various stock prices and volatility levels. This is very useful for scenario analysis. Matrix computation may be somewhat lengthy as the machine has to re-compute the bond price 25 times.

The matrix may be downloaded to a spreadsheet by pressing the "output" key.

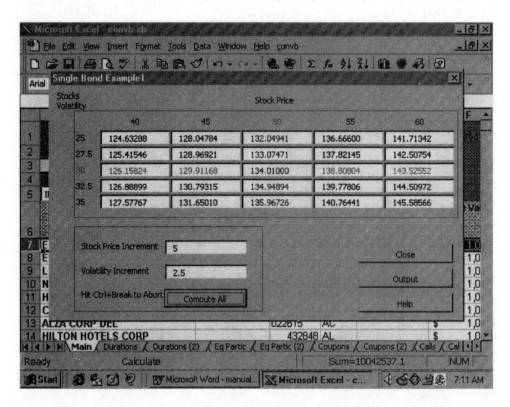

The matrix screen shows how the bond is priced with different stock prices and volatility rates.

By pressing "Output" we obtain this information on a sheet where it can be graphed.

Single Bond Example1

		Stock Price				
		40	45	50	55	60
Stocks	25	124.6329	128.0478	132.0494	136.666	141.7134
Volatility	27.5	125.4155	128.9692	133.0747	137.8215	142.5075
	30	126.1582	129.9117	134.01	138.808	143.5255
	32.5	126.889	130.7932	134.9489	139.7781	144.5097
	35	127.5777	131.6501	135.9673	140.7644	145.5857

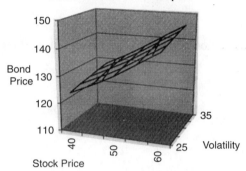

Convertible Bond - Example1

Bond Printout

When the cursor is placed on a specific bond and bond printout is chosen, the bond's details will be downloaded into a special spreadsheet. This can be printed or filed for later use.

Interface to the Value Line Database

When the file **convb.xls** is open, also open the Value Line database file, usually called **convdb.xls**.

A security can be identified in two separate ways:

1. By its code (which may be non-unique).
2. By its CUSIP (which is always unique).

Code

Enter the code of the security (e.g. AUD/Z or AVT/1) in the appropriate field in **convb.xls**.

CUSIP

A CUSIP is made up of a CUSIP number (six characters) and a CUSIP code (two letters). These should be entered in the appropriate fields in **convb.xls**.

The command **Update all securities...** copies the Value Line data from **convdb.xls** into the appropriate fields in **convb.xls**. If a security can not be uniquely identified, a pop up screen asks the user to choose from the possible securities.

Note

Unfortunately, the Value Line database does not contain all of the required information needed for accurate computations by **ConvB**. It is therefore of paramount importance that the user verify that all data has been input correctly.

Connection to Reuters

If the user has a Reuters' terminal connected to the same computer then the machine can automatically be connected to Reuters. Simply **cut** the relevant information from the Reuters' screen and **paste** it into the ConvB spreadsheet. The information is now transferred via a DDE link.

To close the link, simply close the ConvB spreadsheet. When you open it again, answer no to the question: "connect live feed?".

Connection to IDC

ConvB also supports a connection to IDC. Contact us for further information.

Index

Index compiled by Terry Halliday, Indexing specialists, Hove, UK